THE ROSE AND THE THISTLE

Essays on the Culture of Late Medieval and Renaissance Scotland

Edited by
Sally Mapstone and
Juliette Wood

TUCKWELL PRESS

First published in Great Britain in 1998 by
Tuckwell Press Ltd
Phantassie
East Linton
East Lothian EH40 3DG
Scotland

ISBN 1 898410 57 7

British Library Cataloguing-in-Publication Data
A catalogue record for this book is available
from the British Library

Typeset by Carnegie Publishing, Chatsworth Road, Lancaster
Printed and bound by Cromwell Press, Trowbridge, Wiltshire

CONTENTS

PREFACE

The essays in this volume began life in a series of lectures on aspects of national identity in Renaissance Scotland held in the Oxford English Faculty in Michaelmas term 1992 and Hilary term 1993. This is embarrassingly long ago, and the editors can only thank the contributors for their patience and endurance during the compilation and production of the book. One essay has different origins: Nicola Royan's piece on Boece and Bellenden was originally delivered at the 7th International Conference on Medieval and Renaissance Scottish Language and Literature held at the University of Strathclyde in August 1993. We are most grateful to her for agreeing to its inclusion in this collection, where it so naturally fits. Warm thanks are equally due to this book's publishers, John and Val Tuckwell, who look after their authors and their books with a rare kindness and attention.

The illustrations between pp. 84 and 85 are reproduced by permission of The British Library, The Pierpont Morgan Library, The Österreichische Nationalbibliothek, and Staatliche Museen, Berlin. Place of publication in endnote entries is London, unless otherwise stated.

Abbreviations in manuscripts and prints have been silently expanded, unless otherwise indicated; other forms of normalisation or modernisation are specified separately in the essays.

Sally Mapstone
Juliette Wood

ABBREVIATIONS

BL	British Library
CECTAL	Centre for English Cultural Tradition and Language
CSP Scottish	*Calendar of State Papers relating to Scotland and Mary, Queen of Scots, 1547–1747–1603*, ed. J. Bain *et al.*, 13 vols (1898–1969)
DNB	*Dictionary of National Biography*, ed. L. Stephen and S. Lee 63 vols (1885–1900)
DOST	*A Dictionary of the Older Scottish Tongue, from the twelfth century to the end of the seventeenth*, ed. W. Craigie *et al.* (Chicago, Aberdeen and Oxford, 1937–)
EBS	Edinburgh Bibliographical Society
EETS	Early English Text Society
IMEV	*The Index of Middle English Verse*, ed. C. Brown and R. H. Robbins (New York, 1943); *Supplement* (Lexington, Ky, 1965)
IR	*The Innes Review*
JFI	*Journal of the Folklore Institute*
JWCI	*Journal of the Warburg and Courtauld Institutes*
MLN	*Modern Language Notes*
NLS	National Library of Scotland
NQ	*Notes and Queries*
OED	*The Oxford English Dictionary*, ed. J. A. H. Murray *et al.*, 13 vols (Oxford, 1933; 2nd edn, 1989)
PMLA	*Publications of the Modern Language Association of America*
PRO	Public Record Office
RES	*The Review of English Studies*
SGS	*Scottish Gaelic Studies*
SHR	*The Scottish Historical Review*
SHS	Scottish History Society
SLJ	*Scottish Literary Journal*
SRO	Scottish Record Office
SSL	*Studies in Scottish Literature*

STC	*A Short Title Catalogue of Books Printed in England, Scotland, and Ireland ... 1475–1640*, 2nd edn, ed. W. A. Jackson, F. S. Ferguson, and K. F. Panzer, 3 vols (1976–91)
STS	Scottish Text Society
TEBS	*Transactions of the Edinburgh Bibliographical Society*
TGSI	*Transactions of the Gaelic Society of Inverness*
TLS	*The Times Literary Supplement*
TRHS	*Transactions of the Royal Historical Society*
UCL	University College, London

ILLUSTRATIONS

CONTRIBUTORS

Priscilla Bawcutt is Honorary Fellow in the Department of English, University of Liverpool.

Louise Fradenburg is Professor of English at the University of California, Santa Barbara.

Douglas Gray retired in 1997 as J. R. R. Tolkien Professor of English Literature and Language at the University of Oxford.

Alasdair MacDonald is Professor of Medieval English Language and Literature at the University of Groningen and Director of the Netherlands Research School for Medieval Studies.

Sally Mapstone is Fellow and Tutor in Medieval English of St Hilda's College and a University Lecturer at the University of Oxford.

Nicola Royan completed a doctorate at Balliol College, Oxford, on the *Scotorum Historia* of Hector Boece in 1996 and is a teaching assistant in the School of English at the University of St Andrews

Michael Spiller is Honorary Senior Lecturer in English at the University of Aberdeen, and now works in Edinburgh.

Juliette Wood is President of the Folklore Society and Honorary Lecturer in the Department of Welsh, University of Wales, Cardiff.

INTRODUCTION

It is sometimes an advantage to invert a paradigm. The title of this book invokes and inverts the title often assigned to one of William Dunbar's most famous poems, but which of course is not known definitely to have been that bestowed by the poet himself.[1] While risking the obvious charge of chauvinistically putting England first, our concern has been rather to suggest a number of ways in which the traditional perspectives implied in the normal form of that title may benefit from a shift of the kaleidoscope. The essays here afford this on the local level of the 'rose' and the 'thistle' through examinations by Douglas Gray of the pageantry associated with the marriage of Margaret Tudor and James IV in 1503, and by Louise Fradenburg of Margaret Tudor's role in the minority of James V, from Margaret's standpoint, the less than usual view. On the larger, metaphorical level of what those words may imply, they offer together a number of linked perspectives in which the cultural life of late medieval and Renaissance Scotland, and Older Scots literature,[2] can and should be usefully reconsidered.

The eight essays treat material from the end of the fourteenth to the first half of the seventeenth century, with a particular concentration of studies on the sixteenth century. This is a disposition of emphasis that is consonant with the present shift in Older Scots studies from an earlier axis of interest primarily on fifteenth and early sixteenth-century makars to a more extensive appreciation of the differing cultural character of the various reigns or regencies of the sixteenth.[3] Within this framework these studies fall into three overlapping groups, all variously connected with definitions of Scottish identity, both within the texts concerned themselves, and in subsequent historiographical and critical approaches to them. The 'rose' aspect, the part played by English elements, is a recurrent feature. These three groups also cover different sorts of literary material and remind us of the wide range of types of cultural document that scholars in this period should be investigating.

The opening essay, by Douglas Gray, assesses the thematic and iconographic characteristics of the royal entry throughout the sixteenth century in Scotland. The material analysed is primarily written and never neutral, but it constitutes a type of witness to alterations in

cultural and political emphases that has only relatively recently started
to receive the kind of detailed readings it deserves.[4] This essay performs
the especially valuable service of giving both applied discussion of
particular entries and a comparative overview. One of the most attentive
contemporary narratives is that written by John Yonge, the English
herald present at the nuptial celebrations of Margaret and James in
1503. Other written accounts take even more self-consciously literary
form, indeed contribute to the commemoration of the entry itself, such
as Dunbar's poem 'Blyth Aberdeane' or, at the other end of the century,
John Burel's verse description of the arrival in Edinburgh of Anne of
Denmark in May 1590. The entry was of course a European phenomenon, and European and English analogues can provide illuminating
comparative material for artistic and visual evidence lacking for Scottish
examples. Gray's analysis indicates how Scottish entries participate in
inherited practices and work their own distinctive variations on them,
with a 'continuing inventiveness' which inflects both creatively and at
times, notably during the Reformation, controversially, the dialogue
between sovereign and subject which is always at the heart of the
concept of the entry.

As Douglas Gray reconsiders both a range of primary sources for
the Scottish royal entry and previous interpretations of them, so Louise
Fradenburg posits a re-examination both of material reflecting Margaret
Tudor's position in Scotland as a queen and as an Englishwoman and
of previous historical analyses of it. Fradenburg deliberately focuses on
works of 'popular' as well as scholarly historical bent, in order to draw
attention to ideological agendas in Scottish historiography and the
'literary' nature of both documentary evidence and Scottish historical
writing. That this is an American scholar writing should not be ignored
here – the stress in this essay on the primacy of ideas and ways of
seeing over sustained analysis of contemporary and documentary material reflects a particular emphasis in present-day American literary and
historical scholarship. But scholars of both Scottish history and Scottish
literature have been sometimes too ready to foreground the documentary over the interpretative, or to occlude their own ideological
positioning. There is no doubt that Fradenburg is addressing an important issue in opening up the question of how Margaret Tudor's
contribution to the politics of the post-Flodden period should be read.

The next two essays, by Priscilla Bawcutt and A. A. MacDonald,
focus on contrasting aspects of the transmission and reception of Older
Scots material. Priscilla Bawcutt reminds us of the great range of different ways and means by which Scottish material was conveyed into
England or registered itself in texts produced in England. Many of these

have given a significant English dimension to how we have inherited Older Scots literature, from the early English printings of works by the major figures Henryson and Douglas, to the plethora of sixteenth-century Scottish broadside and satirical pieces preserved among English diplomatic papers. From a practical point of view the English taste for Scottish texts provided what in retrospect can be seen often to have been a crucially enlarged catchment area for the eventual survival of editions of works such as Henryson's *Testament of Cresseid*. As A. A. MacDonald notes, the inventory of the estate of the Edinburgh printer Robert Smyth, in 1602, records a striking 1638 'Cressedis', presumably Henryson's poem – but none are now known to survive. By contrast, the earliest printed witness of the *Testament*, in Thynne's 1532 London edition of Chaucer's *Works*, survives in a substantial number of copies.[5] But as important for the cultural historian is an appreciation of the complexity of transmission of the 'Scottishness' of these works in an English context. While it is true, as Priscilla Bawcutt observes, that anglicisation of the language, and even of the sentiments, of Scottish texts was a feature of their English printings, she also points out that this is not absolutely predictably so, as the preservation in Copland's 1555 London print of Douglas's *Palice of Honour* of Scottish phrasing 'modernised out' of the 1579 Edinburgh edition well demonstrates. Bawcutt notes the fact that Wynkyn de Worde's 1499 Westminster edition of *The Contemplacioun of Synnaris* was probably the first printed edition of an Older Scots poem; what is perhaps even less appreciated is that only that edition has the apparatus of accompanying Latin *sententiae*, unpreserved in the four later Scottish manuscript witnesses, and which can be argued to have an important textual relation to the poem and to have probably been an original part of its composition.[6] Scholars today are, rightly, interested in recovering the 'Scottishness' of such texts, in seeking to define, as is sought in this volume, those things that give these works a distinctively national identity. It is equally important, however, to understand their wider resonances in their own day, the manner in which they were received by audiences distanced from their immediate ones, as this in itself may tell us something about how Scots literature was perceived beyond Scotland, a factor brought out in many of the contributions to this volume. This issue perhaps becomes even more relevant as printing assumes greater importance as a means of transmission in the sixteenth century, and some authors, notably those, like Hector Boece, writing in Latin, compose with a sense of a European as well as a national constituency of readers.

The essentially 'public' nature of poems like *The Contemplacioun* and many later works, including those composed in the learned language, and the extent to which their authors assume a speaking role identified with or athwart to the *status quo* forms one of the several areas scrutinised in A. A. MacDonald's essay on defining parameters for Scottish culture across the entire period covered in this book. This is another essay which both places Scottish cultural activity within a European framework and points up its distinctive emphases. It also brings greater light and shade to the changing character of literary production in the course of the sixteenth and seventeenth centuries by isolating the religious, economic and social factors which had significant effects on what could be written and how it might be circulated. The cultural results of the Reformation and the departure of the king and court for London in 1603 are given a depth of analysis which draws attention to the still under-considered issue of their generic implications within the increasingly 'fissiparous' nature of Scottish literary culture in the latter part of this period.

A particular aspect of these political and generic shifts is taken up in Michael Spiller's discussion of what happened to the Scottish sonnet with the Union of the Crowns. He offers an intriguing answer to the question as to why so few Scottish sonnets of the 1580s and 1590s reached print,[7] positing a changing perception of sonnet style, which temporarily polarised Scottish and English modes of expression in the period following the move of the Scottish court to London in 1603. 'Style' in this context means more than modes of expression, relating equally pertinently to the nature of the poetic 'I', an issue also raised by MacDonald and further pursued here, as Spiller sees it, in terms of the opposition of the assured Scots speaking voice in the sonnet to its increasingly more quizzical and discursive English neighbour.[8] A key transitional figure in the shifts at work is the still neglected William Alexander,[9] and a major barometer for their reception, the King himself. The fact that the bulk of James's own poetry was produced during his Scottish rather than his English reign is a well known one, but it is interesting to speculate as to whether his adverse reaction, initially at least, to the nature of English poetic discourse, impeded the cultivation in England of his own poetic voice.[10]

The final group of three essays is concerned with the Scottish chronicle tradition, an area of Scottish historical writing that is coming into increased prominence,[11] but in which certain texts remain insufficiently scrutinised, particularly Hector Boece's *Scotorum Historia* and its 'translation', John Bellenden's *Chronicles of Scotland*, the subjects of the two final essays. The first, by Juliette Wood, performs what for literary and historical scholars should be the immensely valuable service of identifying folkloric material and patterns in a number of chronicles from the fourteenth to the sixteenth centuries, namely those by John of Fordun, Andrew of Wyntoun, Walter Bower, and John Bellenden. One of the factors that has contributed to the less than elevated position assigned to Scottish chronicle writing by historians, both of recent and older vintage, has been the conspicuously 'literary' or 'invented' nature of some of its material, the degree to which chronicle writing can be shown to have served specific ideological purposes, most often concerned with Scottish independence or king-subject relations.[12] That such works thus have to be read as interpretative as well as documentary should not reduce their status as historical texts, and there is evidence that Bower's *Scotichronicon* is starting to receive the kind of informed analysis from this point of view that it so clearly demands;[13] other chronicles are equally worthy of this kind of respect. Part of that process of re-reading, however, also requires an understanding of what material in these texts is formulaic or informed by generic convention from a range of types of source, in which one of the least systematically treated to date, as Juliette Wood notes, is that of folklore. Her analysis of the nature and function of what is nicely termed 'folk logic' within these texts alerts us to the marked degree to which writers of considerable learning, like Bower, were willing to use this kind of material, often in those contexts of key importance in their texts such as Scottish-English relations or issues of kingship. As Juliette Wood suggests, we should take note of the fact that folkloric material was felt to have an entirely acceptable presence within the culture of the literary élite. Like Fradenburg's essay, Wood's work invites us to reassess the kind of prominence we give to different types of literary evidence, reminding us in the process that the current tendency among historians to favour the documentary record over the descendant of oral narrative may create a dichotomy that contains its own danger of anachronism.

John Bellenden is in his own right one of the most neglected six-teenth-century Scottish literary figures,[14] and while his *Chronicles of Scotland* have been more attended to than his translation of Livy, they have too frequently been used as a crib for Boece's *Scotorum Historia*. Nicola Royan demonstrates unequivocally that Bellenden is an un-reliable witness for Boece's work, but that his translation also holds great cultural interest, as a text produced for a different kind of audience from that intended for its Latin original, and as a work some of whose variations from its source reflect its translator's own concerns. This is something brought out at its strongest in the divergences between the manuscript and printed texts of the *Chronicles of Scotland*, and this is the aspect of it concentrated on in the final essay in the volume, by Sally Mapstone. This study returns to the theme of English/Scottish relations by taking as its starting-point the origins of the dialogue between Malcolm and Macduff in act IV scene 3 of *Macbeth*, and tracing this via Holinshed's *Chronicle*, through Bellenden's *Chronicles* to a tradition that ultimately reaches back to Fordun's *Chronica Gentis Scotorum*. The differences between the manuscript and printed versions of Bellenden's translation of this particular scene are shown to be fundamental, and it is argued (building on Royan's work) that they originate with Bellenden rather than with Boece, a point with obviously important implications for the status of Bellenden's 'translation'. The fact that it is to the printed rather than the manuscript version of Bellenden's translation that Holinshed is indebted for this scene is shown to be one surprisingly unappreciated by Shakespearean scholars, at the basic level of citation of editions, but also in its full implications for the shaping that the scene ultimately receives in *Macbeth*.

The 'revisionist' approach which has dominated the study of late medieval Scottish history for the past quarter-century, and which has stressed the extent of stability in Scottish politics and consensus between Stewart rulers and the political community, is itself now beginning to receive reappraisal.[15] But that very reappraisal stems from the existence of a coherent theoretical approach to the study of late medieval Scottish political life. Older Scots literary studies still lack any thorough-going way of seeing the diversity of texts produced in the fifteenth and sixteenth centuries within a coherent cultural overview.[16] A consensus of sorts does exist, however, informed indeed by the work of Scottish historians, on the primacy of situating Scottish literary writing within a full recognition of its participation in political structures, religious movements, and ideological debates, of indeed its essentially public nature.[17] Such an emphasis can still take in less apparently politicised genres, such as the lyric and the sonnet, where the construction of the narrating voice bears a vital connection to the poet's sense of his or her relation to a social nexus.[18] As A. A. MacDonald shows, a developing 'individualised' voice in sixteenth-century Scottish poetry can enhance rather than reduce the importance placed on its connection to social or political mores.

The essays in this volume reflect those and other interdisciplinary concerns; they are also in large part comparative pieces, rather than studies centred on single authors. While extended works on individual figures have an indisputable value, the advantages at this stage in Older Scots studies of contrastive, comparative work are equally great, not least in encouraging constructive thinking on the nature of fifteenth- and sixteenth-century literary production.

'Treuth is, that sendill or nevir ar the Scottis vincust be Inglismen

without sum divisioun amang thaimself', wrote Bellenden in yet another addition to the printed version of his so-called translation of
Boece's *Scotorum Historia*.[19] One of the leading writers of Scotland's
present literary renaissance has recently developed a similar point, 'I
think the Scots oppress themselves by blaming the English and being
obsessed with them. I can understand how it happens, but it's a cul-
de-sac.'[20] It is too much to hope that Older Scots literary studies will
be without division in the next millennium, indeed a little theoretical
skirmishing would be no bad thing for the subject, but the editors of
this volume hope that its partial emanation from England will be taken,
like its title, in the positive spirit in which it is intended. The combination of idealism and realism that informs Dunbar's poem on the rose
and the thistle is a useful template for the continuing redefinition of
their relationship in spheres scholarly as well as political.

1. The poem is untitled in its sole witness, the Bannatyne MS, and the title was
invented by Allan Ramsay in *The Ever Green* (1724), in the form 'The Thistle and the
Rose ... A Poem in Honour of Margaret, Daughter to *Henry* the VII. of *England*,
Queen to James the IV. King of Scots'. It was popularised in the eighteenth century
by a separate printing (Glasgow, 1750) with Bellenden's *Proheme of the cosmographe* and
in anthologies; see P. Bawcutt, *Dunbar the Makar* (Oxford, 1992), p. 92. The spelling
appears to have become 'Scotticised' into *The Thrissill and the Rois* in David Laing's
1834 edition of Dunbar, and this is the form in which it appears in Kinsley's edition
(Oxford, 1979). See also P. Bawcutt (ed.), *William Dunbar, Selected Poems* (1996), p 199.
    2. The term 'Older Scots' came to prominence through the publication of *The
Dictionary of the Older Scottish Tongue* (1937–) and has been consistently promulgated
by A. J. Aitken, e.g. the unpublished paper of 1954 'Sources of the Vocabulary of Older
Scots' (see p. 4 of the introduction in *The Nuttis Schell: Essays on the Scots Language*, ed.
C. Macafee and I. Macleod, Aberdeen, 1987, and more recently 'Progress in Older Scots
Philology', *SSL*, 26 (1991), 19–37). It is used less consistently by literary scholars, but
deserves to be more greatly taken up, as it neatly covers the period from, as the *DOST*
defines it, the twelfth to the end of the seventeenth century. *The Concise Scots Dictionary*
(ed. M. Robinson, Aberdeen, 1985) divides Older Scots up into the following periods:
pre-literary, to 1375; early Scots, 1375–1450; early Middle Scots, 1450–1550; late Middle
Scots, 1550–1700 (p. xiii).
    3. The majority of monographs on Older Scots literature of the 1950–80 period
dealt with the most well-known late medieval makars, e.g. J. MacQueen, *Robert Henryson* (Oxford, 1967); T. Scott, *Dunbar: A Critical Exposition of the Poems* (Edinburgh,
1966); P. Bawcutt, *Gavin Douglas: A Critical Study* (Edinburgh, 1976); D. Gray, *Robert
Henryson* (Leiden, 1979). More recent work has focused on comparative study and on
a far wider range of sixteenth-century material, most notable here are two collections
of essays: *The Renaissance in Scotland*, ed. A. A. MacDonald, M. Lynch and I. B. Cowan
(Leiden, 1994), and *Stewart Style 1513–1542, Essays on the Court of James V*, ed. J. Hadley
Williams (East Linton, 1996).
    4. Seventeenth-century royal entries are also starting to receive greater scrutiny, see

e.g. E. McGrath, 'Local Heroes: the Scottish Humanist Parnassus for Charles I', in *England and the Continental Renaissance*, ed. E. Chaney and P. Mack (Woodbridge, 1990), pp. 257–70, and D. Bergeron, 'Charles I's Edinburgh Pageant', *Renaissance Studies*, 6 (1992), 171–84.

5. See *The Poems of Robert Henryson*, ed. D. Fox (Oxford, 1981), pp. xiv–xv, xcix–c; see *STC* 5068.

6. S. L. Mapstone, 'The Advice to Princes Tradition in Scottish Literature, 1450–1500' (unpublished D. Phil. thesis, University of Oxford, 1986), pp. 282–314.

7. Alexander Montgomerie is not the main subject of Michael Spiller's enquiry, and very few indeed of his sonnets were published during his life-time, but it should be noted that 'Can goldin Titan' appeared in James VI's *Essayes of a Prentise* (1584) and that from Waldegrave's second print of 1597 onwards the 'Supreme essence' sonnet was regularly printed with the editions of *The Cherrie and the Slae* that appeared throughout the seventeenth century.

8. The term 'Castalian' is used in Michael Spiller's essay and in that by A. A. MacDonald to characterise the group of poets around James VI. Spiller quotes indeed from one of the few contemporary references to the term, by the king himself in his sonnet to Sir William Alexander, 'Ful oft alas with comfort and with care/Wee bath'd you in Castalias fountaine cleare'. There is no strong evidence that 'Castalian' or the often cited 'Castalian band' were widely used during the 1580s and 1590s and the phrase seems to have come into present-day critical parlance under the influence of H. M. Shire's *Song, Dance and Poetry of the Court of Scotland under King James VI* (Cambridge, 1969). I am grateful for the advice of Priscilla Bawcutt in this connection.

9. An important recent reassessment is the paper given by David W. Atkinson at the 8th International Conference on Medieval and Renaissance Scottish Language and Literature, St Hilda's College, Oxford, August 1996, '"More than One Voice": The Poetic Accomplishment of William Alexander'. This paper will be published in the proceedings of the conference.

10. For suggestive remarks on the related subject of English 'misunderstanding' of James's political writings see J. Wormald, 'James VI and I, *Basilikon Doron* and *The Trew Law of Free Monarchies*: the Scottish Context and the English Translation', in L. Levy Peck (ed.), *The Mental World of the Jacobean Court* (Cambridge, 1991), pp. 36–54.

11. A major enterprise has been the new edition of Walter Bower's *Scotichronicon*, under the general editorship of D. E. R. Watt, the eight volumes of the text of which appeared between 1989 and 1996. A ninth volume, of critical essays, was published in 1998. Important recent critical discussion of Fordun's *Chronica Gentis Scotorum* is to be found in R. J. Goldstein, *The Matter of Scotland: Historical Narrative in Medieval Scotland* (Lincoln, Neb., and London, 1993).

12. Goldstein, pp. 104–32; C. Kidd, *Subverting Scotland's Past* (Cambridge, 1993), pp. 12–29, 102–7, 256–8.

13. As in the discussion by M. H. Brown, '"I have thus slain a tyrant": *The Dethe of the Kynge of Scotis* and the Right to Resist in Early Fifteenth-Century Scotland', *IR*, 47 (1996), 24–44.

14. Some recent discussion in T. van Heijnsbergen, 'The Interaction between Literature and History in Queen Mary's Edinburgh: the Bannatyne Manuscript and its Prosopographical Context', in *The Renaissance in Scotland* (as n. 3), pp. 183–25 (esp. 191–5); A. A. MacDonald, 'William Stewart and the Court Poetry of the Reign of James V', in *Stewart Style 1513–1542* (as n. 3), pp. 179–200.

15. M. Brown, 'Scotland Tamed? Kings and Magnates in Late Medieval Scotland: a review of recent work', *IR*, 45 (1994), 120–46. The 'revisionist' case was given major

statement in two volumes in the New History of Scotland series: A. Grant, *Independence and Nationhood, Scotland 1306–1469* (1984), and J. Wormald, *Court, Kirk and Community, Scotland 1470–1625* (1981).

16. The most current attempts to open up aspects of this issue have been by R. J. Lyall, e.g. '"A New Maid Channoun": Redefining the Canonical in Medieval and Renaissance Scottish Literature', *SSL*, 26 (1991), 1–18; 'Formalist Historicism and Older Scots Poetry', *Études Écossaises*, 1 (1992), 39–48.

17. As in many of the essays in the collections cited in n. 3, above, the studies by Bawcutt (n. 1), and Goldstein (n. 11), and L. Fradenburg, *City, Marriage, Tournament: Arts of Rule in Late Medieval Scotland* (Wisconsin, WI, 1991).

18. See also T. van Heijnsbergen, 'The Love Lyrics of Alexander Scott', *SSL*, 26 (1991), 366–79.

19. John Bellenden, *The Chronicles of Scotland*, ed. T. Maitland, 2 vols (Edinburgh, 1821), vol. 2, p. 373. His source was Fordun's chronicle. See Johannis de Fordun, *Chronica Gentis Scotorum*, ed. W. F. Skene, vol. I (Edinburgh, 1871), p. 330.

20. M. France, 'The Auld Sangs are the Best', interview with Alasdair Gray, *The Daily Telegraph*, 18 January 1997, p. A5.

1

THE ROYAL ENTRY IN
SIXTEENTH-CENTURY SCOTLAND

Douglas Gray

Scholarly interest in royal and civic pageantry has generally been concentrated on the later sixteenth and seventeenth centuries where a wealth
of material, both verbal and visual, has survived, and, moreover, compared with Europe and England, Scotland, where the documentation
is very much more sparse, has suffered particularly.[1] Indeed it has been
said that it 'barely produced a festival literature at all'.[2] This is an
exaggeration. Although the documentation is not extensive, it shows
that Scotland produced a series of interesting and often spectacular royal
entries from the beginning of the sixteenth century (the 1503 entry of
Margaret Tudor to Edinburgh for her marriage to James IV, the occasion
which inspired Dunbar's *The Thrissill and the Rois*) to the end.

The following analysis is based on the assumption that the choice of
thematic and iconographic material for the *tableaux* devised for a late
medieval royal entry may be both significant and coherent. However,
the analysis of their meanings must of necessity often be speculative.
The difficulties are obvious. In Scotland we do not have full descriptions
of elaborate pageants like those made to welcome Katherine of Aragon
to London in 1501, 'a complex and ingenious intellectual exercise of
considerable originality'.[3] Unlike some later English and continental
descriptions of ceremonial entries, the Scottish accounts usually do not
offer any interpretation of the pageants. So the would-be commentator
is presented with a delicate task. He has to be cautious about claims
for overall coherent patterns. And as to the significance of individual
pageants he must usually restrict himself to tentative suggestions based
on traditional iconography and exegesis and of the particular historical
context. There is also another danger – of a semiotic approach which
is too narrowly focused and simply attempts to find and 'decode' a
single 'message'. The considerable body of anthropological work on
festivals and rituals suggests rather that they have a multiplicity of

meanings and functions: 'a collective ceremony is a dramatic occasion, a complex type of symbolic behavior that usually has a statable purpose, but one that invariably alludes to more than it says and has many meanings at once'.[4] This must certainly have been the case with the civic ceremonies of the fifteenth and sixteenth centuries, which combined, with varying degrees of sophistication, entertainment and instruction, festival and symbolic drama.

By 1503, the royal entry was a well-established feature of European political urban life. It was a magnificent affair, and especially so if it was made into a capital city, and if it was combined with a royal wedding and with international politics. The basic pattern involved a meeting a the gate of the city between the monarch and representatives of the town and of the Church, and then a formal entry and procession by the monarch through the streets to a particular (and often symbolic) goal – a cathedral, a church, or a palace. Along the way he paused to look at a series of scenes or 'pageants', whether painted, acted, mimed or 'posed' as *tableaux vivants*. What was originally a simple procession had gradually become more sophisticated: 'd'abord simple fête, puis aussi spectacle, puis aussi solennité quasi religieuse, une entreé royale est de plus devenue à la fin du xv⁵ siècle un grand théâtre où le sentiment monarchique est de plus en plus exalté et la politique royale de mieux en mieux justifiée'.[5] And the subject-matter of the pageants also developed. Biblical scenes and figures were joined by moral and courtly allegories and then by mythological topics. From Italian humanism came an interest in Petrarch's *Trionfi* and in Roman triumphs, which is reflected in the triumphal arches which became a feature of Italian pageantry and which greeted the invading French armies at the end of the fifteenth century.[6] Royal power was celebrated, royal policy justified, the sacred duties of kingship were recalled, and the hope of the community for peace and prosperity found expression. And at the same time the occasion combined celebration and festivity and was marked by movement, music and noise. It was, in truth, a 'joyeuse et triomphante entrée'.

The essential features of the whole are neatly summarised by Jean Jacquot:

> L'entrée ... c'est d'abord la rencontre de deux cortèges aux portes de la ville, le cortège royale et le cortège civique. L'ordre des personnages et des groupes qui les composent est fixé par un vieil usage, de même que l'itinéraire royal à l'intérieur de la ville, et c'est toujours aux mêmes points que se dressent les décors et les théâtres de rue. Le pouvoir monarchique se donne en spectacle à la cité; la cité se donne

en spectacle au souverain – et à elle-même car elle prend alors conscience de son unité, de son harmonie dans la diversité des
responsabilités, des rangs, des professions. Les sentiments de fidélité
et de protection, l'idée de concorde nécessaire au travail pacifique et
à la prospérité ne s'expriment pas seulement dans un cortège solennel
aux costumes éclatants et accompagné de musique, mais par des dé-
cors, des tableaux vivants commentés par des devises ou des discours.[7]

Three points of special interest here – the traditional nature of the
entry, its spectacular and quasi-dramatic quality, and its significance –
deserve some amplification. The entry was in many ways highly traditional. Not only were the pageants usually placed at the same locations,
but already existing pageants were sometimes re-used or adapted.[8] There
was a traditional route (adapted to the actual and the symbolic topography of the city) along which the cortège passed. In sixteenth-century
Edinburgh the monarch would usually enter at the West Port, go up
the hill to the castle, then down the High Street, and out at the Nether
Bow on his way to Holyrood. But the symbolic topography of the
city might be used in differing ways, and there were changes in the
subject matter of the pageants which are clear reflections of changing
taste or of new political or religious contexts. In short, the entry offered
the possibilities not only of tradition but also of innovation.

The 'dramatic' qualities of this kind of pageantry are equally important. It was not a simple 'tour' of the city, nor a parade. Not only were
the individual pageants themselves 'speaking pictures' or performances,
but the total show was a spectacular piece of street theatre, which was
far from static but had the dynamic quality of a dramatic performance
(and no doubt at some moments something of its unpredictability), and
involved the relationship between actors and audiences. This appears
in a complicated form, in that there were overlapping sets of 'actors'
and 'audiences': the central royal figure and his immediate cortège were
a small moving 'audience' of observers, who paused to watch the
succession of tableaux with their 'actors', whether speaking or silent,[9]
while at the same time the monarch himself was observed, and was
himself an actor as he moved in royal splendour before the larger
audience of the assembled townspeople, who as they applauded also
became in a sense 'actors' in the drama. It was a distinctively communal
drama, involving the various elements of society.

It offered a performance, often of great grandeur, involving movement, sight and sound. The music and the visual effects were especially
important, and the whole was a genuine *Gesamtkunstwerk*, variously
making use of pictures, images, *tableaux vivants*, miming, *tituli* or

speeches. The fifteenth-century Parisian entries contained splendid *tableaux vivants* – the *Journal d'un bourgeois de Paris* describes one of the pageants in the entry of the English regent Bedford in 1424:

> ... in front of the Châtelet there was a very fine Mystery of the Old and New Testaments done by the children of Paris. They did it without speaking or moving, as if they had been statues against a wall.[10]

Another in 1431 evidently entranced the young Henry VI, who paused for a long time to look at the mermaids at the Ponceau St. Denis: 'there were three mermaids there very ingeniously done, and in the middle of them there was a lily whose buds and flowers spouted out milk and wine for everyone to drink who wished or who could. Above, there was a little wood where wild men frolicked about and did very pretty tricks with shields; every one liked watching this.'[11] Elaborate machinery (also found in indoor shows) was used, especially in later pageants. Angels descended from the roof of a cathedral or from an arch across the route; fountains were made to run with wine. (Existing 'features' of the topography were regularly put to use: gates could be decorated and serve as galleries for musicians, whether human or 'angelic'.) For the visit of Charles V to London in 1522 an island (representing England) was devised, surrounded by waves and rocks and containing open country, mountains and woods, 'with dyuers bestes goying abowte the mountayns by vyces [winches]' and flowers that could hardly be distinguished from natural ones, and ponds of fresh water with fish. When the emperor arrived at it, as if by a miracle, 'the bestyes dyd move and goo, the fisshes dyd sprynge, the byrdes dyd synge reioysing the comyng of the ii princes, the emprowr and the kynges grace.' More mechanical marvels followed: two images were raised up, one, in a castle, representing the emperor, the other in an arbour with roses representing Henry VIII, each carrying naked swords: 'the ymages dyd behold eche other, and then cast away the swerdys by a vyce, and with another vyce ioyned eche to other and embrasede eche other in tokennyng off love and pease', whereupon 'an ymage off the father off hevyn all in burnyd gold dyd disclose and appere and move in the topp off the pageant wyth thys scripture wrytyn abowte him – Beati pacifici qui filii dei vocabuntur.'[12]

Such 'speaking pictures' were obviously designed to be attractive and 'affective': they also already seem to be deliberate attempts to achieve what a French historian of later ballet and festival has called 'le merveilleux',[13] to produce moments in which ordinary life is transcended, and the onlookers are transported into a different and enchanted world of dreams ('la liberté du scénario onirique'), a golden age or a fairyland.

Entries were not only splendid and wonderful, they were meaningful symbolic rituals, and quite complex social events (more so than historians of pageantry sometimes allow), affecting social relationships, and involving the participants' social roles and identities. The formal characteristics which are characteristic of collective ceremonies – repetition, acting, or other forms of stylised behaviour – impose an artistic order on the indeterminacy or chaos of ordinary life. Order is central to a collective ceremony (ideally at least, moments of disorder are only permitted to occur at fixed times or places): through its formal procedures it suggests that, in whole or in part, the cosmos and human society is orderly and explicable. But this is enacted dramatically, and this process shows 'order' and 'change' to be interdependent, with a relationship that is dialectal rather than polar. The very occurrence of a collective ritual carries a social message: it has an explicit purpose (the simplest of its meanings to understand) and deliberately uses explicit symbols. It will also make implicit 'statements', sometimes revealing less conscious social and cultural tensions or contradictions, even if it may be designed to deny or disguise them even when it presents itself as an act of affirmation, a declaration of apparent certainties.[14]

The early royal entry is clearly designed to be an 'act of affirmation' in the most positive sense: 'la plupart du temps, la fête paraît sans aucune doute l'occasion d'affirmer des valeurs établies. Elle marque, d'une façon ou d'une autre, un triomphe'.[15] It is an affirmation of political order and presents the image of princely power – the ruler rides as if in triumph, displaying his person to his subjects. This showing of the royal person is a kind of epiphany, and often unites the secular and the sacred, revealing the king as God's representative, and the fount of justice. But the royal figure is not seen in isolation, but in relationship with the town and with the country, and indeed with society as a whole. The 'estates' are always represented, and the monarch's relationship with the Church is symbolically emphasised by the 'blessings' it is seen to give. The public showing of the king in regal splendour is intended to reaffirm the ideal of social order, the bonds of society, the loyalty due from subjects. And such 'messages' are often explicitly emphasised by the various pageants presented along the route.

These will contain elements both of panegyric and of instruction. Often 'a royal entry reflected the achievements of the present and reviewed those of the past while turning an optimistic eye to the future'[16] (expressing, however implicitly, ideals and hopes). As to the 'present', it is not surprising, given the strongly political nature of royal pageantry, to find it being used as a medium of propaganda. This is found both in the wider symbolic messages – the need for harmony, order, etc. – and in more particular or local ones: thus English fifteenth-century pageantry stresses the English claim to the French throne.

But instruction was not addressed simply to the loyal populace. The entry, with its 'two audiences', was a 'dialogue' between the king and his people.[17] The ruler was praised, but (in accordance with Bacon's doctrine '*Laudando praecipere*: when by telling men, what they are, they represent to them what they should be')[18] he was also instructed and exhorted – sometimes implicitly, sometimes explicitly, sometimes generally on the need for virtue and piety, sometimes on the particular duties of the ruler in the manner of the books of advice for princes. Thus at Bruges in 1515 one of the tableaux for the Count of Flanders (later to be the Emperor Charles V) showed Orpheus playing to the animals in an enclosed garden: the significance is that the young prince tunes 'the instrument of his conduct, that is to say the institution of his reign, in perfect consonance and melodious harmony with all excellent virtues'.[19] Such 'Mirror for Princes' material is appropriate to the event as a whole and in no way disturbs its overall coherence. (In a similar way, historical figures or saints with the same name as the monarch appear to welcome and bless him or her, or a series of Biblical and legendary marriages may be portrayed to foreshadow the happy event of a royal marriage.)

Sometimes however the 'messages' addressed to the king may be more particular and local. When the French king Charles VII entered Paris in 1437, the citizens had felt for some time that they had not been well defended against their various enemies. After seeing several fine mysteries, he came to the Hôtel-Dieu, and 'the doors of the church of Notre Dame were closed and the bishop of Paris brought a book to the king upon which he swore as King that he would faithfully and loyally keep all that a good king should. Then they opened the door and he entered the church.'[20] When the victorious Henry VII made a progress in 1486, some English towns with a less than loyal record invented pageants which stressed their loyalty and the need for a king to show mercy.[21] Bristol, which had no such problem, chose to have its legendary founder Brennius lament the decline of its trade. Henry took the message, and soon after sent for the Mayor and leading citizens and encouraged them to develop shipping.[22] At Bruges in 1515 some of the pageants tactfully drew the Count's attention to movement of business and prosperity away from the town to Antwerp.[23] Carefully placed in a context of praise and idealisation, such pageants give implicit expression to deep-seated tensions or difficulties in the community in the hope of resolving them in harmony. The significance of a royal entry was by no means always straightforward or simple.

The Entry was also a popular festival. It requires a positive act of imagination to reconstruct the total effect, with the streets brightly decorated, the crowds and the excitement of a holiday atmosphere. The accounts give only the barest glimpses of this: thus, in Paris in 1424 for Bedford 'the city was decorated everywhere he was to go, and the streets decorated and cleaned', obviously as part of the official organisation, but the chronicler also mentions an acrobat at the corner of the Rue aux Lombards 'performing as cleverly as anyone had ever seen'; in 1437 after the entry had ended 'there were great celebrations that night, pots and pans being thumped, bonfires in the middle of the streets, eating, drinking, dancing, various instruments playing.'[24] Such hints give us some idea of the social richness of these impermanent events. No doubt the festivity was intended, and served, to strengthen the collective bonds of the community. Most people probably just enjoyed a good day out.

For the first – and in many ways the most original and interesting – of the Scottish entries, that of 1503, we are fortunate in having an eye-witness account by John Yonge or Young, the Somerset Herald, who accompanied the English princess to Edinburgh.[25] Young rarely comments on what he sees, and does not attempt to interpret the pageants, but from his full and often quite vivid description a number of dominant ideas and themes emerge. Its distinctive character is clear from the beginning. It is very unusual in having an elaborate 'prologue' before the entry proper, perhaps deliberately devised to complement the queen's long progress north (which Young describes in detail) to which the formal entry and the marriage form a climax. The prologue also establishes the central role of the Scottish king, both as a welcoming spouse and as a chivalric lover. On the morning of 7 August the queen's company, splendidly attired, begins to move from Dalkeith. The king (who had previously gone out to visit her) sends a gentleman to her with a great tame hart 'for to have a course'. The Earl of Surrey, the English commander, courteously defers the course until the king himself arrives. When he does, half-way to Edinburgh, he greets Margaret in a courtly manner, dismounting, and kissing her. He remains with her throughout, mounting her palfrey and riding with her behind him. They then come to a prepared 'scene' rather like something out of the pages of Malory:

And halfe a mylle ny to that, within a medewe, was a pavyllon
whereof cam owt a knyght on horsbak, armed at all peces, havyng
hys lady par amours that barre hys horne. And by avanture ther
cam an other also armed, that cam to hym and robbed fro hym hys

said lady, and at the absentynge blew the said horne, wherby the said knyght understude hym, and tourned after hym, and sayd to hym, 'wherfor hast thou thys doon?' He answerd hym, 'what wyll thou say therto?' 'I say that I schall pryve apon thee that thou hast doon owtrage to me.' The tother demaunded hym iff he was armed. He said, 'ye.' 'Well then, preve the a man and doo thy devoir.'

[fol. 101, Leland p. 228]

(the phrase 'by avanture' suggests that the herald is responding to the romance element). The challenge is accepted, and a joust begins. The king intervenes, and, like a good ruler, asks the cause of their difference and fixes a day for settlement. After this *pas d'armes* we return to the first part of the 'plot' – the hart is released: 'and half a mylle fro thens was the said hert, the wich the kynge caused to be los, and putt a greyond [greyhound] after hym that maid a fayr course. Bot the said hert wanne the towne, and went to hys repayre.' [fol. 101, L. p. 289]. Here, no doubt, the element of 'game' is predominant. The text is too brief to be certain, but symbolic associations with 'hert-huntyng'[26] may not be too far away: there are one or two later hints of hunting as a sub-theme.

We now come to the moment of entry. In the traditional manner it opens with the citizens ('many honest people of the town and of the countre about, honnestly arayd all on horsbak') coming out to meet the honoured visitor. Our illustration (fig. 1) shows how such an event was imagined at the arrival of Helen at the gates of Troy: it is interesting to see how the fifteenth-century artist, unlike the chroniclers, captures a busy crowd scene in which both the musicians and the populace are prominent. Then the king and queen enter the town ('and so by ordre they entred within the said towne the kyng & the qwene'). This moment is, on the one hand, similar to the submission of a conquered town after a siege:[27] here the citizens humbly demonstrate their obedience to the monarch, who will enter the town in triumph and grace it with his presence. On the other, he is 'allowed' to cross its threshold, is given the 'freedom of the city'. The 'dialogue' continues with the arrival of two processions of clerics – the grey friars, and 'a lityll more fourther' the Jacobins – bearing relics for the king to kiss. Again the king twice makes a courtly gesture to his consort – 'he wold not before the qwene' – but the religious significance is uppermost here: the king is demonstrating his obedience to the Church and the faith and is receiving in return its blessing and validation. Yet the festival atmosphere is equally prominent, thanks to 'the mynstrelles, Johannes and hys company, trompettes as well of the one syd as of the other' (though the keen eye of the English herald notes that 'thos of Scotlaund had no baneres new'). As often there was a gate for them to pass through (cf. fig. 2, Bruges 1515): 'at the entrying of the said town was maid a yatt of wod paynted.' It has two 'towrelles' or turrets, and 'a wyndowe in the myddes'. In the turrets and the windows were 'revested [clad in ecclesiastical garments] angelles syngynge joyously for the commynge of so noble a lady, and at the sayd wyndowe was in lyke wys an angell presentyng the kees to the said qwene' [fol. 102, L. p. 289]. This seems to be a *tableau vivant*: quite clearly the new queen is here the centre of attention and homage in a scene in which the heavenly is joined to the earthly. Attention is shifted back to the king by the arrival ('within the town ny to the said yatt') of another procession with a relic, the arm of St Giles, to be kissed: 'wherof he dyd as before, and began to synge *Te Deum Laudamus*' – a nice 'enactment' of his unity with his clerics and the Church, and a further witness to his courtly and regal presence.

The royal party now reaches the Mercat Cross: 'in the myddes of the said town was a crosse, new paynted, and ny to that same a fontayne castynge force [28] of wyn, and ychon drank that wold' [fol. 102^v, L. p. 289]. Fountains running with wine are common in civic entries, and usually suggest abundance and festivity (as in the Golden Age?), and perhaps the combination of cross and fountain might add to this secular symbolism a religious dimension in the image of the 'Fountain of Life', the whole then possibly becoming a glimpse of Paradise.[29] Young's complete silence about significance makes speculation dangerous, but the scene might well express the memory of a Golden Age and the hope for its restoration in a peaceful, harmonious and fruitful reign.

It is more difficult to resist the temptation to speculate about the significance(s) of the pageant which was placed close by. It has three 'scenes' (cf. the double pageant from Bruges 1515, fig. 3).[30] On a scaffold are 'represented' (maddeningly, Young does not say how: the 'scaffold' suggests a *tableau vivant*) (i) 'Paris and the thre deessys [31] with Mercure that gaffe hym th'apyll of gold for to gyffe to the most fayre of the thre, wiche he gave to Venus', (ii) 'the salutacyon of Gabriell to the Virgyne in sayinge Ave gracia' and (iii) 'the sollempnizacyon of the varey maryage betwyx the said Vierge and Joseph'. To a modern historicist eye this may seem an 'odd combination', though a mixture of mythological and biblical material would not have been so unusual in the early sixteenth century.[32] Nevertheless, the three are probably united in offering a compliment to the young queen's beauty and virginity. It seems likely that there are other unifying strands which may form a link with other themes in the entry – the fusion or association of the heavenly and the earthly, and the hope for concord.

The Judgment of Paris is not recorded in English pageantry before this time, and seems not to have been a common subject except in northern France or the Low Countries (Lille 1469, Antwerp 1494, Brussels 1496),[33] whence it may have come to Scotland. It appears in England in the 1533 entry of Anne Boleyn, where it was clearly intended to be a piece of flattery: Paris gave the prize not to a goddess but to Anne herself, and this became a standard Elizabethan compliment.[34] Young's words give a general indication of the iconography. Mercury must have been there as he was in the 1496 Brussels pageant (fig. 4)[35] – indeed the Edinburgh 'scene' may have been similar to this. (Paris is often represented sleeping because the medieval accounts have the goddesses appearing to him in a vision or dream.) It is a pity that we do not know more about the manner of the scene's treatment – whether, for instance, the deviser responded, like some of the artists,[36] to the 'romance', magical elements in these versions of the story (in one Middle English romance they are called 'ladies of elfin land'),[37] which would accord with the spirit of the 'Prologue'. In one popular late medieval account, in Lefèvre's *Recueil*, Paris describes how he went hunting, and was led by a great hart away from his companions deep into the forest where he loses sight of the hart, is overcome by weariness, lies down on the grass, falls asleep and sees the vision of Mercury and the goddesses.[38] How tempting it is to associate this magical hunt with the (symbolic?) hunt of the 'Prologue' – but we do not know if the Edinburgh deviser did. Similarly we cannot be sure about the general significance(s) of the scene. Of the traditional interpretations, those which see it as representing a choice of life (e.g. according to Fulgentius, Minerva is the contemplative life, Juno the active, and Venus the sensual)[39] do not seem obviously relevant, at least without further information. It seems more likely that the scene is panegyrical and that we are to see Venus as the type of beauty and Paris as the ideal combination of beauty, intelligence and strength. In legend, of course, the episode was the ultimate cause of the Trojan war, and the apple, the apple of discord. In some humanist writings we find the idea that this ultimately led to concord, with the foundation of Rome.[40] We do not know if this view was known in Scotland, but the idea of concord growing out of an earlier discord would certainly be very appropriate in this entry, which scrupulously (and obviously deliberately) avoids any suggestion of Scottish nationalism (e.g. the figure of the Bruce, whom we shall meet in a later entry), and by implication expresses a hope for peace and harmony between two nations.

The Annunciation is, by contrast, a very common topic. Young does not give any indication of the iconographic type used – e.g. with the angel gallantly kneeling before the Virgin; the Virgin standing in a church with a ray of light coming to her through a window; the angel appearing in the Virgin's bedroom as she kneels in devotion. In the 'Hours of Margaret Tudor',[41] a book which is almost certainly a gift for the new queen, there is a full-page Annunciation (fig. 5) in which the Virgin is shown sitting in a room with her book of devotion open before her while Gabriel with his hand raised in salutation appears behind her, but it would be rash to assume without further evidence that this was how the pattern was used in the entry. On another page in the same MS,[42] where Margaret prays before an altar (with her Tudor greyhound) the Annunciation is shown on the altar by two standing statues. It might be safe to assume that the Annunciation was known to be a favourite with Margaret. No doubt the pattern adopted by the deviser would reflect the emphasis he wished to give the scene: thus, if he wished to emphasise the theme of love[43] or to point a parallel with the earthly queen and her chivalric lover he might have preferred the type with the handsome angel kneeling before her. What is certain is that the Virgin was taken to be the ideal pattern of maidenly beauty and obedience and devoted motherhood (Mary 'was the bride's model and guide, the paragon of motherhood, and God's consort who had been mystically wed at the Annunciation').[44] Various other patterns and parallels might have been found: the Virgin Mary as a lady chosen for her excellence; the Annunciation as a moment of transcendent joy (and perhaps offering a spiritual example of the *merveilleux* found in Paris's vision) or as a moment of stillness and beauty when the earthly and the heavenly is united in concord, and which produces a new concord for humankind, an image of peace on earth.[45] It might well have been seen as a 'heavenly' parallel and pattern for the queen and her joyful love. This would associate it closely with the third scene.

The Marriage of the Virgin is a less common theme. In the north the solemnisation is usually shown happening in the porch of a Gothic church, with a bishop blessing the pair.[46] In a painting in the Prado by the Master of Flémalle this is combined with another scene showing the choosing of Joseph as in the legend in the *Protevangelium*: it is interesting that the ideas of choice and consent run through the three scenes. Sometimes the miracles of Joseph's flowering rod or the dove flying from it are also depicted. The difference in age (Joseph objects that he is 'an old man, but she is a girl') is usually made evident by the artists. Modern panegyric might tactfully obscure the distinct difference in age between James (b. 1473) and Margaret (b. 1489), but in 1503 it may have been either ignored in favour of a larger symbolic meaning or regarded as part of the scene's *merveilleux*. We have here another great moment of concord and love, and a heavenly parallel for a marriage which, it is hoped, will bring peace and prosperity. Furthermore, this scene by implication brings back the king 'into the picture', and presents him and his queen as united in a love which is both earthly and heavenly.

King and queen together move on to the next, and apparently final pageant. On a gate are represented the four Virtues on seats:

> Justice holdynge in hyr haund a swerd all naked, and in the tother a paire of ballaunces, and she had under hyr feet the kyng Neron; Force, that was armed, holdyng in hyr haund a shafte, and under hyr feet was Olofernes, all armed; after, Temperaunce, holdyng in hy[r] haund a bitt of an horse, and under hy[r] feette was [E]pe-curus; after, Prudence, holdynge in hy[r] haund a syerge [candle], and under hyr Sordenopalus [Sardanapalus]. With thos was tabrettes [timbrels] that playd merely whill the noble company past thorough that same, and under was [a] licorne and a greyond that hel[d] a dif-ference of one chardon [thistle] florysched and of a red rose entrelassed.
>
> [fol. 103, L. pp. 289–90][47]

Allegorical pageants like this are frequently found. One in Paris (1514) had an upper stage with four maidens – Pity, Truth, Force, Clemency – with a crown and a fleur-de-lis, and beneath a garden with the king and the pope, guarded at the gate by Peace with Discord under her feet.[48] Again we are not explicitly told that it is a *tableau vivant*, but it rather looks as if the timbrels were played either by the Virtues or by musicians close to them. However, the iconographic pattern of the Virtues trampling beneath their feet the Vices in the form of exemplary historical figures is familiar from the fourteenth century on [49] (see fig. 6, from the Hours of Simon Vostre). The pairing of the Virtues and the examples of Vice (with Tarquin sometimes standing in for Epicurus), and the attributes of the Virtues are traditional and common – with the possible exception of Prudence's candle rather than her usual ser-pent.[50] This of course is 'advice to princes' material, and probably not only didactic but 'prophetic' in expressing a hope for an ideal reign. It is a nice dramatic enactment of the allegorical message that the princes pass through the gate (as if into a Tower of Doctrine) escorted by the joyous music of the timbrels. And as they do, they find the visual culmination of the series in the heraldic and political images above them. Of the animals, the Greyhound is a Tudor badge (which we have seen depicted with Margaret in her Book of Hours – and perhaps earlier as a hunting dog), and the Unicorn is a badge of James (two unicorns appear as the supporters of his arms in the Hours of Margaret Tudor).[51]

The Unicorn also carried a notable symbolic charge and was also associated with hunting, being a fierce animal which could only be captured by a virgin. The 'mystic hunt of the unicorn' shows the angel Gabriel as a hunter blowing an Ave from his horn, while the unicorn rests in the lap of the Virgin Mary. Secular versions of this allegorical depiction of what Rosamund Tuve rightly calls 'power captive to purity'[52] are found in tapestries made for weddings.[53] Whether such suggestions are meant here in addition to the literal heraldic imagery we cannot say. The intertwining of the Thistle and the Rose – a motif repeated in the windows of Holyrood and elsewhere – symbolises the union and the harmony of the two kingdoms.[54]

The cortège finally moves out of the town to its *telos*, Holyrood Abbey, and to a magnificent religious service, which Young describes in great detail (and yet further examples of gallantry from the king).[55] And for a moment Young allows us to catch a glimpse of the crowd and to feel the festival atmosphere of an entry: 'the said town of Edinburgh was in may places haunged with tappissery, the howses full of lordes, ladyes, gentylwomen and gentylmen, and in [the][56] streyttes so grett multitude of people without nombre that it was a fayr thynge to se. The wich people was very glad of the commynge of the sayd qwene; and in the churches of the said town belles rang for myrthe' [fol. 104v, L. p. 291]. This is, incidentally, a nice indication of the successful collaboration – though we know little of its practical details – between the court and the burgh.[57]

This is a most intriguing opening to our series of Scottish entries. An habitué of entries in London or Paris might have thought the pageants rather few in number, but the whole affair is very successful for what seems to be the country's first attempt at an elaborate entry. It sets a pattern in providing a fascinating blend of the traditional and the new. The English visitors would have recognised familiar themes and motifs, but would have found other things strikingly different and probably innovative – the choice of the Judgment of Paris for instance, or the unusually prominent rôle taken by the king himself, displaying himself as a chivalric prince and as a magnificent European monarch. The entry has a remarkable inner coherence, blending celebration, welcome and advice, deliberately avoiding nationalism and any memory of the bloody past, but stressing peace and concord between the king-doms.

In May 1511 Queen Margaret made a ceremonial entry into Aberdeen, The Burgh records reveal civic pride – the queen is to be received 'als honorablie as ony burgh of Scotland, except Edinburgh allanerlie' –

and generous expenditure. For a description of the entry we have to rely on the poem 'Blyth Aberdeane, thow beriall of all tounis' by Dunbar, who seems certainly to have been present at the occasion.[58] The traditional pattern was followed, with the queen being met at the Port by 'ane fair processioun' and conveyed through the streets 'all hung with tapestrie', filled with a great 'pres of peopill' acclaiming her, past a number of pageants and a fountain at the cross running wine, to her lodging, where she was presented with a rich goblet. It is obviously more domestic that the 'international' pageantry of 1503, but it sounds impressive. The queen is welcomed by the sound of artillery, and a rich pall is carried above her head by four strong young men in velvet gowns, 'as the custome hes bein'. There seem to have been six pageants or shows. Dunbar's 'mycht be seine' is not very specific, but his later remark 'pleasant padgeanes *playit* prattelie' might suggest *tableaux vivants* rather than painted scenes. The first three are Biblical and could well have been already in use in processions or plays: the Salutation of the Virgin (with 'the sound of menstrallis blawing to the sky'); the Magi offering their gifts to Christ; and the angel driving Adam and Eve from Paradise 'with sword of violence'. This last, man's punishment 'for innobedience', may possibly link the preceding scenes, which represent the reversal and redemption of man's disobedience, to the next two political pageants. There is first a statement of national identity notably absent from the 1503 entry – the figure of the Bruce 'as roy cum rydand under croun' (*cum* might suggest an actual rider rather than a depiction of one) – and then what seems to be (the text is incomplete) the family tree of the Stewarts 'with branches new and greine'.[59] Finally the queen is met by a company of twenty-four maidens, appropriately arrayed as for a maying, with green clothes, white hats, playing 'timberallis' and singing – a nice festival touch.[60]

For a full description of an Edinburgh entry we have to wait until 1561, but there is evidence of the preparations of what are called 'triumphs' for monarchs. James V married Madeleine, the daughter of the French king, Francis I, on 1 January 1537. David Lindsay, who had been to France for the wedding, was to devise a joyous entry, but her sudden death (7 July) soon after her arrival in Scotland meant that instead a solemn funeral had to be arranged. In his eloquent *Deploratioun of the Deith of Quene Magdalene*[61] he alludes not only to the splendid festivities in Paris, where James was received 'with laud & glorie,/Solempnitlie, throw arkis triumphall', but in some detail to the preparations for the entry into Edinburgh – Death, he says, saw

... makand rycht costlie scaffalding,

> Depayntit weill with Gold and asure fyne,
> Reddie preparit for the vpsetting,
> With Fontanis flowing watter cleir and wyne,
> Disagysit folkis, lyke Creaturis deuyne,
> On ilk scaffold, to play ane syndrie storie ...

Besides these examples of the *merveilleux*, he describes the citizens who would have met and/or escorted the queen: craftsmen dressed in 'schort clething of grene' carrying bows, burgesses, the Provost and baillies, lords of Parliament, all in splendid garments, and the 'Lordis of Religioun' and the 'cunnyng Clerkis honorable' who would have walked 'full plesandlie in thare Processioun'. Passing through the town, under a pall of gold carried by the burgesses 'clothit in silkis fyne', and accompanied by the heralds and the mace-bearers 'vpon ather of thare handis,/To rewle the preis, with burneist siluer wandis', Madeleine in her resplendent attire ('of Gold, and perle, and precious stonis brycht/Twynkling lyke sterris in ane frostie nycht') would have heard 'the din of instrumentis, the cries of '*Vive la Royne*' 'with ane Harmonious sound Angelicall,/In euerilk corner, myrthis Musicall', and listened to orations saluting her before her coronation in 'the fair Abbey of the Holy rude'. 'The day of her entrace' would have been a veritable triumph. In these twelve stanzas another herald with first-hand experience gives us what is the most impressive evocation of a splendid Scottish entry in the period, and invaluable information to help flesh out the brief accounts, such as the attendants keeping order with their 'wandis' and the formal giving of 'greit propynis' or presents to the visitor. In this idealised scene burgh and court and religion exist in joyous harmony.

Although the cruel tyrant Death swept all this festivity away, it is likely that much of it was reproduced for the entry of the king's second wife, Mary of Guise, in 1538,[62] since Lindsay is among the persons directed to 'answer for' the various stations. But we do not know anything more about the 'disagysit folkis' and their pageants. Lindsay was clearly skilled in such things, for it is recorded that when Mary landed on the Fife coast and was received at St Andrews there was a show devised by him:

> quhilk caussit ane greit clude come out of the heavins done abone
> the ʒeit quhair the quene come in, and oppin in two halffis instant-
> lie and thair appeirit ane fair lady most lyke ane angell havand the
> keyis of haill Scotland in hir handis deliuerand thame into the quens
> grace in signe and taikin that all the heartis of Scotland was opnit
> to the ressawing of hir grace; witht certane wriesouns and exorta-
> tiouns maid by the said Schir Dawid Lyndsay into the quens grace

instructioun quhilk teichit hir to serue her god, obey hir husband, and keep hir body clene according to goddis will and commandement.[63]

This is the traditional opening pageant of welcome which was to live on; the uplifting 'exortatiouns' were also to flourish. 'The triumphe and play at the Marriage of the Quenis Grace' at Edinburgh in 1558 celebrating Mary Stewart's wedding to the Dauphin seems to have included a play or a masque involving the seven planets and Cupid (William Adamsoun was paid for writing a part of the play and William Lawder for 'the making of the play and wrytting thairof').[64] But there were also, it seems, some traditional elements (suggested by payments for wine to run from the Cross and for the 'players of the skafferts') beside some intriguing ones – payments for two leather skins for a pair of breeks for the grey friar, for a fool with a coat, for fireballs, and for summer trees with 'birkis about thame' on the Nether Bow and Butt and the Nether Tron. Even these scraps of information suggest a continuing inventiveness.

New developments in religion and religious politics were soon to be reflected in civic pageantry. The reformers had had hopes of favour from Madeleine, but Mary of Guise was 'all papist' as was her daughter Mary Stewart. There are signs of the changing 'climate of opinion' in London entries in 1533 and 1554. The first, of Anne Boleyn, was by implication celebrating a change in religious politics, but the pageants themselves were in no way tendentious – though there is a notable absence of the old traditional religious pageants (only St Anne, with her progeny the three Maries, appears in one of the many praising the new queen) and a cautiously secular tone (with a number of classical subjects, including the Judgment of Paris). In the 1554 welcome for King Philip of Spain, the husband of Queen Mary, we have clear evidence of religious tension. In one pageant in which Henry VIII and Edward VI were shown together with the Nine Worthies, Henry was shown with a sceptre in one hand and a book 'whereon was wrytten *verbum Dei*' in the other. According to one chronicler this implied slight 'agaynst the quenes catholicke proceedinges' provoked the fury of Bishop Gardiner, who threatened the painter and made him repaint it with a new pair of gloves instead of the book (or – in the elaborated version of Foxe the martyrologist – the unfortunate painter in his fear wiped out a part of Henry's fingers as well!).[65] This reminds us of the dramatic moment in Lindsay's *Ane Satyre of the Thrie Estaitis* (1552) when Dame Veritie brings in the New Testament 'in Englisch toung' (ll. 1100 ff.)

Religious strife made the 'ambiguous triumph' for Mary Stewart in Edinburgh in 1561 [66] a less harmonious affair than the entry of 1503. The opposition of civic power and royal power was reflected even in the topography, since the palace of Holyrood was not, like Notre Dame or St Paul's in the 'heart' of the city: 'the basic sequence was that of castle, burgh and palace, and the civic part of the event was in a sense an interlude within an otherwise royalist occasion'. [67] Mary's influence in France had disappeared with the death of her husband Francis II in December 1560, and her power in Scotland was uncertain. The internal situation was uneasy: the Protestants had apparently triumphed in 1560, but much of the pre-Reformation hierarchy was still in place. In 1561 there was an enactment for the 'destruction of all places and monuments of idolatry', and although Mary declared that she 'meant to constrain none of her subjects' in religion, her practice of having mass said in her private chapel alarmed and infuriated Knox, who preached a fierce sermon in St Giles on the Sunday before the entry was due to be held (Tuesday 2 September) denouncing 'idolatry'.

In traditional manner, Mary entered at the West Port and went up the hill to the castle. She was met by fifty young men dressed as 'Moors', their arms and legs coloured black, wearing black visors, black hats, and gold chains on their arms and legs. Possibly they 'symbolised exotic forces of disorder which had to be tamed by the authority of a Christian ruler'; [68] possibly we should (in the absence of further information) simply regard them as exotic – like the Black Lady in James IV's tournament of June 1507, at which some attendants were dressed as 'wild men' with harts' horns and goatskins. She was also met by sixteen citizens in velvet gowns who were to carry the pall over her. A 'propyne' was presented, which was placed in a cart and accompanied her. At the Butter Tron (weighing machine) there was a wooden port, brightly coloured and hung with arms, and children singing 'in the most hevenlie wyis'. As she passed through, a cloud opened and a 'barne' descended 'as it had bene ane angell,' who delivered the keys of the town to her before ascending again. This traditional example of *merveilleux*, however, differed strikingly from its equivalent in 1503. The queen was not greeted by processions of clerics with relics, and with the keys she was presented with 'ane bybill and ane psalme buik'. [69] According to the verse speech of welcome these two books, which showed 'the perfytt waye vnto the heavens hie', were 'trewlie translated'. Clearly the presentation of vernacular scriptures was an unusually pointed 'comment' – according to Knox, 'the verses of hir awin praise sche heard and smyled', but 'when the Bible was presented, and the praise thairof declared, sche began to frown' but 'for schame she could not refuise it'.

At the Tolbooth there were two scaffolds, one above the other. In the upper was Fortune, beneath were three virgins – Love, Justice, and Policy. There was also 'ane litell speitche'. We are back into the advice to princes material, though now placed in a very different context. At the Mercat Cross were four fair virgins 'cled in the maist hevenlie clothing': they were probably the four cardinal virtues, as in 1503, but no details are recorded. Wine ran 'in greit abundance' from the spouts, and 'thair wes the noyiss of pepill casting the glasses with wyne' – the traditional expression of the hope for good governance and prosperity. However the next pageant, at the Salt Tron, seems to have been particularly forthright. There were some speeches and something was burnt on the scaffold in 'the maner of ane sacrifice'. Accounts differ, but it seems to have been directed against the Mass. According to one, an effigy of a priest in vestments ready to say Mass was thrown into a fire; according to another 'thei were mynded to have had a priest burnt at the altar, at the elevation', but 'the Erle of Huntly stayed that pagient', and what was represented were the wicked Korah, Dathan and Abiram (punished by being swallowed in the earth according to Numbers 16), presumably as an exemplum of 'idolatry'. Whatever happened it was an audacious and to some an offensive piece of Reformation propaganda: 'a pageant that seemed to many ridiculous, but to the French it seemed contemptible'; 'diverslie constructed, according to men's humours, either to derision, contempt, or presumption; and everie man thought it needles'. In the final pageant at the Nether Bow there were speeches, and a dragon burnt on a scaffold, and afterwards a psalm was sung. The dragon was most certainly the dragon or one of the beasts of the Apocalypse (esp. chapters 12–13, 17), taken as a figure of Antichrist, and often in Reformation propaganda representing the Pope or the Roman Church.[70] In an illustration in the 1534 Luther Bible (fig. 7) it wears a papal tiara. If the 'woman clothed with the sun' appeared with the seven-headed dragon (as in the Luther Bible, fig. 8), it might have even more offensively suggested Mary herself and her future progeny – but there is no record of this, and if the previous pageant was indeed modified it would suggest that this would have been too extreme. Even at the end, at Holyrood, the unfortunate queen had to endure yet another speech 'concernyng the putting away of the Mass'.

The 'triumph' of 1561 is perhaps the most extraordinary royal entry recorded.[71] It would be hard to find a more extreme or intense example of a tendentious 'message' being given to a monarch. It is a remarkable display of self-confidence on the part of the burgh: here the monarch, though praised (Knox sourly says that 'whatsoever mYght sett furth hir glory, that sche heard, and glaidlye beheld'), is – in striking contrast to James IV – cast in a passive role. The traditional co-operation of court and burgh seems virtually to have vanished. Compared to 1503 there seems also to have been a shrinking of intellectual boundaries: this is a civic rather than a national festival. And not only have the Catholic pageants disappeared, so have the classical ones. But what has been lost in subtlety and suggestiveness is balanced by an audacious originality. And that in 1561 it was still a magnificent show in the French manner is strongly suggested in the critical remark of Knox: 'in ferses, in masking, and in other prodigalities, faine wold fooles have counterfooted France.'

Different again is the entry of the young James VI to Edinburgh in October 1579, though the accounts are brief, and much of the detail remains unknown.[72] The city was cleaned and decorated as usual, and the 'violeris' and 'sangsteris' performed above the Overbow. At the West Port the king was met by the 'honest men of Edinburgh' in black gowns with a pall (there is no mention of the Moors of 1561, though we cannot be certain that they did not appear – as they did in 1590), and saw a tableau (of an unspecified kind) of the 'wisdom of Solomon'. This apparently new subject was a depiction of the Judgment of Solomon [3 Kings 3: 16–28]: King Solomon 'was representit with the tua wemen that contendit for the young childe', and after the judgment was presented with the sword 'for one hand, and the scepter for the uther.'[73] It is clearly related to the advice to princes pattern in entries. A more traditional scene followed at the Overbow: there appeared out of a globe 'ane bony boy' (presumably an angel?) who delivered the silver keys of the town to James to the accompaniment of 'melodious singing'. At the Tolbooth were four ladies – Peace, Justice, Plenty and Policy – who spoke to the King. After a brief church service (at the instigation of Dame Religion, according to one account), he moved on to the Mercat Cross, where not only did wine pour 'abundantly' from all the spouts, but 'the storie of Bacchus' ('distributing of his liquor to all his passingers and behalders') was represented. At the Salt Tron was painted the genealogy of the Kings of Scotland. At the Nether Bow were the Seven Planets, who 'rang the tyme of the kingis birth', and 'King Ptolomaeus' who interpreted the scene. The stairs of the houses along the way were adorned with 'images and fine tapestries' and the streets were spread with flowers. Finally at Cannon Cross was a pageant tantalizingly entitled 'ane breiff fabill for abbolisching of the paip and of the mess'.[74] This is the only relic of the strongly Protestant material which had been deployed eighteen years earlier. Its final position perhaps suggest that it is meant as a warning against the perils and disharmony which might still threaten. Bergeron's criticism that it is difficult to perceive any thematic unity in the entry is hard to sustain. In the usual manner it combines advice for the prince with a festive welcome celebrating his fortunate birth and expressing the hope for prosperity and peace. And it has the happy combination of old and new which we have seen in the earlier entries.

The last Scottish entry of the century was held in May 1590 to welcome James's new queen, Anne of Denmark, whom he had married by proxy in Copenhagen in August 1589.[75] To the disappointment of the Provost and the burgesses, apparently, it was postponed for two days after the coronation on Sunday 17 May because some of the ministers argued that the pageants and devices would profane the Sabbath, but apart from this there is little evidence of Kirk influence. The traditional route and the traditional pattern were followed. The Queen was welcomed with a great volley of shot from the castle. As she passed under the West Port, she paused to hear a Latin oration given by John Russell, whose son played the role of the angel in the first pageant: he 'being placed uppon the toppe of the Port head, and was let downe by a devise made in a globe [perhaps that of 1579], which being come somewhat over her Maiesties heade, opened at the toppe into foure quarters, where the childe, appearing in the resemblance of an angell, delivered her the keyes of the towne in silver; which done the quarters closed, and the globe was taken uppe agayne, so as the childe was no more seene there.'[76]

This example of the *merveilleux* was the prelude to an entry of great splendour. Six ancient townsmen held a canopy of purple velvet over her, while she was escorted by the Provost and baillies riding, and 'three score young men of the towne, lyke Moores'. These Moors were evidently dazzling, though since the accounts of this entry give much more detail than in 1561, it would be rash to claim that they were more so than their predecessors. We are told that they were 'clothed in cloth of silver, with chaines about their neckes, and bracelets about their armes, set with diamonds and other precious stones, very gorgeous to the eie', and 'went before the [queen's] chariot, ... everie one wiith a white staffe in his hande, to keepe of the throng of people' (here, apparently, acting as agents of order rather than disorder). Another source says that they wore black visors and danced before the queen. The 'Moirs' ('quha dois inhabit in the ynds'), 'thir savagis', says the enthusiastic verse account of John Burel, 'fra top to tae I you assure/ Thair corps with gold wes birnist bricht.' They led her to a new pageant at the Bow Street. It continues the interest in the world outside Britain: there 'was erected a table, whereupon stoode a Globe of the whole Worlde, with a boy sitting thereby, who represented the person of a King, and made an oration.'

At the Butter Tron 'were placed nine maidens, brauely arraied in cloth of silver and gold, representing the nine Muses, who sung verie sweete musicke, where a brave youth played upon the organs, which accorded excellentlie with the singing of their psalmes; whereat her Maiestie staied a while.' This pageant, apparently making its appearance for the first time, presents her with an image of harmony, both heavenly and earthly. From here she passed down the High Street, which was all decked with tapestry. For the first time we have an account which tells us something about the house decorations which seem to have been a feature of earlier pageants also: Burel mentions both classical subjects – Venus enclosing Achates and Aeneas with a 'mekill mistie clud', Anna 'wondrous wrath' deploring 'hir sister Didos daith', Poly-phemus, Janus with double face, Icarus, Medusa, Achilles, Mercury and Argus – and Biblical – Jephtha, Jael and Sisera. At the Tolbooth she encountered the old favourite 'advice to princes' pageant of the four virtues, presumably depicted now in a more Renaissance style,[77] but with the traditional iconography: Justice with the balance in one hand and the sword in the other, Temperance with a cup of water in one hand and a cup of wine in the other, Prudence with a serpent and a dove 'declaring, that men ought to bee as wise as the serpent ... but as simple as the dove', and Fortitude, holding a broken pillar, 'repre-senting the strength of a kingdome.'

After a church service, the party came to the Mercat Cross. On the top was a table 'whereupon stood cups of gold and silver full of wine, with the Goddesse of Corne and Wine[78] sitting thereat, and the corne in heaps by her, who, in Latin, cried that there should be plentie thereof in her time; and on the side of the crosse sate the god Bacchus upon a puncheon of wine,[79] winking and casting it by cups full upon the people, besides other of the townsmen, that cast apples and nuts among them' while the cross ran with claret wine. The traditional hope for prosperity and the return of a golden age is here given visual and aural form in a way which combines the popular and the learned. The next pageant, at the Salt Tron, stressed the national identity of Scotland. It showed the earlier kings of Scotland seated, 'one of them lying along at their feete, as if he had been sick, whom certain souldiers seemed to awake at her Majesties comming, whereupon he arose, and made to her an oration in Latine ...' – a nice panegyrical and complimentary welcome, suggesting perhaps the revival of the past glories of the kingdom. Finally, at the Nether Bow was a pageant showing the marriage of 'a king and his quene', with a child giving an explanatory speech relating it to that of James and Anne. Here the town's gift was presented to the queen in a more poetic and magical way than in 1561: a box 'esteemed at twentie thousand crownes' was lowered from the scaffold on a silken string, and all was brought to an end with the singing of psalms, 'with verie good musicke.'

Once again it is noticeable how the claims of religion have been relegated to the background, and how its retreat is marked by the advance of secular and classical topics. This entry is a magnificent and an ingenious climax to the century's pageantry. It is difficult to agree with Bergeron's criticisms, that 'this royal entry resembles in so many details the earlier ones made by Mary and James into Edinburgh: it is as if the pageant imagination is bankrupt', and that it appears 'disjointed'. The 'continuity' between one entry and the next is both traditional and in itself meaningful, but it is not a slavish repetition: there are new pageants, and new emphases. And it is, in fact, completely coherent, combining in the traditional manner celebration and 'advice', and coming to a natural climax in the portrayal of the royal marriage.

Scottish entries may not have been as elaborate as some English and European examples, but they seem to be well thought out and well presented. In them we can see some very interesting variations on the traditional pattern of ideas and in the 'dialogue' between monarch and subject. They are diverse and genuinely original. Scotland quite clearly produced its own distinctive 'festival literature', and its entries, while never heavily nationalistic, discreetly and proudly reveal a sense of national identity.

1. On entries in general see the following: S. Anglo, *Spectacle, Pageantry and Early Tudor Policy* (Oxford, 1969); D. M. Bergeron, *English Civic Pageantry 1558–1642* (1971); D. A. Bullough, 'Games People Played: Drama and Ritual as Propaganda in Medieval Europe', *TRHS* 5th ser. 24 (1974), 97–122; J. Chartrou, *Les entrées solenelles et triumphales à la Renaissance (1484–1551)* (Paris, 1928); B. Guenée and F. Lehoux, *Les entrées royales français de 1328 à 1515* (Paris, 1968); J. Heers, *Fêtes, jeux et joutes dans les sociétés d'occident à la fin du moyen-age* (Montreal and Paris, 1971); J. Jacquot (ed.), *Les fêtes de la Renaissance*, 2 vols (Paris, 1956, 1960); G. R. Kernodle, *From Art to Theatre: Form and Convention in the Renaissance* (Chicago, 1944); G. Kipling, 'Triumphal Drama: Form in English Civic Pageantry', *Renaissance Drama*, 8 (1977), 37–56; R. Strong, *Splendour at Court* (1973), and *Art and Power: Renaissance Festivals 1450–1650* (Woodbridge, 1984); G. Wickham, *Early English Stages 1300 to 1660*, 2 vols (London and New York, 1959, 1963): R. Withington, *English Pageantry. An Historical Outline*, 2 vols (Cambridge, Mass, 1918–20). On Scotland, see A. J. Mill, *Mediaeval Plays in Scotland* (Edinburgh and

London, 1927); L. Fradenburg, *City, Marriage, Tournament: Arts of Rule in Late Medieval Scotland* (Madison, 1991); A. A. MacDonald, 'Mary Stewart's Entry to Edinburgh: an Ambiguous Triumph', *IR*, 42 (1991), 101–10.

2. Strong, *Art and Power*, p. 176.

3. Anglo, p. 3, and pp. 56–97. See also *The Receyt of the Ladie Kateryne*, ed. G. Kipling, EETS, 296 (1990).

4. *Secular Ritual*, ed. Sally F. Moore and Barbara G. Myerhoff (Assen, Amsterdam, 1977), p. 5.

5. Guenée and Lehoux, p. 29.

6. At Lucca, for instance, Charles VIII saw a 'portal triumphant a lançienne façon' (*Mer des Histories* (1500), fol. cclxxvi^v). Such arches, like those devised by the emperor Maximilian (see *The Triumph of Maximilian I. 137 Woodcuts by Hans Burgkmair and Others*, New York, 1964), became more common in the north during the sixteenth century.

7. Jacquot I, p. 4.

8. The *Journal d'un bourgeois de Paris*, for instance, says that when the French king entered Paris in 1437 one of the things he saw was 'a representation of the Passion, as it was done for the little King Henry when he was consecrated in Paris' (trans. Janet Shirley, *A Parisian Journal 1405–1449*, Oxford, 1968, p. 319; French text ed. A. Tuetey, Paris, 1881).

9. And sometimes they saw themselves impersonated. In Paris in 1431, Henry VI saw himself represented by a boy of his age and build *(Journal* trans. Shirley, p. 270). See also *L'entrée de Henri II à Rouen 1550*, ed. M. M. McGowan (Amsterdam, 1979). In Scotland this happens in the 1590 entry of James VI and Anne of Denmark, p. 31 above.

10. Shirley, p. 201.

11. Ibid., p. 269.

12. Anglo, p. 197.

13. Marie-Françoise Christout, *Le merveilleux et le théâtre du silence* (The Hague, 1965).

14. Moore and Myerhoff, pp. 16–17.

15. Heers, p. 11 (in a chapter entitled 'La Fête, affirmation des valeurs sociales et politiques').

16. Strong, *Splendour at Court*, p. 23.

17. Guenée and Lehoux, p. 8.

18. 'Of Praise', quoted by Wickham, I, p. 80. Earlier, in 1504, Erasmus writes to Desmarez, arguing that panegyrics are not 'nothing but flattery': their aim 'consists in presenting princes with a pattern of goodness, in such a way as to reform bad rulers, improve the good, educate the boorish, reprove the erring, arouse the indolent, and cause even the hopelessly vicious to feel some inward stirrings of shame' (*The Correspondence of Erasmus – Letters 142–297*, trans. R. A. B. Mynors and D. F. S. Thomson, Toronto, 1975, p. 81.)

19. R. Wangermée, *Flemish Music and Society in the Fifteenth and Sixteenth Centuries*, trans. R. E. Wolf (New York, London, 1968), p. 176 and fig. 6 (from the account of the historiographer Rémi du Puys). It nicely combines two traditional images – the garden of the realm, and music as the image of harmony in the state.

20. Shirley, p. 320.

21. See Anglo, pp. 22–32.

22. Ibid., pp. 32–4.

23. Kernodle, p. 69.

24. Shirley, pp. 200, 201. Our rather 'official' accounts do not reveal much about

cases where 'indeterminacy' or the chaos of life were not successfully ordered, where things went wrong (a rare glimpse is the description in the *Journal d'un bourgeois* of a dinner after the entry of Henry VI to Paris in 1431 at which the common people got in and misbehaved, and 'the food was very bad' – 'the English were in charge of all this', Shirley, pp. 271–2). Nor do we know how much of the more elaborate symbolism people understood. At Rouen in 1550 the Queen was absorbed, but some of the onlookers seem not to have understood the significance of what they were watching (McGowan, pp. 23–4). Sometimes, too, people might find unintended interpretations: the Protestant Foxe satirically identifies Orpheus (London, 1554) with Philip of Spain and 'all English people resembled to brute and savage beasts following after Orpheus's harp, and dancing after king Philip's pipe' (Anglo, p. 334).

25. John Yonge or Young (d. between 4 March and 21 May 1516), Falcon pursuivant (1 March 1486), Somerset Herald (1493), Norroy Herald (1511). In 1502 he was with an embassy to Hungary and attended the wedding of Wladislas II and Anne de Foix. For his journey to Edinburgh new tabards were supplied for him and for Bluemantle at a cost of 33s 4d (note his comment p. 18, above); he apparently stayed in Edinburgh for two years after the wedding. His account is printed in Hearne's additions to Leland's *Collectanea* (2nd edn., 1774) IV, pp. 265–300. There are two MSS, one a seventeenth-century copy (see Kipling, *Receyt*, pp. xxxi–xxxv). My quotations are from the College of Arms MS 1 M. 13, fols 76–115^v (with the punctuation modernised and abbreviations expanded). I am grateful to the College of Arms for allowing me to consult this MS. For a detailed and interesting, though speculative, discussion of this entry, see Fradenburg, pp. 91–122.

26. Chaucer, *Book of the Duchess*, l. 1313. See M. Thiébaux, *The Stag of Love: The Chase in Medieval Literature* (Ithaca, N. Y., 1974). R. van Marle, *Iconographie de l'art profane au moyen-age et à la Renaissance* (La Haye, 1932) II, Allégories et Symboles, fig. 125, shows a stag pursued by the hounds Desio and Pensier.

27. See Guenée and Lehoux, pp. 20–3. In 1503 this may have been at the site of the Bristo Port: see I. Campbell, 'James IV and Edinburgh's First Triumphal Arches' in *The Architecture of Scottish Cities and Towns*, ed. D. Mays (East Linton, 1997), pp. 27 and 33, n. 9.

28. L. reads forth, but I think the MS has force (*OED* sb^1 sense 10a 'plenty, large quantity').

29. As in London, 1432. See D. Gray, 'The Five Wounds of Our Lord', *NQ*, 208 (1963), 166; H. N. MacCracken, 'King Henry's triumphal entry into London, Lydgate's poem, and Carpenter's letter', *Archiv*, 126 (1910–11), 89–92. But it is perhaps rash to say that Edinburgh is representing itself 'as a heavenly place' (Fradenburg, p. 109).

30. On the left Moses is giving the tables of the Law, on the right Louis de Nevers is giving privileges to the city of Bruges.

31. Fr. *deessys* probably came easily to a herald (cf. *chardon, vierge,* etc.) and probably does not represent a Fr. *titulus.*

32. The Brussels entry of 1496 combined a profusion of Biblical pageants with scenes from history and antiquity (see Max Herrmann, *Forschungen zur deutschen Theatergeschichte des Mittelalters und der Renaissance*, Berlin 1914, pp. 367 ff.). 'This mixture of pagan and Christian themes is characteristic of the entrées of the early sixteenth-century' (F. Wormald, 'The Solemn Entry of Mary Tudor to Montreuil-sur-Mer in 1514', *Essays presented to Hilary Jenkinson* ed. J. Conway Davies, 1957, p. 473). Cf. Chartrou, pp. 22–4, 43. For a Venetian example, see E. Muir, *Civic Ritual in Venice* (Princeton, 1981), pp. 172–3.

33. Kernodle, p. 66. James IV had hangings or tapestries with the 'history of Troy town' (L. pp. 295–6).

34. Anglo, pp. 255–6. T. S. Graves '*The Arraignment of Paris* and Sixteenth-Century Flattery', *MLN*, 28 (1913), 48–9. See E. Wind, *Pagan Mysteries in the Renaissance* (1958; enlarged and revised edn., Harmondsworth, 1967), p. 82. ('Our Lorenzo', according to Ficino, adored all three goddesses according to their merits, 'whence he received wisdom from Pallas, power from Juno, and from Venus grace and poetry and music'). For an earlier (eleventh-century) connection with the panegyric, see Margaret J. Ehrhart, *The Judgement of the Trojan Prince Paris in Medieval Literature* (Philadelphia, 1987), pp. 174–5.

35. Berlin, Kupferstichkabinett, MS 78 D 5, fol. 57 (the MS has illustrations of the Brussels pageants, shown as scenes (*lebende Bilder*) on raised stages or scaffolds). It is impossible to know if part of the attraction was the 'naive, popular sensuality' of such scenes (J. Huizinga, *Herfstij der Middeleeuwen*, 2nd edn., 1921, pp. 550–1): he quotes Jean de Roye's appreciative description of the naked mermaids in a pageant in Paris in 1461, and Molinet (*Chronique*, ed. Buchon, *Collection des chroniques nationales françaises* V, Paris, 1824, p. 15) who notes that at Antwerp in 1494 the pageant of the three goddesses represented by nude girls excited the most interest among the people; at Lille they also seem to have been nude, wearing golden crowns (though there was apparently a parodic element here, with a fat Venus, a gaunt Juno and a hunch-backed Minerva).

36. See M. R. Scherer, *The Legends of Troy in Art and Literature* (New York, 1964), figs 11, 12.

37. *The Seege or Batayle of Troye*, ed. M. E. Barnicle, EETS, 172 (1927), l. 508.

38. In Caxton's version (*The Recuyell of the Historyes of Troy*, ed. H. O. Sommer 1899, pp. 520–2). The dream after the hunt is in Dares and is widely found.

39. On these interpretations, see Ehrhart, chapter 5, Fradenburg, pp. 110–14, Anne Moss, *Poetry and Fable. Studies in Mythological Narrative in Sixteenth-Century France* (Cambridge, 1984), esp. chap. 2.

40. See Wind, pp. 197n., 270–1, for a woodcut by Burgkmair, invented by the humanist Conrad Celtes, in which Discordia gives the apple of strife to Paris, while on the other side Mercury 'lifts the caduceus as the emblem of concord', with the inscription *errando discitur philosophia*, and for Raphael's design of the scene as 'an epiphany, a mysterious communion between mortal and gods', where concord arises out of discord, but only for a fleeting moment. On Ficino's Venus as 'the pleasure principle underlying all human endeavour' and Jean Lemaire des Belges, who takes the scene as instruction for young princes in general, and sees Venus as beneficent, associating her with the concord of the elements, since the 'machine totalle' of the world would fall in ruin if it were deprived of her loving harmony, see Moss, esp. pp. 20–5. Possibly the Edinburgh devisers may have been more familiar with the older versions of these ideas, of Venus working in harmony with Nature (as she proclaims in the Judgment scene in Lydgate's *Reason and Sensuality* (1847 ff.) or as a principle of power and concord in the universe (see Chaucer, *Troilus and Criseyde* III, 8–30).

41. See the full description of the MS (now in Vienna) by Leslie Macfarlane 'The Book of Hours of James IV and Margaret Tudor', *IR*, 11 (1960) 3–20 and the facsimile *Das Gebetbuch Jakobs IV von Schottland und seiner Gemahlin Margaret Tudor*, ed. Franz Unterkircher (Graz, 1987).

42. Macfarlane, pl. III.

43. As in Henryson's poem on this subject.

44. Muir p. 142.

45. The Montreuil entry of Mary Tudor (1514), which also stresses the restoration

of peace and concord between two previously warring nations, also uses the Marriage of the Virgin and the Angelic Salutation, explicitly linking heavenly and earthly peace: 'ou estoit escript Fiat michi secundum verbum tuum. Le gendre humain delivré; qui representoit le mariage du Roy a la Royne Marie par lequel le poure peuple estoit delivré de la subgection de la guerre mere de tous maulx' (Wormald, p. 477).

46. A handsome French example in a Book of Hours made for Isabel Stewart, the daughter of King James I, who married the Duke of Brittany in 1445 (Fitzwilliam Museum MS 62), is reproduced by M. R. James in his Catalogue (Cambridge, 1895, plate xiii, no. 307). In Raphael's 'Lo Sposalizio' (Brera, Milan) the scene takes place in front of a temple.

47. hy[r] MS hys; MS ?Opecurus; MS and deleted; MS helded.

48. Kernodle, fig. 37 (BL MS Cotton Vespasian B ii); see also fig. 36 from the same series, showing musicians behind. The four cardinal virtues are common: see, for instance, Lydgate's *Mumming at London* (*Minor Poems* II, ed. H. N. MacCracken, EETS, 1934, pp. 682–91).

49. See M. Evans 'Tugenden und Laster' in *Lexikon der Christlichen Ikonographie* IV (1972), cols 388–9; R. Tuve, 'Notes on the Virtues and Vices', *JWCI*, 26 (1963), 264–303. R. van Marle, II, fig. 12 shows Justice crushing Nero.

50. See above, p. 30. That Young misinterpreted the image is unlikely, since he is very precise here, and Prudence has a candle in a fourteenth-century Italian poem on the Virtues (*La Canzone delle Virtù e delle Scienze di Bartolomeo di Bartoli da Bologna*, ed. L. Dorez, Bergamo, 1904). Dr J. S. and Mrs P. H. Richardson point out to me that Aquinas (*Summa Theol*. 2.2 qu. 47 art. 1) refers to Isidore's relevant etymology: 'prudens dicitur, quasi porro videns, perspicax enim est, et incertorum praevidet casus.'

51. See Macfarlane, Plates I and II. Unicorns support the royal arms in the treaty of the marriage (which has an adorned margin composed of roses, thistles, and marguerites entwined, and below the arms the letters I. M. in gold entwined with a love-knot beneath a jewelled crown); *Accounts of the Lord High Treasurer of Scotland AD 1500–1504*, ed. Sir James Balfour Paul (Edinburgh, 1900), p. lviii.

52. R. Tuve, 'Notes on the Virtues and Vices', *JWCI*, 27 (1964), 42–72 (62–3).

53. Surviving examples are in the Musée de Cluny and the Cloisters Museum (the latter thought probably to be for the marriage of Anne of Britanny and Louis XII in 1499).

54. Young (L. p. 295). It seems that James IV was the first Scottish monarch to make extensive use of the thistle as badge; see P. Bawcutt, 'Dunbar's Use of the Symbolic Lion and Thistle', *Cosmos* 2 (1986) 83–97. Campbell, p. 29, argues that this gate was a triumphal arch.

55. See Young, L. p. 290.

56. the] MS the, deleted.

57. *The Treasurer's Accounts* list payments for splendid clothes, for the furnishing of the queen's apartment, tapestries, pavilions, gold for the royal arms on the gate at Holyrood; payments for minstrels including (p. 387) 'the thre menstrales of Berwik', 'the Inglis spelair, that playit the supersalt', 'the bere ledair of Inglond', 'the five lowd menstrales', etc.

58. *The Poems of William Dunbar* ed. J. Kinsley (Oxford, 1979), no. 48; see P. Bawcutt, *Dunbar the Makar* (Oxford, 1992), pp. 89–92.

59. The words 'gart upspring', if taken literally, might suggest a mechanical marvel. Guenée and Lehoux note a Jesse tree turning on an axle at Lyon in 1476. As they say, this originally religious subject became 'un des thèmes favoris de la religion royale' (p. 28n.). It is found at London in 1432 with two other trees demonstrating the young

king Henry's descent from St Edward and St Louis. In 1554 for Philip of Spain a 'most excellent' pageant was devised showing the English royal genealogy from Edward III: there was 'a great arboure or tree'; under its root lay an old man with a long white beard, wearing a crown and carrying a sceptre, who represented Edward III; on the branches above sat his descendants depicted as children, and at the very top a king and a queen representing Philip and Mary (Anglo, pp. 334–5).

60. In 1515 when Albany was 'received' into Edinburgh Leslie mentions 'sindrie farcis and gude playis' put on by the burgesses in his honour (*The History of Scotland*, ed. E. G. Cody, 2 vols, STS, Edinburgh, 1895, II, pp. 156–7). Other towns staged royal entries during the century, but the records do not give details; see Mill, p. 78. In January 1561/2, Queen Mary was 'honourably received' in Aberdeen 'with spectacles, interludes, and other things as they could best devise' (Mill, pp. 159–60).

61. See *The Works of Sir David Lindsay*, ed. D. Hamer, 4 vols, STS (Edinburgh, and London, 1931–4), I, pp. 106–112.

62. Mill, pp. 82, 179–80.

63. Ibid., p. 287.

64. Ibid., pp. 183–8.

65. Anglo, pp. 329–30.

66. See esp. MacDonald, 'Mary Stewart's Entry to Edinburgh' (which contains the text of the verse speech of welcome); see also Mill, pp. 189–91.

67. MacDonald, 103.

68. Ibid., 105. Moors and (Highland) wild men figured in the 1566 celebrations at Stirling (see M. Lynch, 'Queen Mary's Triumph: the Baptismal Celebrations at Stirling in December 1566', *SHR*, 69 (1990), 1–21). Here the Moors seem to have worn bonnets made of lambs' skins. This was an outdoor show: Moors frequently appeared in indoor festivities where (with blackened faces) they often danced 'moresques' (see Wangermée, p. 158 and fig. 63, Anglo p. 177). Edward VI himself took part in a masque of Moors in 1548 (Anglo, p. 301–2). At Rouen in 1550 there was an elaborate scene involving fifty naked Brazilians in a replica of a jungle island (see the illustration in McGowan). On the Black Lady, see Fradenburg, pp. 229 ff.

69. Mill, pp. 189–90.

70. See, for example, R. W. Scribner, *For the Sake of Simple Folk* (Cambridge, 1981), figs 143–5, 149.

71. In striking contrast is the baptismal celebration of 1566 (a court rather than a civic festival), which was a triumphant Renaissance *magnificence* involving an assault on an enchanted castle and various classical pageants, and which presented Mary as hero and reconciler (Catholic and Protestant noblemen carried white staffs, 'the traditional emblem of reconciliation of feud,' Lynch, 101).

72. See Mill, pp. 193–5; Bergeron, pp. 66–7.

73. See Mill, p. 193, n. 2.

74. It is impossible to say what this consisted of: for early sixteenth-century German Protestant prints, see Scribner figs 45, 135; see also John N. King, *Tudor Royal Iconography* (Princeton, 1989), fig. 53. The sixteenth-century English painting in the National Portrait Gallery called 'Edward VI and the Pope' or 'An Allegory of the Reformation under Edward VI' (King, figs 22–3) shows the Pope at the boy king's feet with a book above his head (which has apparently knocked him down) with the *titulus* 'The Worde of the Lord endureth for ever', while in the right hand top corner can be seen men pulling down an image of the Virgin and Child. (perhaps c. 1570; see M. Aston, *The King's Bedpost: Reformation and Iconography in a Tudor Group Portrait* (Cambridge, 1993).

75. See Mill, pp. 201–4, Bergeron, pp. 67–9. The most detailed account is a tract (1590), printed in J. T. Gibson Craig, *Papers Relative to the Marriage of King James the Sixth of Scotland with the Princess Anne of Denmark* (Bannatyne Club, Edinburgh, 1828); this contains the verse account by John Burel, the text of which also appears in *Watson's Choice Collection* ed. H. H. Wood, STS (1977), 1, Part II, pp. 1–15.

76. Another source (Johnston; see Mill, p. 202n) says that with the keys she was presented with 'ane bybill and psalme buik' – if so, this is a rare vestige of the earlier entires' insistence on the Reformed religion.

77. See, for instance, Van Marle, figs 51, 64–67, 74.

78. For sixteenth-century depictions see *Reallexikon zur deutschen Kunstgeschichte* ed. O. Schmitt *et al.* (Stuttgart, 1937–) s.v. Ceres, figs 2–3.

79. See *Reallexikon* s.v. Bacchanal, fig. 1 (Melchior Bocksberger, *c.* 1560).

2

TROUBLED TIMES: MARGARET TUDOR AND THE HISTORIANS

Louise O. Fradenburg

The history of the concept of 'nation' has often been linked to that of 'sovereignty'; to be identifiable as such, a nation has needed to possess or at least to demonstrate sovereignty. One way of 'narrating the nation,' to use Homi K. Bhabha's phrase, has accordingly been to feature as protagonist a single sovereign national identity, whose emergence is figured as depending upon its power to subordinate particularities of region or affiliation or ethnicity to the interests of a higher unity. As is suggested by the work of cultural critics like Bhabha and Sara Suleri, however, such a developmental narrative conceals a nonetheless legible history of the nation not as an emergent sovereign subject but as a shifting and permeable field of exchanges and dependencies.[1]

Developmental accounts of the nation's sovereignty – and loss thereof – have their own histories. This essay explores the workings of a 'statist' historiography in accounts of James V's minority and Margaret Tudor's political career. By 'statist' I mean an historiography that constructs an opposition between private and public interests, privileging the latter with respect to ethics and historical agency: certain interests are defined as public and represented as responsible for significant change, others are defined as private and represented as obstructive or even destructive with respect to the history of the nation.

The celebration of statist administration – of its ability to order disorder, to pacify passion,[2] to demand the sacrifice of local interests to a greater unity – has been a recurrent theme in colonial history. English historiography has often linked England's national identity and imperial power to the superior strength of its administrative culture; the theme of the centralisation of power also appears in Scottish political historiography, chiefly in the form of the story of the crown's efforts to pacify its over-mighty subjects.[3] The historiography of nationhood, moreover, makes over-mighty subjects highly visible during the king's minorities. The minorities of kings are troubled times, when factions, children, women rule, when particular desires disrupt the dispassionate administration of justice and threaten the integrity of national boundaries and identities.[4]

In his chronicle account of James V's minority, written in the 1640s, William Drummond of Hawthornden linked the perils of internal disorder and vulnerability to foreign interests; in doing so he developed themes pursued by earlier as well as later historians.[5] He explains the Duke of Albany's return to Scotland from France in 1515 as follows: when Albany

> understood the great discords of the Nobility of *Scotland*, persons of
> Faction being advanced to places, dangerous immunities being
> granted to the Commons, *France* and *England* beginning to be tyred
> of their Peace, and preparing for a new War: to curb the *Scottish* Fac-
> tions, keep the Nation in quietness in it self, by giving the Subjects
> other work abroad, whilst common danger should break off particu-
> lar Discords,

he returned to Scotland, and set himself 'to amend the enormities committed in his absence'.[6]

The compression of Drummond's account is in itself suggestive of the political intricacies of minorities. Its rhetorical purpose is to accumulate and intensify peril, to make us feel 'enormity' in the form of broad-ranging discords focused, despite their diversity, on the Scottish 'Nation'. And despite Drummond's partiality to Albany's rival Archibald Douglas, Albany is a mender of 'enormities' and the subject of a reflection on 'common danger' and 'particular Discords'. Drummond's rhetoric of 'enormity' illustrates the dramatization of disorder identified by William Kevin Emond as central to chronicle accounts of the minority; and we glimpse here, too, the outlines of an identification of Scotland – in particular, of 'the Nobility of Scotland' – with partiality and violence, an identification elaborated also by other chroniclers.[7]

The story of Scotland's struggle with order has, however, been revised in recent years. Jenny Wormald has pointed to the dangers of applying to Scotland concerns about centralisation appropriate to English history. Her work has thus both exposed and illustrated the extent to which the narratives told by Scottish political historiographers have been shaped by the nationalisms of England and Scotland. Emphasising the difference of late medieval Scottish politics from those of England, Wormald has argued that Scotland's kings ruled *through* – not despite – a decentred polity.[8] In her view, the minorities of the later Middle Ages, far from threatening good order, 'provided a safety valve' that reduced 'the threat of autocracy'.[9]

But Wormald's account of the differences between late medieval English and Scottish styles of rule raises the question of how such differences are to be explained. If we consider that, by the early sixteenth century, Scotland had for centuries been part of a shifting colonialist ecology mapped decisively, though even then perhaps not 'originally', by the Roman conquest of Britain, we cannot deploy notions of a Scottish preference for decentralised political work or of an English preference for centralisation without nuancing what is meant by 'Scottish' and by 'English' in this context. Only in the framework of a nationalist historicism can certain apparatuses of centralisation be identified as distinctly English; and though Scotland may not have needed such apparatuses, it may still, in some ways, have been prevented from developing them. We must thus read the troubled minority of James V – and the narratives that have recounted it – as part of a long history of colonisation and conquest, during which those regions that would become Scotland and England shaped and reshaped one another.[10]

Wormald's notion that minorities actually inhibited oppression also requires further scrutiny if we are to understand the role played by constructions of violence in Scottish historiography. The view that minorities, by hampering 'developments in central government', provided a kind of a safety-valve, has the advantage of implying that violence is often a 'public' as well as a private phenomenon; only from certain perspectives will the violence of the centralised state be seen as an improvement on the private exercise of arms. To this extent, Wormald's formulation helps to undo unthinking equations of centralisation with peace and order.[11] But for my purposes, the formulation takes as too self-evident the difference between centre and locality, public and private. The argument that troubled times may be less violent than they have sometimes seemed is both true and highly significant – significant partly because we need to understand the workings of a statist projection of passion onto those agents who seem not to have 'public' interests at heart. But trouble-making and rule, I would argue, are often mutually implicated; and the boundaries of the public and the private do not precede politics, but are decided upon – temporarily – in the course of political struggles over who can claim to speak for the community and who cannot.

The difficult political agency of queenship illustrates the mutual implication of trouble-making and rule. The complicated loyalties of medieval queens enjoined upon them a particularly challenging marital politics; the critical role of queens in alliance-formation presented both opportunities and dangers to statecraft.[12] As 'interstitial' or 'liminal' figures, queens threatened the unity of families, lineages, classes, nations; but they also embodied unity, because their very 'outsideness' to particularised interests could make them seem 'above' or 'beyond' such interests.[13] This indeterminacy – the intense association of queens with the concepts *both* of division and of unity – is what made queenship so valuable, if so risky, a practice. Queens performed kinds of cultural and political work that might be described as boundary-forming. As the agents of new alliances, they reshaped the complex of regional and global relations in which their countries were immersed, and thus redefined the identities of those countries. And they were closely associated with kinds of time marked as extraordinary: with regencies, minorities, absences, dynastic transition.

Throughout the fifteenth and early sixteenth centuries in Scotland a series of mishaps produced not so much orderly succession as a succession of lengthy minorities, during which times Scotland had to wait for its seventeen-month-old or six-year-old kings to grow up, and had to endure the political intricacies of long regencies, in which the activities of Scotland's queens were prominent.[14] Despite these facts, many of the important histories of the ruling élites of fifteenth- and sixteenth-century Scotland rely almost exclusively on the organising principle of kings' reigns or kings' activities, and neglect the importance, during the minorities of Scotland's kings, of the activities of Mary of Gueldres, Margaret Tudor and Mary of Guise – all foreign queens who served, however briefly, as regent.[15] Donaldson is helpful on the minorities: for example, he notes that 'the resolution of the Queen Mother to meet the challenge and continue her husband's policy may well have helped to shape the situation' in the minorities of James II and III.[16] But even Donaldson does not fully appreciate the broad significance of the minorities for the changing character of rule (which proved often enough to be the character of queenly rule) in later medieval Scotland.

The minorities threw Scotland's queens into situations both of heightened opportunity and peril, and gave them a leading role in Scottish politics. Re-marriages to Scots noblemen caused resentment and ended queens' official regencies. After James I's murder in 1437, Joan Beaufort governed for two years, but her marriage to Sir James Stewart of Lorne and the rise to power of the Livingstons brought an end to her effective power and caused her to lose custody of the young king.[17] When James II was killed in 1460, his queen, Mary of Gueldres, took over the rule of the country, and managed the complexity of Scotland's foreign affairs during the time of the English Wars of the Roses. According to Donaldson an alliance with Hepburn of Hailes and an ensuing attempt to 'gain control of the young king's person ... discredited [her], in much the same way as Joan Beaufort had been by her marriage with Stewart of Lorne,' but Norman Macdougall has questioned such parallels, arguing that Joan Beaufort and Mary of Gueldres were actually confused by chroniclers too dependent on oral tradition.[18]

It seems that neither the foreignness nor the gender of Scotland's queens prevented their accession to powers of regency; at the same time, at least in the case of Joan Beaufort and later that of Margaret Tudor, remarriage or factional alliance could call their fidelity into question, and end their official regencies and control of the heir. Certainly the complexities of Margaret Tudor's position during the minority of James V proved almost impossible to negotiate. She was widow of James IV; mother of James V, at the time likely heir to the throne of England; and sister to Henry VIII, whose army killed her husband. The early Scottish chroniclers of the minority rarely castigate Margaret for its disorders, reserving most of their opprobrium for various of the Scottish nobility whom they wished, for factional reasons of their own, to defame.[19] Despite such a tradition of restraint, however, the contradictions of Margaret's position were not much appreciated by nineteenth- and early twentieth-century historians, who instead applied to Margaret many of the stereotypical character flaws – selfishness, fickleness – also associated in medieval political literature with 'bad' queens. Green delights in calling her 'the inconstant queen', 'the ever-changing queen'; J. M Stone describes her as 'cruel, vindictive, unscrupulous, sensual and vain', a treacherous woman whose 'history is one series of intrigues, the outcome of her ruling passions – vanity and greed'.[20]

More recently, Gordon Donaldson writes that Margaret 'differed from' Joan Beaufort and Mary of Gueldres because

> ... she was the sister of the reigning King of England and she was conspicuously unstable in her affections. Indeed, her matrimonial adventures came near to rivalling those of her brother, Henry VIII ...
> This was the woman who, in terms of James IV's will, was tutrix to her son as long as she remained a widow, and therefore head of the government.[21]

Donaldson's rhetoric – 'This was the woman' – seems designed to make us feel the folly of anyone's giving power to Margaret (that her husband did so in his will remains a mystery to those historians who speak confidently of Margaret's waywardness).[22] But Margaret's 'matrimonial adventures' hardly come near 'rivalling those of her brother'. She had none of her husbands executed. Moreover, matrimonial adventurism was standard practice for the day – even, given the example of Joan Beaufort, not altogether unusual for fifteenth-century Scottish queens.[23] Historians have tended to repeat and embellish, rather than analyse, complaints about Margaret made by the powerful and scarcely selfless men whom she undoubtedly annoyed and whose purposes she undoubtedly frustrated. It is ironic that some of the most strident contemporary complaints about Margaret come from her brother and his agents, Wolsey and Thomas Lord Dacre, Warden of the English March, whose remarks have too often been accepted at face value by historians of Scottish politics.[24]

Margaret speaks of her isolation, of how easily support could melt away, in an angry letter to Dacre:

> ... I have nen here that vyl helpe me of my complaynt, nor doo me
> justys; so that I may not lyf to my honowr; and my lyfeng is here, I
> man cast me to plesse thys raulme; ... my Lorde I pray you remem-
> byr that an ye var in a nother Rawlme vhare ye schuled lyf your
> lyfe, ye vould doo that ye myght to ples them soo that thay schuld
> not have eny mystrust of you.[25]

In another letter she writes to her brother of her second husband's ill-treatment of her, saying '"As to my part, your Grace sal find no fault, but I am a vhaman [woman], and may do little but by friends."'[26] Margaret's letters suggest that she understood the risks involved in the work of queenship; they suggest also that we ought to consider whether accusatory representations of her might seek to discipline her agency, and to occlude, by making into vice, features of the very queenly interstitiality that served her powerful male rivals in the first place. Though Dacre and Wolsey did not acknowledge the fact, Margaret's presence in Scotland was unquestionably helpful to Henry, even if she often also frustrated his purposes. Accusations of self-seeking and shiftiness (made liberally by Dacre as well as by more recent historians) conceal political *dependence* on favours and factions and 'outsiders'. And the rhetorical conflation of Margaret with a troubled Scotland has helped to conceal this dependence.

Hester Chapman, in *The Sisters of Henry VIII* (1969), presents the following image of the Scotland in which Margaret Tudor lived:

> ... although Scotland was entering upon a period of comparative
> prosperity, and had begun to show signs of civilized learning – even
> of concern for learning and the arts – it remained, as ever, impover-
> ished, commercially backward and in that state of internal chaos
> which was part of the national way of life.[27]

Scotland 'remained, as ever, impoverished'. The phrase 'as ever' – like Chapman's claim that '[t]he clans were not subdued ... by James's authority, because his government was not, and never became, centralized' – insists upon a timeless, unchanging Scotland, an obdurate *nature*, one that can only be brought into the forward march of history through outside intervention.[28] Chapman's logic is as follows: given its internal, essential incapacity for order, Scotland can only be rescued from itself by a foreign power; according to Chapman, it was 'obvious to all but themselves that the Scots were incapable of rule, and that only conquest and colonization could bring them peace and prosperity' (p. 111).[29]

Chapman's view of Margaret seems initially more sympathetic than her view of early sixteenth-century Scotland. She rejects the image of Margaret as the 'evil woman of Scottish legend,' 'the treacherous instrument of English policy'. Her Margaret is, instead, indomitable – she 'refuses to admit defeat' despite having 'more to endure ... than falls to the lot of most young women' (p. 95). And yet Chapman does see Margaret as, if not precisely 'treacherous', still the 'instrument of English policy', helping Henry VIII 'to colonize Scotland through her regency' (p. 90). Finally, Margaret's 'strength of purpose ... forced out of one channel into another', 'whirled into a maelstrom', she became, 'not so much the victim of the tempest, as the tempest itself' (p. 94).

Thus Margaret is given no ethical or political responsibility for bringing Scotland into its 'future'. The story of her obduracy, moreover, though valorised by Chapman as her resistance to defeat and despair, finally resembles Chapman's depiction of Scotland. Margaret's tempestuousness develops in the course of her 'struggling on', a forward movement quite different from the march of imperial progress. The determined *and* tempestuous Margaret bears a suspicious resemblance to those unsubduable, atavistic Scottish nobles, so willing to betray their country as it suited them.[30] Like the Scottish nobility, Margaret is both too changeful and too resistant to change. At stake here is the construction of an inadequate subject of history, too variable to be trusted with responsibility, therefore incapable of sovereignty, too obdurate and therefore too regressive to have any hope of global competitiveness. In the midst, then, of the troublesomeness of the minority, we find an unruly English queen of Scotland and an unruly Scottish nobility, their futures determined by the interventions of a 'better-organized country' (p. 123).

William Kevin Emond's revisionist treatment of James V's minority, the most comprehensive to date, seeks to undo the preoccupation with violence that marks the minority's historical tradition, and presents Margaret Tudor's role in nuanced and scholarly fashion. In explicating the disorders whose extent and intensity he also seeks to minimise, Emond has stressed the international dimension of the troubles of the minority, remarking on the 'unprecedented opportunities presented to England and France for interference through the rival claims to authority' made by Margaret Tudor and the Duke of Albany (abstract, n.p.) and the resulting importance of Scotland's role in international politics (p. x). The 'personal nature of Scottish government' made especially significant the international loyalties of the personalities (p. ix); Margaret Tudor's difficulties in negotiating her links with England were the 'principal reason' for the downfall of her second regency (p. 435).

Despite, however, the complexity of Emond's treatment of the violence of the minority, his work remains committed to a statist construction and valuation of impartial governance. This double movement may be seen even in Emond's handling of the question of sources. He cites Lesley's obsession with factionalism (p. 583); Pitscottie's uncritical acceptance of stories and local traditions; Drummond and other chroniclers' belief in the high level of political violence during the minority (p. 596). He writes:

> The chroniclers are a useful source of rumour and oral tradition concerning the minority of James V ... the basis of these stories is demonstrable in fact, but the stories remain dramatic narrative illuminating the bare bones of contemporary evidence without adding to that evidence. (p. 602)

And one of Emond's chief sources for the minority is the *Acta Dominorum Concilii*, the *Acts of the Lords of Council* – i.e. the records of that very body in which, along with Albany, Emond locates the minority's chief experience and development of 'government'.[31] But the picture of Scottish politics provided by these records is particular to them and to the fledgling administrative culture that was seeking to establish itself in part through their generation. Emond's fine appraisal of the sources for the minority needs to be further nuanced, through a recognition that the documentary cultures that have produced historical records have until now been, and indeed perhaps remain, closely intertwined with statist ideologies and political practices – with, that is, the very concept of administrative power we have seen as central to colonialist and post-colonial British historical narrative. Documents are not useless or valueless – they are enormously helpful – but neither are they neutral objects; they have histories, and the notion that they are inherently more valuable witnesses to historical truth than, for example, oral narrative, is itself part of a colonial historiography that places a high value on the products of statist administration.[32]

In critiquing the chronicles' preference for dramatic narrative, Emond follows the lead of Norman Macdougall, whose brilliant essay reappraising the legend of James III regrets the fact that

> ... the traditional picture of fifteenth-century Scotland, still broadly accepted today ... should be founded much less on information obtainable from the public records than on the stories purveyed by sixteenth-century chroniclers, whose motives in writing varied from a desire to glorify a particular political power group or family to blatant post-Reformation bias.[33]

The chroniclers' accounts were also skewed because they 'saw their function ... in setting forth a series of moral tales on the virtues and vices of kingship' (p. 11). Finally, they lacked 'reliable contemporary written accounts', and 'turned to oral evidence, ballads or prose tales, to fill out their narratives' (p. 14), providing 'dramatic tableaux' (p. 17) rather than 'serious history' (p. 30). 'True historical scholarship ... did not really begin until the publication in 1729 of Thomas Innes's *Critical Essay on the Ancient Inhabitants of Scotland*', writes Macdougall, and 'a spirit of critical enquiry into sources ... is not to be looked for in sixteenth-century Scotland' (pp. 10–11). The contributions made by scholars like Macdougall and Emond to our understanding of early sixteenth-century Scotland have been inestimable, and it is not my purpose either to obscure their achievement or to question their commitment to a critical historical method. Rather, my point is that all sources, and all methodological positions, benefit from scrutiny. Macdougall's apparent willingness to accept at face value the trustworthiness of 'information obtainable from public records' forms a striking contrast to his careful analysis of factionalism in the chronicles.

Moreover, even practitioners of 'serious' history like Macdougall and Emond purvey their visions from the standpoint of a documentary culture itself invested in certain notions of (good) government and versions 'of moral tales on the virtues and vices of kingship': Macdougall's characterisation of James III's brother Albany as a 'squalid conspirator' (p. 18) is scarcely dispassionate. And it is, again, *from* the standpoint of this documentary culture that chroniclers can be figured as inadequately documented, excessively dramatic, excessively reliant on oral tradition and obsessed with violence – in fact, as atavistic, since true historical scholarship does not begin until the Enlightenment. In the view of Emond and Macdougall, the sixteenth-century chroniclers are, like Chapman's Scotland, too fascinated with the very violence they deplore, and too much of the past.

The Duke of Albany, in contrast, is Emond's hero, because 'Albany alone had no personal motivation. Margaret had started out that way, but all too soon developed political ambitions. Albany acted as the embodiment of the will of the estates' (p. 615). And Albany 'brought about the provision of the impartial Council, perceived to be providing justice', an institution whose documents are central to Emond's argument that, despite chroniclers' theatrical treatments of the chaotic violence of the minority, government evolved and provided peace and justice (p. 627). Like Macdougall, then, Emond has some quite strong notions about 'the virtues and vices of kingship'; and too often in his account Margaret Tudor is the foil to Albany's selflessness.

Emond's treatment of Margaret Tudor eschews the hysteria of some nineteenth- and early twentieth-century accounts of her reign. But Emond has his own list of adjectives – Margaret was 'politically inept, greedy, impulsive, and lacking in sound judgement' (p. 628); and she appears in Emond's account as partial to her own interests, unwilling to be the 'figurehead' he thinks James IV intended her to be when he provided for her regency in his will (p. 11). Instead she desired – with disastrous consequences – 'real power' (p. 37). Her regencies failed because she failed to foster unity (p. 13), and neglected the common weal (p. 39); when, for example, she set up a secret code that would allow her brother Henry to know, or think he knew, which letters bearing her signature were in accord with her mind and which were not, her action is interpreted by Emond as a denial of compromise among Scotland's contending interests. The 'stubbornness' (p. 428) of Margaret's 'personal antagonism' toward her second husband, Archibald Douglas (p. 419), limited her 'policy objectives' (p. 421); she 'wantonly' abandoned the opportunity of national coalition to ensure that Angus would have no influence (p. 408), though Emond notes that opposition to Angus was in fact broad (p. 428).

One of the reasons given by Emond for the downfall of Margaret's second regency is the 'failure of Margaret's government to provide justice' (p. 426). Of such a failure there is indeed evidence, chiefly in the form of a 'remarkable rider' attached to the recommendation of the August parliament that the Lords appointed to the Council Session carry out their duty to '"Be impartial even when the king or queen ask them otherwise"'.[34] Emond also gives as evidence for Margaret's failure to administer justice the treatment of the murderers of Lord Fleming (p. 426). '[P]rivate justice seems to have prevailed' in the case of Fleming's murder by Tweedie of Drumelzier (p. 427). But Emond's account does not show that this instance of 'private justice' was regarded by contemporaries as one of the 'failings' of Margaret's administration (p. 427).[35] What seems to be at stake in Emond's presentation of this story is a preference for official justice and administrative intervention, despite his recognition of 'the personal nature of Scottish government'; and it is indicative of the statism at work in Emond's account that he associates Margaret with feud, a subject frequently addressed in the chronicles' at times almost ethnographic discourse of atavistic Scottish violence.[36]

Emond's presentation of the role of the Chancellor, James Beaton, in the downfall of Margaret's second regency is another case in point. According to Emond, Beaton withdrew support from Margaret because he was persuaded that, owing to 'Margaret's mismanagement of government', 'the best interests of Scotland lay in a renewed admittance of Angus' to power (p. 435). But there is little evidence of Scotland's 'best interests' having been on Chancellor Beaton's mind. His relation to Margaret had been turbulent for years, owing in part to his support for the pro-French policy that led to the disaster of Flodden, and to his subsequent support of Albany; and there are indications of Beaton's own intrigues with England.[37] Moreover, the evidence for Margaret's mismanagement, when compared with the evidence of the difficulty of her situation, is hardly striking. On this score Emond's narrative is split by a hesitation between the impulse to locate Margaret's defeat in her personal incapacity to order disorder (Margaret's 'initiative' was 'swept away from her to Angus and Beaton by the failure of her government') and by the impulse to locate her defeat in England's power to disorder her ('The downward spiral of control stemmed from her reliance on England while the English were determined to promote Angus ... The failings of her internal administration seemed hardly to matter in the face of this vicious circle'[p. 440]).

Rarely does one find Emond ascribing to Margaret's enemies anything other than *reasons*. His project of minimising and reframing the violence of the minority needs to be understood as both product and enactment of a certain historiographic rationalism. For while it is, again, crucial to see that this minority – and by extension, perhaps other minorities – were not necessarily evil times in which a (peculiarly Scottish) pursuit of atavistic private interests broke apart the peaceful, progressive, public time of the state, but were instead times of significant peacefulness and governance, such a logic repeats rather than dislodges the figuration of passion and fantasy as always outside or obstructive of political history.

What does it mean for contemporary historians to insist that the truth of late medieval Scotland can only be known through sources and methods committed to a rationalism bent on purging a pre-Enlightenment fascination with the irrational? And thus to some degree at least participating in narratives that link pastness to the colonialist romance of unruly ethnicities? I do not want to insist on a yet purer conception of historical truth-telling than that advanced by Macdougall and Emond. Rather I want to suggest that we foreground the question of violence and fantasy, and ask what the proscribed register of the legendary might tell us about the construction of Scottish violence in relation to administrative culture. Only by doing so will the role of documentary culture in colonial and post-colonial historiography emerge. For, as has been noted, violence, in later 'serious' accounts as well as in early chronicles of the minorities, is frequently part of a discourse of Scottish identity. And if we are to analyse such discourses, it is important to explore how dialectical are the relations between national and regional identities, how, even when power differentials are striking, the history of regional struggle is always one of mutual transformation.

I want to turn again to Margaret's own role in such transformations. Margaret complained to her brother about Lord Dacre as follows:

> Also I complain to the King my brother of what my Lord Dacre does and says to my hurt, for he says to Scottish folk, 'that he marvels that *they will let any woman* have authority, and especially ME'. Quhilk words should come of others, not of Englishmen. For, the more honor I get, England will have the more; and such words as these may do me mickle ill.[38]

While Margaret may have incurred displeasure simply because, despite her gender, she refused to retire from the pursuit of power, her letter reminds us of how much the men who sought to manage and calibrate her power actually made political use of her gender. It is perhaps not so much because she declined to bow out, as because she declined to be docile to the purposes of men like Beaton and her brother – thus revealing her usefulness to them – that she earned so much opprobrium. Margaret has been accused of disturbing the peace not because she politicked (even dowager queens in convents politicked) but because she did so too explicitly. For example, she writes to Dacre:

> ... great business and labour has been betwixt the governor and you, to what effect I know not, whereof I marvel: for I think, an if any way should be made betwixt these two realms, I think I should have been advertised, and have had my part therein.[39]

Something is being laid bare here – namely, that politics on behalf of the 'common weal' are very difficult to distinguish from politics on behalf of what Margaret herself referred to as 'particular pleasure'. My point here is not a cynical one. I mean simply to stress that contending political interests are always struggling to legitimate themselves as public, or official, or tending to the common weal; and what, at a given moment in history, may appear to be an obvious public good (strong dynastic succession, for example) will at another moment be rendered in political discourse as merely a particular pleasure.

Even at a given historical moment, it is not always easy to determine what is particular and what is not. For example, Margaret seems to have worked hard on behalf of her son. Did she do so because it was in her interest to do so? Insofar as her son was king of Scotland, did she protect him because it was in Scotland's interests to do so? Did she do so for Henry VIII, her brother, in the thought that he wanted to see his nephew crowned king of Scotland? Is doing something for Henry also doing something for herself, or for the alliance with England, or for peace? Such uncertainties cannot usefully be reduced to the moral categories of waywardness and selfishness, in part because the question of whether someone is serving 'public' or 'private' interests relies on a reinscription of the very categories that require scrutiny. This is the case not least because one of the most indeterminate, as well as over-determined, figures at stake in Margaret's tempestuousness is nation itself. Margaret is a borderline figure, the unreadability of whose purposes has troubled and assisted the nationalisms of historiography as much as the calculations of princes.

In the figure of Margaret, conventionally opposed positions meet: coloniser and colonised, English and Scottish. She becomes an image of the perilous transformations that characterise the colonial encounter: the potential sameness of the enemy, the potential of the other to be transformed into oneself or of the self to be transformed into the other. Hence the discourse that links Margaret's fickleness to the fickleness of the Scottish lords; hence, too the endless distrust of Margaret's motives on the part of Henry VIII, Wolsey, and Dacre, or for that matter the concern of some Scots that she might, as it were, help to transform Scotland into England, by gaining support for the English alliance. Yet the aversiveness displayed in representations of Margaret's power to destabilise should not blind us to the usefulness of that very power to all parties involved. It is not merely ironic that both Henry VIII and the Scottish council seem to have thought it best to keep Margaret in Scotland.

As a figure for the destabilisation of national identity, Margaret is also a figure around whom the very question of national identity could be articulated. She not only wrote grandiloquently about the 'common weal' but spoke about the Scottish commons.[40] She reports to the Earl of Surrey that, at a time when the Duke of Albany was making arrangements to separate Margaret from her son and to surround James with Albany's own supporters,

> ... to eschew more evil appearing, I thought for that time I would not contrary them ... I said before the lords then, that it that was for the good of the king my son's person I would be contented with, and that I should be a good Scotswoman.[41]

Being a 'good Scotswoman' is here expressed as a loyalty to 'the good of the king', as an ability to be content with whatever conduces to that good. It is not clear that this definition of a 'good Scotswoman' would have been acceptable to the likes of the Earl of Murray and Lord Fleming; and yet they could scarcely have argued against it. That the king of Scotland himself should have been so tied by birth to England, and so vulnerable to anglicisation, was indeed partly what was at stake in the struggle to mitigate Margaret's influence; but even though the instability of such national identities is clearly brought out by Margaret's story (in what sense other than adoptive could Margaret be a 'good Scotswoman'? if nationality is a matter of will, with what ease might it be unwilled?), the story nonetheless suggests the extent to which nationality, precisely because of its indeterminacy, has the power to transform identity – to make, for example, the grandson of Henry VII into the very touchstone of good Scottishness.

Margaret was an outpost of England; she was an outpost of English vulnerability. Margaret was a veritable media phenomenon, a prolific letter-writer, Henry's eyes and ears in Scotland: 'Now I will advertise you what [the Duke of Albany] hath brought with him, ... he hath eight-and-twenty cannons', she wrote to Surrey, despite the fact that 'all things is kept from me as far as the duke may'.[42] Her position differed from Henry's – she was not at 'home', she constantly struggled to repossess herself of the allowances and rents which were withheld from her, as a woman she could only seek favour from her friends, and so on. Nonetheless her position mirrored Henry's: each sought to deceive the other, to bind the other's fidelity. More, each came to depend on the other, Henry on Margaret just as much as she on him; she could see what he could not see, and hear what he could not hear. English policy feared its dependence on her and sought to mitigate it by discrediting her, thus making her service less effective and paradoxically less reliable: Wolsey instructs an ambassador to Scotland that it was '"right to use the Queen of Scots ... *but not so as all shall depend on her*. I mistrust threads wrought by woman's fingers"', says the upright and honourable Wolsey.[43]

The anomalousness of Margaret's national identity was a function of her gender and her status as queen, and was crucial to her management of and by power. Her 'wantonnes' was sensationalised and made politically useful. Despite his and his agents' endless epistolary preoccupation with Margaret's 'shamefulness', it was the very promulgation of her transgressiveness that Henry VIII set in train. In 1520, when '[a] report was current in Scotland that the duke [of Albany] intended to divorce his own wife to marry Margaret ... Wolsey especially requested the rumour to be farther circulated, that it might injure Albany in the estimation of the Scots'.[44] The preoccupation of Henry VIII with his sister's sexual and marital history was at once political and 'private'; his attempts to control and calibrate the disposition of Margaret's body and pleasures were in part an extension of his designs on Scotland. The management of her body, and the disciplining of her conscience, were instruments whereby Henry could pursue the annexation of Scotland.

Like Margaret's ungovernability, the Scottish 'state of internal chaos' to which Hester Chapman refers was also, as Emond notes, to some degree produced as well as represented. It is difficult to read Henry VIII's support of the widely disliked Earl of Angus in any other way. Henry may have been credulous with respect to Angus's representations of his prospects; he may have so desired an agent effective in ways that Margaret, to his mind, could not be, that he distrusted Margaret's repeated explanations that Angus's intervention on behalf of Henry would damage rather than enhance the English cause.[45] But such possibilities only suggest that reason and reasons do not always adequately explain history. Given the evidence available to Henry that Angus was distrusted in Scotland, and that his return from exile would cause 'chaos' rather than resolve it, it would seem that England's wish at this time was precisely to trouble Scotland – to destabilise, just as much as, perhaps even more than, to 'pacify.' Two points are at issue here: that rational calculation of the interests of one 'common weal' can produce a *desired* chaos and violence in another; and that rational calculation of interests may not always be the most useful way of understanding the workings of political desire.

England's policies toward Scotland during the time of the minority succeeded in exacerbating Scottish conflicts and in 'undermining' Margaret's authority (Emond, p. 408); but, as Emond also notes, Henry's support of Angus produced little in the way of real influence (p. 613). Plans such as Wolsey's to kidnap Chancellor Beaton, and the voluminous evidence for Dacre's *fomenting* of disorder among the Scottish nobility, indicate both the lengths to which England was prepared to go in the production of chaotic violence, and the workings of powerful fantasies and desires in so doing.[46] The aggression and hostility of Henry VIII was not lost on the early chroniclers; on the troubles leading to the battle of Flodden, Lesley comments simply that Henry was 'de[s]ierous to haif weires' (p. 83). J. S Brewer notes, in reviewing the correspondence of this period, how 'curious' it was that Henry's policies so often had the effect of causing Margaret to throw herself 'into the arms of those who were opposed to England' (p. 514); regarding the failure of Margaret's first regency, Brewer remarks that '[i]t has appeared strange that in so critical a period Henry should have rendered such ineffectual aid to Margaret'.[47] Margaret's letters reveal a clear awareness of the nature of English activities: she writes to Dacre:

> I know well ye have done your part to hinder me at the King's
> grace my brother's hand. Why may ye not fail to me, whe ye fail to
> the King's grace my brother? And better mend in time ne to be
> worse. Which an ye do not, it will be occasion to this realm and my
> lord Governor [Albany, into whose arms Margaret had recently been
> thrown] to do such like as ye have done; which is receiving of rebels
> and maintaining of them ...[48]

The 'curiousness' of Henry's treatment of Margaret is also registered in the puzzlements of watching nations, who, Emond notes, could not believe that Margaret was not pro-English (p. 406).

The image I am offering of Anglo-Scottish relations during the minority of James V is thus not one of a powerful imperialistic nation coolly destabilising the peace and prosperity of a poorer neighbour. It is, instead, one of an imperialistic power practising and participating in violence and chaos. In some ways England profited from its policies, but it did itself little real good. It produced a Scottish king, James V, stubbornly resistant to Douglas and English influence; and it produced an English queen mother, Margaret Tudor, equally distrustful of Henry's intentions. Margaret's own intrigues, betrayals and affairs likewise need to be evaluated from a standpoint that recognises the extent to which calculation may be impelled by desire. Passion is embedded in the structures and practices of power that both obstruct and instantiate historical change.

1. Homi K. Bhabha, *Narrating the Nation* (New York, 1990); Sara Suleri, *The Rhetoric of English India* (Chicago, 1992).

2. I will use the term 'passion' in this essay not only because of its association with strong emotion, but even more particularly because of its association with the production and enduring of violence, and with notions of control and rule: a passionate emotion is one that can overwhelm or master us. The term points to the long-standing construction of powerful emotion as a threat to rule, whether self-mastery or public governance.

3. See Jennifer M. Brown [Wormald], 'The Exercise of Power,' in Brown [Wormald], ed. *Scottish Society in the Fifteenth Century* (1977), pp. 33–65, for a critique of this formulation, and Ranald Nicholson's *Scotland: The Later Middle Ages* (Edinburgh, 1974), for the formulation; also Louise Olga Fradenburg, *City, Marriage, Tournament: Arts of Rule in Late Medieval Scotland* (Madison, WI, 1991), pp. 274–5, n. 1.

4. Ernst H. Kantorowicz, *The King's Two Bodies: A Study in Medieval Political Theology* (Princeton, 1957) includes a study of kings' minorities.

5. On the continuity of Drummond's ideological preoccupations with those of certain sixteenth-century chroniclers, see Thomas I. Rae, 'The Historical Writing of Drummond of Hawthornden,' *SHR*, 54 (1975), 22–62.

6. William Drummond of Hawthornden, *The History of Scotland, From the year 1423, until the year 1542* ... (1681), p. 265.

7. On the chroniclers' belief in the high level of political violence during the minority, see William Kevin Emond, 'The Minority of King James V: 1513–1528, unpublished dissertation (University of St Andrews, 1988), p. 596, hereafter cited in the text, and discussion above. Drummond refers to the Scots as mutinous and ungovernable (p. 244); according to Pitscottie, Albany himself remarked to the King of France that the Scots 'could not be contentit witht no ciwell man to be thair governour'; *The Historie and Cronicles of Scotland*, ed. Æ. J. G. Mackay, STS, 3 vols (rpt. 1966), I, p. 301.

8. See Brown [Wormald], 'The Exercise of Power', and Jenny Wormald, *Court, Kirk and Community: Scotland 1470–1625* (1981), pp. 12–14.

9. Wormald, p. 13. Emond follows her lead, proposing that 'in general, minorities acted as a safety-valve in the development of Scottish government, preserving a balance between the interests of crown and magnates' (abstract, n.p.).

10. See Michael Hechter, *Internal Colonialism: The Celtic Fringe in British National Development 1536–1966* (Berkeley, 1977). For studies on nationalism and related topics in late medieval Scotland, see R. James Goldstein, *The Matter of Scotland: Historical Narrative in Medieval Scotland* (Lincoln, Neb. and London, 1993); Alexander Grant, *Independence and Nationhood: Scotland 1306–1469* (1984); Fradenburg, esp. pp. 67–122 for work on Margaret Tudor and the minority of James V.

11. Wormald, p. 13. This view of a largely non-violent and dominantly consensus-based relationship between Stewart kings and their magnates has recently been challenged in an article by Michael H. Brown that appeared after the completion of this essay, 'Scotland Tamed? Kings and Magnates in Late Medieval Scotland: a review of recent work', *IR*, 45 (1994), 120–46.

12. The notion of queen as peace-weaver is common in medieval and early modern texts. Margaret Tudor made use of it when she asked Cardinal Wolsey to help her ambassadors to Henry VIII bring their matters to a good end, so that there may be sure love and amity betwixt these two realms; considering them so near as they are of

blood, and that I am the labourer betwixt them'. See Letter 129, d. 1524, in *Letters of Royal and Illustrious Ladies of Great Britain, from the Commencement of the Twelfth Century to the Close of the Reign of Queen Mary*, ed. Mary Anne Everett (Wood) Green, 3 vols (1846), I p. 357; hereafter cited in the text. See also Pauline Stafford's influential book *Queens, Concubines and Dowagers: The King's Wife in the Early Middle Ages* (Athens, GA, 1983), pp. 29, 46, on the queen's power to personify 'old grievances'; and *Women and Sovereignty*, ed. Louise Olga Fradenburg, *Cosmos* 7 (Edinburgh, 1992).

13. The term 'liminality' has been used by Victor Turner, and by a host of scholars of ritual influenced by his work, to indicate a specially marked cultural condition, one that suspends everyday rules and hierarchies either by substituting new ones or by emphasising the (usually temporary) equality of those persons who have crossed the threshold of this condition. Carnival is one example; the distinctive locations and ritual practices of initiation would be another. 'Liminality', then, can indicate specially bounded states that, however set-apart, nonetheless give expression to central cultural values. Turner, however, has also, and problematically, used the term to indicate the more permanent, structural liminality or 'inferiority' of conquered groups, foreigners, and women; see *The Ritual Process: Structure and Anti-Structure* (Ithaca, 1969, repr. 1977), pp. 99, 114, 166–8. With respect to queenship, I prefer the term 'interstitial' to 'liminal' because the former permits greater emphasis on the daily intimacy of queenly alliance-formation with more clearly 'official' practices of rule. For further discussion see *Women and Sovereignty*, ed. Fradenburg, pp. 4–7.

14. Helpful summaries of the histories of these minorities may be found in Gordon Donaldson's *Scottish Kings* (1967, 2nd edn, 1977).

15. The table of contents in Nicholson's *Scotland: The Later Middle Ages* mentions not a single queen, presenting instead chapter titles like 'The Minority of James II and the Little Schism'. Norman Macdougall's books are biographies of kings: *James III: A Political Study* (Edinburgh, 1982) and *James IV* (Edinburgh, 1989).

16. Donaldson, p. 96.

17. See Donaldson, pp. 64 and 80–1; there are striking parallels between the political consequences of Joan's and Margaret Tudor's second marriages, though Margaret fought long and hard to retain influence.

18. Donaldson, pp. 96–8; Macdougall argues that 'sixteenth-century chroniclers, drawing on oral tradition for their information about the activities of queen mothers following their husbands' deaths confused [Mary of Gueldres and Joan Beaufort]' and thus 'the claims that Mary of Gueldres was a wilful woman endangering the minority government by her low amours … cannot be sustained' ('Bishop James Kennedy of St Andrews: a reassessment of his political career,' in Norman Macdougall, ed. *Church, Politics and Society: Scotland 1408–1929* (Edinburgh, 1983), pp. 1–22, at p. 5).

19. The sixteenth-century chroniclers are, for example, not especially critical of Margaret's second and third marriages. Pitscottie remarks of one of Margaret's shifts in loyalty away from Albany and of her third marriage only that 'the quenis grace tyrit of him and pairtit witht him, and ane lyttill efter marieit Harie Stewart brother to my lord of Annerdaill' (p. 307). Lesley describes the queen's second marriage as '[s]uddan …, quhilk [s]ho did [s]ore eftirwart repent', and notes that Margaret married Angus 'for her ple[s]our', but this is the extent of his moralising; Margaret's decision to take 'the hole governement of the realme apon hir' was 'be the proud con[s]ell of her hu[s]bandis friendes' (*History of Scotland*, Edinburgh, Bannatyne Club, 1830, p. 99). Buchanan, because of his post-Reformation stance, is of the earlier chroniclers the most impatient with Margaret, and the most defensive: 'when she herself by marrying, had of her own accord retired from the regency, there could be no indignity in substituting

another, to fill the situation she had deserted, and which, indeed, the ancient laws refused her; for they did not suffer women to administer the government, even in times of tranquillity, much less in such turbulent times as these, when men of the greatest wisdom and authority, could scarcely apply remedies to so many pressing evils'; see *The History of Scotland ... of George Buchanan*, trans. James Aikman, 4 vols (Glasgow and Edinburgh, 1827), II, p. 265.

20. Green, pp. 264, 342; J. M. Stone, *Studies from Court and Cloister* (Edinburgh, 1905), pp. 4–6. Agnes Strickland's study of Margaret, in *Lives of the Queens of Scotland and English Princesses Connected with Regal Succession of Great Britain* (New York, 1859) was decisive for the Victorian image of Margaret as a spoiled, vain, avaricious, self-centered child and woman, covetous of power and careless of common decency. See Priscilla Bawcutt's *Dunbar the Makar* (Oxford, 1992), p. 88, on Margaret Tudor's harsh treatment by historians; and cf. Patricia Hill Buchanan, *Margaret Tudor, Queen of Scots* (Edinburgh, 1985), pp. 34–6. A brief but refreshingly thoughtful treatment of Margaret's situation as queen mother may be found in Leslie J. Macfarlane, *William Elphinstone and the Kingdom of Scotland 1431–1514: The Struggle for Order* (Aberdeen, 1985), at pp. 433–5. Little extended discussion of her is given in two more recent studies, Carol Edington, *Court and Culture in Renaissance Scotland: Sir David Lindsay of the Mount* (Amherst, 1994) and *Stewart Style 1513–1542: Essays on the Court of James V*, ed. Janet Hadley Williams (East Linton, 1996).

21. Donaldson, p. 148.

22. See Buchanan, p. 71. Emond asserts without evidence that James meant her to be a 'figurehead' (p. 11).

23. It is not clear whether Donaldson regards Margaret as 'conspicuously unstable in her affections' because she was married three times rather than two or because she once sought a divorce. For an excellent article on the 'complicated social reality' and creativity of late medieval marriage transactions, see Robert C. Palmer, 'Contexts of Marriage in Medieval England: Evidence from the King's Court circa 1300' (*Speculum*, 59, 1984, 42–67).

24. Henry VIII levelled similar accusations at his sister, charging her with deceitfulness and making herself 'a shame and disgrace to all her family' because she tried to divorce a man (the Earl of Angus, whom she had married in 1514) favoured by Henry for his apparent friendliness to English interests. See Strickland, pp. 139–40.

25. Letter 79, d. 1520, in *Original Letters, Illustrative of English History*, ed. F. R. Ellis, 2nd Series, 4 vols (1827), I, pp. 277–8. Margaret is responding to the charge that she co-operated in soliciting the return of the Duke of Albany from France to Scotland; Henry VIII opposed his regency.

26. The letter was written in July of 1524; cited by Strickland, p. 176.

27. Hester W. Chapman, *The Sisters of Henry VIII* (1969), p. 36, hereafter cited in the text. Chapman's history is a 'popular' one, and deserves scrutiny for that very reason. In the writing of Scottish political history there has been something of a sharp divide between 'academic' histories of kings and 'popular' histories of queens, and the reputations of figures like Margaret Tudor have been shaped significantly by the latter. Rosalind K. Marshall's *Virgins and Viragos: A History of Women in Scotland from 1080 to 1980* (1983) is an important exception.

28. Like the contrast made by Chapman (and so many other historians) between the forward-looking Henry VIII and the backward-looking James IV: 'The contrasting behaviour of James and Henry illustrates the Gothic as opposed to the Renaissance attitude, in spite of certain resemblances' (p. 67).

29. Chapman importantly qualifies, perhaps without meaning to, her emphasis on

Scotland's internal incapacities when she points out that 'Parliament, the civic authorities and the wealthy burgesses were helpless in the face of the nobles' and their followers' bestial savagery, and the support of the English kings, who paid them to betray their country' (p. 36).

30. Chapman, p. 36. See also Green, pp. 322–3: 'The fickle Scottish lords again wavered in their fidelity'; only a few lines later 'such was Margaret's fickleness'.

31. Emond, p. viii, citing SRO CS 5/26–38; see also *Acts of the Lords of Council in Public Affairs 1501–1554. Selections from Acta Dominorum Concilii*, ed. R. K. Hannay (Edinburgh, 1932).

32. A good cautionary example of the privileging of documentary technologies may be found in the work of the nineteenth-century scholar J. S. Brewer, who disparages even the letters of James IV as sources that add little 'to the scanty information we have of the state of Scotland in those turbulent times. With the exception of these few facts, the history is nothing more than the turbulent doings of an intractable nobility, who "laid about them at their wills and died"' (J. S. Brewer, *The reign of Henry VII from his accession to the Death of Wolsey*, ed. James Gairdner, 1884, I, pp. 27–8). He contrasts the rich detail of 'the [English] State papers' with 'the meagre and unsatisfactory narrative of Scotch historians in general' (p. 207). For Brewer, the inability of Scottish historians to produce narratives richly documented by public records is the result of Scotland's barbarism – for example, its 'barbarous and unlettered nobility, hardly able to write their own names' (p. 28).

33. Norman A. T. Macdougall, 'The Sources: a Reappraisal of the Legend', in Brown [Wormald], *Scottish Society in the Fifteenth Century*, pp. 10–32, hereafter cited in the text.

34. Emond, p. 426; *The Acts of the Parliaments of Scotland* ed. T. Thomson and C. Innes (Edinburgh, 1814–75), XII, cap. 7.

35. Emond notes that on 23 November 1529 an interim agreement was made between the Laird of Drumelzier and Malcolm, Lord Fleming; the decreet arbital between the two parties was agreed on 4 March 1530 (p. 427).

36. The chroniclers do not make any particular association of Margaret with feud. Pitscottie ascribes the 'great troubill in Scotland' in part to 'auld feid and slaughter that had bene befoir in King James the fourtis tyme' (p. 280); Drummond describes how John Hepburn, Prior of St. Andrews, instructed Albany 'how the great houses of *Scotland* were so joined and linkt together, by kindred, Alliances, Bonds of service or Homage, that no Gentleman of any quality, although a Malefactor and a guilty person, could be presented to justice without some stir, commotion, tumult of the Grandees and their factious friends' (p. 244).

37. Emond cites a letter from Wolsey to Beaton hinting that Beaton might be made a Cardinal; Dacre assured Beaton that Henry would want him to have the chief ruling of James once he was in full control. See Emond p. 443, n. 28, citing *Letters and Papers, Foreign and Domestic, of the Reign of Henry VIII*, vol. I, pt. ii, ed. R. H. Brodie (2nd edn, 1920); vol. II, pt. i–iv, ed. J. S. Brewer (1864–70), no. 526, Wolsey to the Chancellor of Scotland (21 July); and n. 27, citing no. 520, Dacre to the Chancellor of Scotland, 20 July.

38. Cited by Strickland, p. 178.

39. Green, Letter 117, d. 1524, p. 317.

40. In a letter to Surrey she speaks of the importance of the 'poor commons' to successful political calculation (Green, Letter 105, d. 1523, pp. 277–8); in another letter dated the same year (1523), she urges Henry to take advantage of the moment before Albany's return to Scotland: 'you will have all the hearts of the common people in

this realm; for they would never see the governor' (Green, Letter 103, d. 1523, p. 274). The early chroniclers are sometimes quite flattering on the subject of Margaret's service to the common weal of Scotland; see Pitscottie on how, attempting to dissuade James IV from going to fight the English, 'this nobill woman did her dewtie and labouris sa far as scho might for the weill of hir husband and the commone weill of the contrie and also for the lufe that scho buire to her brother the king of Ingland desyrand no discord to be betuix the two realmes in hir tyme' (p. 261).

41. Green, Letter 112, d. 1523, p. 300.

42. Ibid., Letter 107, d. 1523, pp. 283–4.

43. Cited in Chapman, p. 130.

44. Green, p. 236.

45. In one of many letters arguing against the return of Angus, Margaret contends that the 'coming of the said earl in this realm, should rather be to the king my son's great apparent damage, making of break and trouble within this his realm'; she contrasts the 'particular pleasure of the said earl' with the 'combination, unity, and pacifying of these two realms and common weal of the same' (Green, Letter 127, pp. 350–1, to the Duke of Norfolk).

46. Emond notes Wolsey's plan at p. 414; on Dacre, see Brewer, p. 212 ff.; Brewer portrays Dacre as 'an inimitable agent of mischief and destruction' (p. 218), and cites Dacre's description of the 'evil disposed or discontented of the Scottish nobility' as '"the fiddling stick ... to hold Scotland in cumber and business"' (p. 511). Brewer's emphasis on the havoc wrought by Dacre on the borders is suggestive in the light of Emond's argument that Margaret's failure to bring peace on the borders was a significant factor in the defeat of her political ambitions (pp. 424–5). Stone's statement that Dacre, Lord of the English March, was 'bent on maintaining peace, and would probably have succeeded but for Margaret' (p. 10), is nothing less than astonishing.

47. Brewer, p. 209. Brewer suggests, not very compellingly, that Henry regarded himself as bound by treaty with France to refrain from overt interference with Albany's regency.

48. Cited in Brewer, p. 520.

3

CROSSING THE BORDER:
SCOTTISH POETRY AND ENGLISH
READERS IN THE SIXTEENTH CENTURY

Priscilla Bawcutt

This paper is concerned with a neglected topic. There have been in-numerable discussions of the literary relations between England and Scotland up to about 1600, but they tend to be one-sided; they are concerned chiefly with the influence upon Scotland of English poetry, particularly that of Chaucer and his followers. Many recent critics, of course, deny or minimise such signs of English cultural dominance – the term 'Scottish Chaucerians' is now politically incorrect [1] – yet there have been only a few attempts to investigate whether Scottish poetry made any impact south of the Border.[2] We are thus left with a vague impression of English hostility, ignorance or indifference, in line with the common slur about English cultural insularity.

The reality seems to me more complicated, and much more interes-ting. Anglo-Scottish relations in the later Middle Ages, according to historians, consisted of mutual hostility and intermittent warfare. But we should not assume that political hostility was necessarily reflected in cultural attitudes, nor that it was felt at all times or by all persons. The Border between England and Scotland was not an Iron Curtain but a highly permeable zone; across it flew arrows and bullets, accom-panied by verbal missiles – insults, flytings, and propagandistic pamphlets. But there was also, despite the attempts of English and Scottish governments to prevent it, more peaceful and sociable 'inter-communing';[3] the causes included exile, pilgrimage, marriage, trade, diplomacy, and education. One small pointer to this is the number of Scottish authors who are known to have visited England: John Barbour, Richard Holland, William Dunbar, Gavin Douglas, John Mair and Sir David Lindsay.

The sixteenth century witnessed growing English awareness of Scot-tish books and writers. Of the various factors responsible for this, I would single out three: new technology, in the shape of the printing press; the Reformation, that added fresh motives for crossing the Border, such as religious persecution; and most important of all, the marriage of James IV of Scotland to Margaret Tudor in 1503. This led ultimately to the accession of James VI to the English crown in 1603, and its dynastic consequences were vividly present to English minds throughout the century. As Keith Brown remarks, the Elizabethans 'paid serious attention to Scotland'.[4]

The topic of Anglo-Scottish literary relations is both vast and bedevilled by preconceptions. There has been an obsession with seeking influences, or finding them (as in the case of Robert Henryson upon Sir Thomas Wyatt) where none exists. Most modern readers particularly admire the trio of vernacular poets, Henryson, Dunbar and Douglas. But one has to beware of a preoccupation solely with what we now consider the great names and the literary masterpieces. Obscure and anonymous poems, perhaps surviving only in manuscript, have escaped critical scrutiny, yet have much to tell us about the cultural relations between Scotland and England; others that may today seem dull and tedious were once best-sellers. We have to beware also of erecting mental frontiers as well as geographical ones: verse cannot be wholly dissociated from prose, nor vernacular writings from those in Latin. I cannot here explore all the complicated ramifications of this topic, and do not propose to mention prophecies, for instance, or the court poets associated with James VI. What I wish to discuss might be grandly labelled questions of dissemination and reception: put more simply, which Scottish poems travelled south, how did they get there, and how did the English respond to them?

I will begin with the man who made the first, rudimentary attempt to catalogue Scottish writers: John Bale, Carmelite friar turned Protestant controversialist. 'Bilious' Bale may not be of high repute as a dramatist, but he was a genuine scholar and bibliophile, whose work marks the beginnings of British literary history. His *Scriptorum Illustrium Majoris Britanniae ... Catalogus* was the precursor of great modern bibliographical tools, such as the *Short-title Catalogue of Books Printed ... 1475–1640*. The second part of the *Catalogus*, published in 1559, devotes many pages to Scottish writers, and mentions some seventy-six names. This startlingly large figure, of course, lists only a few vernacular poets among a vast body of Latin prose writers. What is more, Bale includes any author ever labelled *Scotus*, even when he undoubtedly originated in Ireland. Bale has often been criticised, notably for a propensity to multiply authors and titles; he certainly got things wrong when he took Stephen Hawes to be Scottish. But what he achieved was remarkable, especially when one recalls the appalling vicissitudes of his life, and the loss of his precious library.

Bale was extremely influential. For good or ill, he long helped to shape Scotland's image of its literary past.[5] He mentions most of the early Scottish poets who are famous today (apart from Barbour), although how familiar he was with their work is open to question. Some of his knowledge is clearly second-hand. His brief account of blind Hary and *The Wallace* (which is tucked away in an entry for William Elphinstone) undoubtedly derives from John Mair, to the Latinised form of whose name he gives a precise reference: *de quo Maior lib. 4. cap. 15*. His account of James I and *The Kingis Quair* also comes from the same source.[6] Bale seems to have known no more than the names of Dunbar and Kennedy, whom he mentions in the *Index* (his manuscript notebook unpublished till the twentieth century), along with *Rolandus Harryson* and *Quintinus*.[7] I suspect that he derived part of this information either from Douglas's *Palice of Honour* (923–4) or Lindsay's *Testament of the Papyngo* (10–54). I take *Rolandus* to be either a typographical error for Richard Holland, or possibly the minor poet, John Rolland. *Harryson* may well be Henryson. *Quintinus* seems to derive from Douglas's mysterious 'Quintine with ane huttok on his heid'.

Bale had better knowledge, however, of three other poets, Douglas, Bellenden, and Lindsay. His account of Douglas's life draws upon the recollections of a friend, Polydore Vergil, and he mentions both *The Palice of Honour* and *The Eneados*, supplying incipits for both, in a suitably Latinised form: not 'Quhen paill Aurora with face lamentabill', for instance, but *Dum aurora pallida lamentabili facie*. The manuscript notebook correctly gives the number of books in the *Eneados* as thirteen, but in the printed *Catalogus* this has changed to twelve, perhaps from lapse of memory, or a feeling that it ought to have the same number as the *Aeneid*.[8] The account of Bellenden in the *Catalogus* illustrates Bale's weaknesses as well as his virtues: basically accurate on Bellenden's life and the verse appended to his prose translation of Hector Boece's *Scotorum Historia*, it nonetheless contains a curious list of extra works: *Super litera Pythagorae* (of the letter of Pythagoras), *De virtute & voluptate* (of virtue and pleasure), and *Super quodam somnio* (of a certain dream). All three titles, in effect, constitute notes on the advice-poem addressed to the youthful James V, rather confusingly known as 'the Proheme to the Cosmography', and reveal one of the processes by which Bale multiplied works. Perhaps separated from his books and after the passage of years, he seems to have misinterpreted his notes on a single poem as describing three separate ones.[9] In the case of Lindsay Bale refers specifically to some minor works, *The Testament of the Papyngo*, which he nicely calls *Psittacum Loquacem*, or 'The Talkative Parrot', *Cardinal Beaton*, and *The Dialogue of Experience and the Courtier*. Lindsay's editor, Douglas Hamer, also argues that Bale's mention of *Acta sui Temporis* is a valuable clue to the existence of a lost work, and that it corroborates Scottish references to Lindsay as a historian of his own times.[10]

How did an English reader, like Bale, acquire knowledge of Scottish writers? He himself, in an interesting letter to John Knox and Alexander Alesius,[11] laments that he had not visited Scotland or investigated its libraries; indeed, if he had, we might be better informed about Scottish medieval manuscripts. Unfortunately, although he had intended to sail to Scotland when fleeing from Ireland on the accession of Mary Tudor in 1553, Bale was abducted by Flemish pirates and eventually landed in the Netherlands, penniless and bookless. Bale, in fact, seems to have had access chiefly to printed Scottish books, and his notes imply that he borrowed them from friends, such as the poet and lawyer, Nicholas Brigham, or purchased them from a shop, such as that of the London printer and bookseller, John Day. It should be recalled that Day published English editions of several of Lindsay's works, including the *Tragedy of Cardinal Beaton* in 1548.

It is not always appreciated that the very first printed edition of a Scottish poem (as far as we know) was published, not in Edinburgh by Chepman and Myllar, but in Westminster in 1499 by Wynkyn de Worde. This was *The Contemplacioun of Synnaris*, a devotional work by Friar William of Touris.[12] The earliest surviving editions of other important Scottish poems were printed in London: Douglas's *Palice of Honour* and *Eneados* (1553), and Lindsay's *Testament of the Papyngo* (1538). I stress 'surviving', because in some cases there is evidence that these editions derive not from manuscripts but from lost Scottish prints. But another work very famous in its own time, George Buchanan's *Baptistes*, was first printed in London (1577) rather than Edinburgh, largely because of the enthusiasm felt for Buchanan by Thomas Randolph and other English admirers.[13]

Printed books travelled across the Border particularly quickly when they had well-known authors or touched on controversial issues. A generation after Bale Gabriel Harvey purchased James VI's *Essayes of a Prentise* not long after it had been published (Edinburgh, 1585), noting the price he paid (2s. 4d.), and the day he read it (24 February 1585/6). In the margins he wrote enthusiastic comments, such as 'How much better then owr Gascoignes Notes of instruction for Inglish Verse and Ryme!' In a letter to Arthur Capel (*c.* 1573), thought to have been one of his Cambridge students, Harvey vividly conveys how books circulated among friends and were eagerly discussed: 'M. Capel, I dout not but you haue ere this sufficently perusid ... thos tragical pamflets of the quen of Scots ... there is a frend of mine that spake unto me yesternight for mi book of the Quen of Scots ...' [14]

In times of peace some Englishmen purchased books in Scotland itself; one example is the British Library copy of the 1594 edition of Lindsay's *Squire Meldrum*, which has an inscription showing that it was bought in Edinburgh on 2 March 1597/8, for 30 'Skottis' pence, by Thomas Arrowsmith, servant to Henry Bowes, Esq.[15] But other Scottish books left Scotland less legitimately. At the end of his reign Henry VIII attempted to bring about the betrothal of his son and the infant Mary Queen of Scots – an episode sometimes known as the 'Rough Wooing'. In 1544 the Earl of Hertford invaded Scotland and sacked Edinburgh. Among the English forces was a knight, Sir William Norris, who brought unusual plunder back to his home, Speke Hall, near Liverpool: fifteen substantial volumes of law and theology, that had belonged to the abbots of Cambuskenneth. Inscriptions in the books record precisely where and when they were acquired, and proudly instruct that they should remain at Speke forever 'as an heirloom'.[16] Curiously, another book-loving Englishman was also present on this occasion, John Thynne, ancestor of the Marquess of Bath; in the flyleaf of the Longleat manuscript of Bellenden's translation of Boece is an inscription: 'Found in Edenburgh at the wyninge and burninge therof the viith maye', etc.[17] In September 1547 Thynne was again fighting the Scots, and was knighted on the field of battle. It has been suggested that it was then that he acquired an even more important manuscript, the Longleat copy of Douglas's *Eneados*. But this seems unlikely, since this copy was not completed until 22 November 1547.[18] It should be noted that by European standards Norris and Thynne were but petty thieves compared to Louis XII, who in 1499 seized and brought back to France a large part of the splendid library formed by the Visconti rulers of Milan.

A surprising number of Scottish works travelled south in what today might be called 'the diplomatic bag'. In the sixteenth century there was a great expansion of diplomatic activity. Legations had long been sent abroad for specific missions, to negotiate a marriage or a treaty. But the custom of maintaining a resident ambassador, along with a network of sympathisers or paid informers, was increasingly prevalent throughout Europe. English governments – often with good reason – were almost as suspicious of Scotland as of France, and wished to know not only what was happening, but what was being said and written. This had extremely interesting literary consequences. Preserved among the English State Papers, in the Public Record Office and the British

Library, is much precious information about contemporary Scottish verse and drama. If it were not for the detailed report sent to Thomas Cromwell by the English envoy, Sir William Eure, we would know nothing of the moral interlude performed at Epiphany 1540 before the Scottish court in the palace of Linlithgow. Sir William Eure was chiefly concerned with the light this performance shed on the Scottish king's attitude to the Reformation and to 'the bussope of Rome'. But for us his report has a different importance. Not only does it help flesh out the skeletal dramatic annals of Scotland; the interlude's striking resemblance to parts of Lindsay's *Satyre of the Thrie Estaitis* (a work thought to have been first performed on 7 June 1552) poses a fascinating and much-debated problem for literary historians. Was this Linlithgow interlude an early draft or first version of the *Satyre*? [19]

Even more important is the fact that among these diplomatic papers are preserved actual poetic texts, both in manuscript and print. Not surprisingly, since what the English were interested in was Scottish public opinion, their subject matter is highly topical. Some pieces are official in character, such as the admonitory poem that welcomed Mary Queen of Scots on her entry into Edinburgh in 1561.[20] But the majority are polemical and satirical, and deal with such sensational events as the murder of Darnley (1566), the murder of the Regent Moray in 1570, or the siege of Edinburgh Castle in the early 1570s. Dozens of copies, particularly of the printed broadsides, must once have circulated in Edinburgh, but almost the only ones now surviving are those sent to William Cecil, Lord Burghley. Many were dispatched by Thomas Randolph, English agent and investigative reporter, who had a wide-ranging interest in Scottish affairs. His career and friendships, especially with Buchanan, and his letters from Scotland in the 1560s and early 1570s require closer attention than they have yet received from literary scholars.[21] The poems have been preserved in remarkably good condition, and often bear the endorsements of Cecil's clerks: 'an exhortation to ye L. of Scotland in metre', or 'a lewd ballet, taken with ye L. Setons writings'.[22] Why did so few survive in Scotland itself? One answer might be that they suffered the usual fate of popular but flimsy leaflets: read to pieces, discarded when no longer topical, or – worse – consigned to the 'privy' purposes envisaged by Thomas Nashe in *The Unfortunate Traveller*.[23] A more cogent explanation is that many were deliberately destroyed. In April 1567 an act was passed, proscribing 'tickittis of defamatioun set up under silence of nycht in diverse publict places' (Cranstoun, I, lvii). Robert Lekpreuik, who printed many of these poems, was repeatedly fined and imprisoned; in 1571 his house was searched for copies of *The Chamaeleon*, George Buchanan's notorious satire on William Maitland of Lethington.[24] It is not surprising that the earliest extant text of this work is among the Cotton Manuscripts in the British Library.[25]

Why is this important? If this material had not been preserved in England, Lekpreuik's recorded output as a printer would be much diminished, and our knowledge of early Scottish printing would be sadly impaired. As for the poems themselves, it seems to me that they call out for re-investigation and a more sympathetic evaluation. At the moment they are available only in James Cranstoun's useful but out-dated nineteenth-century edition; there exist more texts, in prose and verse, and more information about them than he realised. The intensity of English interest in the murder of the Earl of Moray, for instance, is indicated not only by the London location of the three surviving copies of *The Regent's Tragedy* (Cranstoun, no. xii), but also by its rapid publication in an English broadside version: 'Lately set forth in Scottish ... And now partly turned into English'.[26] Again, it has long been known that the Public Record Office possesses the only copy of a printed poem attacking William Maitland, called *The Bird in the Cage* (Cranstoun, no. xxii); but until recently little interest has been shown in an unpublished manuscript that it possesses, also attacking Maitland, and sent to London at the same time as the poem. This short prose dialogue between two Edinburgh women is political in nature, but has a highly literary framework – its narrator spies on the women as they are carousing one night – and clearly owes much to the tradition of Dunbar's *Twa Cummaris* and *Twa Mariit Wemen and the Wedo*.[27] Cranstoun's commentary is also at times curiously misleading. In the 'lewd ballet', mentioned earlier, he interprets the repeated phrase 'chaist forett' as 'chased forward', when it is clearly a sarcastic reference to an adulterous Protestant minister by the name of Forett. This particular poet has a caustic wit, vigorously developing the 'world upside down' topos: the plough goes in front of the oxen, the beast guides the man, and 'The soutar is the grett prechour; the gray freir moks [makes] the shone' (Cranstoun, no. xxix, 13).

Metrically, these poems are extremely varied, ranging from ballad metre to rhyme royal. Stylistically, they can be crude but are often lively and vigorous, more interesting than much of the modish but dull verse associated with James VI's court. But they offended nineteenth-century notions of the poetic: Cranstoun, comparing them with the Border Ballads, found they lacked 'poetic sentiment', and he later complained that 'we look in vain for a fresh glimpse of nature. We have murder ... but no cool grove or grassy mead'.[28] Even today they are undervalued: condemned for their 'bitterness', or dismissed by a historian as 'vehicles of anti-Marian propaganda'.[29] Yet they are precisely the sort of work that another historian, Roger Mason, has rebuked critics for ignoring;[30] their authors engage, covertly or directly, with the great political and religious issues of their time. New Historicists and those who call for the expansion of the canon should turn their attention to these poems. They illustrate not only the strength of the flyting tradition in Scotland, but the new politicised directions that it was taking. The influence of Dunbar is clear in the diction of some pieces, such as the boisterous and alliterative 'Reingat rapfow, thocht thow raif' (Cranstoun, no. viii): phrases like 'Blasphemus baird' and 'carlingis pett' derive from *The Flyting of Dunbar and Kennedy* (63, 247).[31] But there are also new techniques that recall Lindsay rather than Dunbar – one of these is the use of satirical personae, such as 'Maddie, prioress of the Caill mercat', who signifies rumour or the gossip of the streets (see Cranstoun, nos iii, viii, xii, and xxii). Robert Sempill is undoubtedly a real person, who found his name useful as a symbol for the simple, honest plain-speaking man. To possess and disseminate such poems could be as dangerous as to be their author; is it perhaps significant that they are largely absent from the Bannatyne Manuscript, which was compiled in these tumultuous times (*c.* 1568)? It throws an interesting light on George Bannatyne; he has recently been called 'devious', but perhaps a kinder epithet would be 'circumspect'.[32]

I shall now turn, briefly, to a different medium of transmission, the oral. There are several vivid accounts of the way in which one Scottish poem reached an English audience: this was 'London, thou art of townes A per se', and the occasion was a dinner party, given by the mayor of London at Christmas 1501 to visiting Scottish envoys. The accounts are highly circumstantial: the 'balade' was made by 'a Scottysh preyst syttyng at oon of the syde tablys', and afterwards he received 'much money of dyuers lordes for hys indyting'.[33] On this occasion the poem appears to have been recited, but when words are sung or accompanied by music they cross national boundaries even more easily. One has only to recall how rock music penetrated the former USSR, or how 'Lili Marlene' became a favourite of the Allied troops in the second world war. There is growing evidence that, long before the age of Burns, some Scottish songs travelled south. One of these, together with its music, is preserved in a famous Tudor song book, along with other pieces undoubtedly English, such as 'Westron wynde when wyll thow blow'.[34] This song, 'Now fayre, fayrest off every fayre', is certainly Scottish, despite its anglicised spellings (e.g. 'dofter' for 'dochter'). It welcomes the Rose, both red and white, to be queen of Scotland, and its occasion can be identified as the wedding of Margaret Tudor to James IV in 1503.

A herald's account of the wedding festivities mentions the singing of ballats, and this one was presumably brought back to England by an English guest. This song is well known, because it – like the poem in praise of London – has often been included in editions of Dunbar. Yet there is no conclusive evidence that he was author of either.

My second example is less familiar, but intriguing. At the end of the sixteenth century there are many English allusions to a very popular song on a theme that is usually known as 'the night visit'; the earliest of these is an entry in the Stationers' Register on 4 March 1588 for a ballad 'intituled *Goe from the windowe goe*'. This title derives from the refrain, the words addressed by a girl to her over-ardent lover, 'Go from my window, go!' But no English text of such a song seems to be recorded until the seventeenth century.[35] It is interesting therefore that there exist two related texts, of an earlier date, and that both come from Scotland. One of these is the curious version, found in the mid-century *Gude and Godlie Ballatis*.[36] In this incongruously moralised piece it is God who says

> Quho is at my windo, quho, quho?
> Go from my windo, go, go.

And the lover is now a type of sinful man:

> Lord, I am heir, ane wratcheit mortall,
> That for thy mercy dois cry and call.

It is less well known that there exists an even earlier version of the song in a very famous Scottish manuscript, now in the Bodleian Library, which contains the *Kingis Quair*. Unfortunately this is what its discoverer called a 'flyleaf scribble', probably of the early sixteenth century, and very difficult to read. But enough has been deciphered to confirm that it is an erotic dialogue, and possibly a carol.[37]

> [Go fro my] vindow, go, go fro my window ...
>
> [...]   ȝour seruand, madame.
> quhateuer ȝe be, go hens schir, for scham,
> [...]   scath not my gud name
>   go fro my vindow, go.

These words resemble phrases in later versions of the song.

It is often difficult to map the routes by which Scottish poems travelled to England; it is no easier to assess English responses to what they read. The sixteenth century was not a great age of criticism, and explicit critical comments are sparse, just as in contemporary Scotland.

What seems to have been of primary interest to English readers was subject matter. This is most obviously the case with the satiric broadsides, which brought south sensational 'News out of Scotland'. But this criterion also explains the remarkable popularity of 'London, thou art of townes A per se', which was a poem of a very different type. There are at least five English copies, all from the reigns of Henry VII and VIII, whereas no genuine poem by Dunbar survives in so many early manuscripts.[38] I would attribute the popularity of this particular piece largely to the vanity of Londoners. It pays glowing tribute to the Thames, the Tower, London Bridge, the wealth of the merchants and the beauty of their wives, tactfully concluding with the excellence of the Mayor. Perhaps the same motivation explains the choice of this piece, a few years ago, for the excellent 'Poems on the Underground' series.

There can be no doubt that Buchanan enjoyed the greatest prestige of all Scottish writers at this time, but Lindsay was the best-known vernacular poet. What appealed, however, was less his wit or humour than his excellent docrine, and the widespread belief that he was a committed Reformer. In 1564 William Bullen thus pictured him 'with a hammer of strong steele in his hande, breakyng a sonder the counterfeicte crosse kaies of Rome, forged by Antichriste' (see Geddie, p. 301). There is no sign that Lindsay was esteemed in England for the work that is now acclaimed as 'a theatrical masterpiece', performed at the Edinburgh Festival, and a set text for the Open University. *A Satyre of the Thrie Estaitis* was slow to be printed; the earliest extant Scottish edition is dated 1602, and reached London two years later. If this play had been known to an English audience in the 1550s, it might have had great impact; but in 1604 it must have seemed incredibly old-fashioned to theatre-goers acquainted with Marlowe and Shakespeare. An early seventeenth-century English annotator of one copy of *A Satire*, although not unsympathetic, conveys this vividly: 'I think their theatre was the bare ground'.[39] Lindsay's most successful work – in England as in Scotland – was the encyclopedic, highly didactic *Dialogue between Experience and a Courtier*. This had several English editions, and that of 1566 contains a remarkable preface by Thomas Purfoote, eulogising Lindsay, and noting that the work was 'profitable for all estates, but chiefly for gentlemen'. Two years later a part of this same poem, describing the Siege of Jerusalem (3952–4125), was incorporated in a ballad, printed in Fleet St (1568–9), and designed to be sung 'to the tune of the Queenes Almayne'. As late as 1605 a copy of this 1566 edition was of interest to a haberdasher called William Ruskatt, who records that he bought it 'of Mrs Stow the cronicklers wife'.[40]

Religious bonds and sympathies, as the case of Lindsay illustrates, were very important; they frequently outweighed national allegiances. This was no less true for Catholics than for Protestants. It probably explains how Lord William Howard (1563–1640), an English nobleman and devout Catholic, came to possess a Scottish collection of prayers and verse meditations, compiled on the eve of the Reformation (BL, MS Arundel 285).[41] The importance of religious loyalties is illustrated also in the little-known but interesting figure of William Forrest, an Oxford poet, priest and Catholic controversialist, who flourished *c.* 1530–81. Into a work of his own, devoted to the honour of the Virgin Mary (BL, MS Harley 1703, dated 1571–2), he inserted a delightful Scottish poem on the same subject that begins 'Rose Mary, most of vertue virgynall'. How Forrest came across this piece is not known, but he includes four stanzas in Scots not recorded in other copies, and he also praises the poet enthusiastically:

> This salutation, much eloquentlye
> A devout Scotte, of love most entire
> Longe time sithen dyd yt edyfye ...[42]

Both the eloquence and the piety of the Scottish poet are here celebrated by Forrest. Aesthetic values were commonly interwoven, in this way, with other factors. Buchanan thus impressed a small group of Englishmen – the so-called Sidney circle – both by his political ideas and also his mastery of Latin style and versification. Harvey praised his 'Invective veine, for elegant style none nearer owre Ascham'.[43] Gavin Douglas's reputation was at its zenith in the sixteenth century: his fame was not confined to Scotland, but spread, as he predicted, 'throw owt the ile yclepit Albyon'. In 1563 Barnabe Googe, himself now largely forgotten, commended Douglas's 'famous wit in Scottish ryme'. But I suspect that this fame was due in part to the sheer usefulness of Douglas's *Eneados* among those who were not fluent in Latin; until 1573 it was the only complete translation of the *Aeneid* available in England.[44] Yet this alone is not sufficient to account for the extraordinary influence of this work upon Henry Howard, Earl of Surrey, who incorporated striking words, phrases and whole lines into his own translation of Virgil.[45]

Perhaps most interesting of all is the English response to Henryson. *The Testament of Cresseid*, paradoxically, was the most influential of all Scottish poems; it profoundly modified the Chaucerian image of Criseyde, and contributed largely to the widespread Elizabethan conception of her as a 'lazar kite'. (So essential did it seem to the story, that a seventeenth-century reader added it to the famous manuscript of *Troilus and Criseyde* at St John's College, Cambridge.) Yet Henryson received no credit, since the poem was included in William Thynne's 1532 edition of Chaucer; henceforth it was widely believed to be Chaucer's, though not by discerning readers, such as Sir Francis Kinaston (d. 1642), who translated both *Troilus* and *The Testament* into Latin.[46] In much the same way numerous English poems were mistakenly included in editions of Chaucer at this time, and absorbed into his canon.

All this, of course, is very well known. Probably less familiar, however, is the response to Henryson's *Fables* of an Englishman called Richard Smith. In 1577 he published a work, said to have been composed by him a few years earlier in the Vale of Aylesbury, whose title page reads: 'The Fabulous tales of Esope ... Compiled moste eloquently in Scottishe metre by Master Robert Henrison, & now lately Englished ... Euery tale Moralized most aptly to this present time'. The balance here between eloquence and morality would surely not have displeased Henryson himself; and it reappears in Smith's later comments on Henryson's powers of 'invention' and his 'doctrine both pleasant and profitable'. The table of contents spells out the moral of each tale: *The Lion and the Mouse*, for example, shows 'the reuerence we owe to our Princes person'; *The Fox and the Wolf* reveals 'the great hypocrisie of the Popish prelacie'; and *The Parliament of Beasts* 'sheweth our duetie at all assemblies commaunded by our Prince or superiors'. The Protestant updating of Henryson's criticism of the church is obvious, yet not wholly perverse. Smith frames the text of the Fables within other material, including a lightly humorous and self-mocking dialogue between Aesop and the translator that is clearly modelled on Henryson's own practice. In it he speaks in glowing terms of Henryson as 'this Scottish Orpheus'. As Denton Fox noted, Smith's remarks constitute the 'earliest literary criticism of the Fables'.[47] It is remarkable that no Scot is recorded as saying a word about them until Allan Ramsay in the eighteenth century.[48] The earliest critical comment on *The Testament of Cresseid* is likewise English: Gabriel Harvey's perceptive note, 'In the beginning of the Testament of Creseide a winterlie springe'.[49] It is one of the minor mysteries of literary history how rapidly Henryson was forgotten in his own country. When Kinaston tried to discover something about his life from 'diuers aged schollers of the Scottish nation', they gave him the patently erroneous information that Henryson flourished at the end of Henry VIII's reign.[50]

It would be anachronistic to term the anglicised versions of Henryson and other Scottish poets 'appropriation' or 'piracy'. A similar practice of Scotticising English verse had long been prevalent in Scotland. The great manuscript miscellanies of Asloan, Bannatyne, and Maitland all contain poems by Chaucer, Lydgate, and other English poets, wearing

Scottish dress, and usually with no hint of their authorship.[51] A piquant but less familiar example is the vivid description of winter, found in an Aberdeen manuscript that represents the first four stanzas of Sackville's Induction to *The Mirror for Magistrates*.[52] Such practices continue the medieval habit of translating from one dialect into another. As in Middle English, there was no sense of infringing copyright; and, as in Middle English, it is sometimes only the nature of rhymes or the survival of distinctive vocabulary that gives a clue to the original dialect. The treatment of William of Touris' devotional poem, *The Contemplacioun of Synnaris*, illustrates this continuity. Its publication in 1499 by Wynkyn de Worde, in an anglicised version, is not so strange as first appears. De Worde printed northern English prose works, chiefly by mystical writers; he also printed a northern alliterative poem, *The Quatrefoil of Love*. All of these were revised and adapted for a southern audience: 'the driving force was a desire to eradicate the Northern dialect forms, to modernize ... and to make the poem suitable reading matter for a sixteenth century Londoner'. This is Norman Blake's comment on the print of *The Quatrefoil*; but much the same might be said of De Worde's *The Contemplation of Sinners*.[53]

Few scholars have closely inspected these English editions of Scottish poets, and the usual response is unfavourable. Discussing Smith's rendering of Henryson, Fox sadly concurs with his modest 'Verdict on his labour':

> His harpe alas I make to iarre,
> And both his name and mine do marre.

As early as 1568 Henry Charteris reviled the English printers of Lindsay: 'thai haif gane about to bring thame to the southerne langage, alterand the vers and collouris ... quhairfoir the natiue grace and first mynd of the wryter is oftentimes peruertit'.[54] Language goes to the core of most people's perception not only of national identity but of poetic identity. We might well agree that the 'native grace' of this passage from Henryson's *The Two Mice* (*Fables*, 330–33):

> Fra fute to fute he kest hir to and fra,
> Quhylis vp, quhylis doun, als tait as ony kid.
> Quhylis wald he lat hir rin vnder the stra;
> Quhylis wald he wink, and play with hir buk heid.

is diminished by Smith's rendering:

> From fute to fute he cast hyr so with pusches,
> Now vp now downe, now suffir hir to creepe,

> Now would he let her run vnder the rushes,
> Now would he winke and play with hir bo peep.

Yet it is as well to remember that Smith and his southern readers faced real linguistic obstacles, as with this line (*Fables*, 1414): 'Sum tirlit at the campis of his beird'. One might argue that there is wit and ingenuity in Smith's solution: 'Some twirled at the muchachos of his beard'.

We should, in any case, beware of indiscriminate, blanket condemnation of these English editions, since they vary considerably, in purpose and merit. The London print of Douglas's *Palice of Honour* (*c.* 1553) was neglected for centuries, because it was considered 'southron'; yet in the preparation of an edition for the Scottish Text Society I discovered many authentic readings and distinctive Scottish words that had been modernised out of the long preferred Edinburgh edition of 1579.[55] To compare these anglicised texts with their originals, when extant, is often linguistically rewarding; it highlights areas of difference between Scots and southern English, and also the growing obsolescence of words once current in both tongues. By the end of the sixteenth century Douglas's archaism was increasingly felt, not only in England but in Scotland also. It should be noted too that some styles and genres travelled south more easily than others. Comic verse, as A. J. Aitken has shown, was 'much the most densely Scottish of any kind of writing in older Scots'.[56] This must have made it harder for English readers to comprehend. Moral and devotional poems, however, tended to employ more words from the common core of the language. Such verse travelled easily, and its nationality is occasionally difficult to ascertain.

One illustration of this is a verse Complaint of Christ from the Cross, preserved in two Scottish witnesses and three English. The best and fullest version is that in MS Arundel 285, and there is a strong probability that the poem is Scottish or northern English in origin.[57] Another intriguing problem is posed by the anonymous proverb poem, found in the Bannatyne Manuscript (f. 134ᵛ) and the Maitland Folio (p. 139), that begins 'Mony man makis ryme and luikis to na ressoun'. A later Scottish copy in an unpublished seventeenth-century manuscript is there unconvincingly described as 'King James the fyft his pasquill'.[58] At first sight this poem is chiefly interesting as the earliest collection of proverbs in Scots, and for its ingenious interlaced rhyme-scheme, in which the last word of each line rhymes with one in the middle of the next. But it is intriguing to find that there exist two English copies of this poem, both belonging to the mid-sixteenth century. One is in Cambridge (Corpus Christi College, MS 168); the other is in Oxford (Bodleian, MS Digby 145). The bulk of the latter manuscript is known to have been copied *c.* 1532 by Sir Adrian Fortescue, who was executed in 1539; there is a difference of opinion as to whether the proverb poem is in his hand. Where then did this work originate? Some scholars consider the proverbs 'of Fortescue family provenance'; but there are many rhymes (e.g. *seik: meik, wirk: kirk*) that suggest a Scottish or northern English origin. This was noted by B. J. Whiting, yet he found it puzzling that Sir Adrian should show 'a special interest in things Scottish'.[59] One possible explanation lies in the fact that he was the great nephew of Sir John Fortescue, who in the 1460s had been exiled to Scotland along with the deposed Henry VI; this would suggest one means of trans-mission to the Fortescue family, although it does not, of course, account for the poem's presence in the Corpus Christi manuscript.[60] Further linguistic and textual analysis may shed light on this and other 'debat-able' poems.

I have touched briefly on many topics in this paper. Some, such as the English admiration for Douglas and Lindsay, have already received much scholarly attention. Other areas, however, which seem interesting in their own right, are neglected and deserve further study. The satirical poems clearly need re-editing, together with a searching investigation of their political context. There is more material of this type, I suspect, awaiting discovery in the British Library and the Public Record Office. It would also be rewarding to explore the existence and implications of cross-Border friendships, particularly those of a literary and human-istic character. It is evident that the cultural contacts between England and Scotland in the sixteenth century were numerous and extremely varied. With hindsight, however, probably the most important English responses to Scottish verse, whatever their motivation, were to collect, transcribe, or print it, thus preserving for posterity much that might otherwise have perished.

1. Objections to the term (coined *c.* 1900) have occurred throughout the century; for recent ones, see R. J. Lyall, '"A New Maid Channoun"? Redefining the Canonical in Medieval and Renaissance Scottish Literature', *SSL*, 26 (1991), 1–18, especially 12–13; and R. James Goldstein, *The Matter of Scotland* (1993), pp. 144 and 257–8.

2. Two valuable studies are Gregory Kratzmann, *Anglo-Scottish Literary Relations 1430–1550* (Cambridge, 1980), and A. A. MacDonald, 'Anglo-Scottish Literary Relations: Problems and Possibilities', *SSL*, 26 (1991), 172–84.

3. On the Border in particular, see Anthony Goodman, 'The Anglo-Scottish Marches in the Fifteenth Century: a Frontier Society?', in *Scotland and England 1286–1815*, ed. Roger A. Mason (Edinburgh, 1987), pp. 18–33.

4. 'The Price of Friendship: the "Well Affected" and English Economic Clientage in Scotland before 1603', in Mason, p. 139.

5. On Bale as scholar and antiquary, see W. T. Davies, 'A Bibliography of John Bale', *Proceedings of the Oxford Bibliographical Society*, 5 (1940), pp. 203–79; on his multiplying of works, see A. G. Rigg, 'Antiquaries and Authors: the Supposed Works of Robert Baston, O. Carm.', in *Medieval Scribes, Manuscripts and Libraries: Essays presented to N. R. Ker*, ed. M. B. Parkes and A. G. Watson (1978), pp. 317–31. Rigg notes that *poemata et rhythmos* is Bale's 'way of saying "etcetera"' (p. 330). Bale's knowledge of Scottish writers and his influence upon subsequent cataloguers is documented in William Geddie's excellent *A Bibliography of Middle Scots Poets*, STS (Edinburgh and London, 1912), esp. pp. xlii–liii.

6. For exact citations from the *Catalogus*, see Geddie, pp. 149–50; and 111–12.

7. See *Index Britanniae Scriptorum*, ed. Reginald L. Poole and M. Bateson (Oxford, 1902); rpt. with Introduction by Caroline Brett and J. P. Carley (Cambridge, 1990), p. 496.

8. *Index*, p. 83; Geddie, p. 234.

9. Geddie, p. 260.

10. *Index*, p. 60; *Catalogus*, pp. 223–4; Geddie, p. 300; *The Works of Sir David Lindsay*, 4 vols, ed. D. Hamer, STS (Edinburgh and London, 1931–6), IV, pp. 19–20.

11. The letter is quoted in part by Geddie, p. xliv.

12. See A. A. MacDonald, 'Anglo-Scottish Literary Relations', 174–6, and his article, 'Catholic Devotion into Protestant Lyric: the Case of the *Contemplacioun of Synnaris*', *IR*, 35 (1984), 58–87.

13. See James E. Phillips, 'George Buchanan and the Sidney Circle', *Huntington Library Quarterly*, 12 (1948–9), 23–55.

14. See Eleanor Relle, 'Some New Marginalia and Poems of Gabriel Harvey', *RES*, n.s. 23 (1972), 401–16; and Virginia F. Stern, *Gabriel Harvey: his Life, Marginalia and Library* (Oxford, 1979), p. 223 and p. 251.

15. BL pressmark: C39.d.23; cf. Hamer, IV, p. 64.

16. See Robert Donaldson, 'The Cambuskenneth Books: the Norris of Speke Collection', *Bibliotheck*, 15, no. 1 (1988), 3–7.

17. For a facsimile, see [John Collins], *A Short Account of the Library at Longleat House, Warminster, Wilts.* (1980), pp. 6–7. Cf. also R. W. Chambers, 'Bellenden's Translation of the History of Hector Boece', *SHR*, 19 (1922), 196–201 (198).

18. Cf. *Virgil's Aeneid Translated into Scottish Verse by Gavin Douglas*, 4 vols, ed. D. F. C. Coldwell, STS (Edinburgh and London, 1957–64), I, pp. 99–100. Dr Kate Harris, Librarian to the Marquess of Bath, informs me that 'the earliest firm reference' to this MS is in the 1702 catalogue of books owned by the Thynne family, although the 1577 inventory refers to what seems to be the 1553 print of the *Eneados*.

19. The description is printed in Lindsay, ed. Hamer, II, pp. 1–6; see also R. J. Lyall, 'The Linlithgow Interlude of 1540', in *Actes du 2ᵉ Colloque de Langue et de Littérature Ecossaises*, ed. J-J. Blanchot and C. Graf (Strasbourg, 1978), pp. 409–21. Our knowledge of the Twelfth Night masques in 1564 depends similarly on the reports sent to London by Thomas Randolph; see I. D. McFarlane, *Buchanan* (1981), pp. 231–2.

20. The text was first printed in Robert S. Rait, *Mary Queen of Scots* (2nd edn, 1900), pp. 21–2. For discussion and an improved text, see A. A. MacDonald, 'Mary Stewart's Entry to Edinburgh: an Ambiguous Triumph', *IR*, 42 (1991), 101–10.

21. Randolph's curiosity and care for detail are seen in his account of an altar to Apollo, discovered at Musselburgh in May 1565; cf. *Treasurer's Accounts*, XI (1559–66), ed. Sir J. Balfour Paul (Edinburgh, 1916), pp. lii–liii. K. P. Frescoln, 'Thomas Randolph: an Elizabethan in Scotland' (Ph.D. dissertation, West Virginia Univ. 1971), pays little attention to Randolph's cultural interests.

22. See *Satirical Poems of the Time of the Reformation*, ed. James Cranstoun, 2 vols, STS (Edinburgh and London, 1891–3), nos v and xxix. For more recent bibliographical information about the prints, see Carole R. Livingston, *British Broadside Ballads of the Sixteenth Century: A Catalogue of the Extant Sheets and an Essay* (New York, 1991).

23. *The Works of Thomas Nashe*, ed. R. B. McKerrow (1966), II, p. 207.

24. Cranstoun, I, p. lvi. Cf. also *CSP: Scottish*, III, no. 242 (16 May 1570), where Randolph says that the printer of an unnamed book is 'lyke to smerte' for it.

25. BL, MS Caligula C. iii, fol. 280; for discussion, see McFarlane, pp. 336–7; *CSP: Scottish*, III, p. 456.

26. Now in the Huntington Library: Britwell No. 77/HEW 18337. See Livingston, no. 138; *STC*, 22210.

27. PRO, SP. 52/17 (item 70). Cf. M. Loughlin, 'The Dialogue of the Twa Wyfeis: Maitland, Machiavelli and the Propaganda of the Scottish Civil War', in *The Renaissance in Scotland*, ed. A. A. MacDonald, M. Lynch and I. Cowan (Leiden, 1994), pp. 226–45.

28. Cranstoun, I, pp. xi and xxxv.

29. Cf. *History of Scottish Literature I: Origins to 1660*, ed. R. D. S. Jack (Aberdeen, 1988), pp. 6–8, and M. Lynch, 'Queen Mary's Triumph', *SHR*, 69 (1990), 15. For searching criticism of these poems, see Gregory Kratzman, 'Sixteeenth-Century Secular Poetry', in *History of Scottish Literature* I, pp. 116–18; and 'Political Satire and the Scottish Reformation', *SSL*, 26 (1991), 423–37.

30. R. A. Mason, in *SHR*, 69 (1990), 101–2.

31. On the Scottish flyting tradition, see Priscilla Bawcutt, 'The Art of Flyting', *SLJ*, 10, no. 2 (1983), 5–21.

32. Cf. A. A. MacDonald, 'The Bannatyne Manuscript: a Marian Anthology', *IR*, 37 (1986), 36.

33. See Priscilla Bawcutt, *Dunbar the Makar* (Oxford, 1992), p. 82; and C. Bühler, 'London thow art the Floure of Cytes all', *RES*, 13 (1937), 1–9.

34. BL, Royal MS, Appendix 58, fols 17^v–18^r; dated in the first quarter of the sixteenth century. The most accurate transcript is in E. Flügel, 'Liedersammlungen', *Anglia*, 12 (1899), 256–72.

35. See C. R. Baskervill, 'English Songs on the Night Visit', *PMLA*, 36 (1921), especially 580–5.

36. *The Gude and Godlie Ballatis*, ed. A. F. Mitchell, STS (Edinburgh and London, 1897), pp. 132–6.

37. See P. J. Frankis, 'Some Late Middle English Lyrics in the Bodleian Library', *Anglia*, 73 (1955–6), 299–304. For the text, see *The Works of Geoffrey Chaucer and The Kingis Quair: a Facsimile of Bodleian Library, MS Arch. Selden. B.24*, ed. J. Boffey and A. S. G. Edwards (Cambridge, 1997).

38. Copies are preserved in BL, Cotton Vitellius A xvi; BL, Lansdowne 762; Guildhall Library, MS 3313; Oxford, Balliol College, MS 354; and Pierpont Morgan, MA 717.

39. The note refers to the stage-direction, 'Pauper sal ... cast the relicts in the water'. See Marie Axton, '*Ane Satyre of the Thrie Estaitis*: The First Edition and its Reception', in *A Day Estivall*, ed. Alisoun Gardner-Medwin and J. H. Williams (Aberdeen, 1990), pp. 21–34.

40. For fuller information, see Hamer, IV, pp. 38–9; IV, p. lv; and IV, p. 44. A sixteenth-century owner of a manuscript of Lydgate's *Fall of Princes* included in an interesting list of his books 'A dyaloge betwene experyens and the courter. Davyd Lyndseye' (Lydgate, *Fall of Princes*, ed. H. Bergen, EETS (1924–7), IV, pp. 22–3).

41. The manuscript is published in *Devotional Pieces in Verse and Prose*, ed.

J. A. W. Bennett, STS (Edinburgh and London, 1955). It is perhaps relevant that Lord William's home at Naworth was close to the Scottish Border.

42. See the *DNB* article on Forrest; and Louise Imogen Guiney, *Recusant Poets, with a Selection from their Work* (New York, 1939), pp. 137–45. Harley MS 1703, like another copy of Forrest's poems, was once in Welsh ownership; see *History of Grisild the Second*, ed. W. D. Macray, Roxburghe Club (1875), p. xxii. On the Scots poem, see H. N. Mac-Cracken, 'New Stanzas by Dunbar', *MLN*, 24 (1909), 110–11; and Ian C. Cunningham, 'Two Poems on the Virgin: (National Library of Scotland, Adv. MS. 18.5.14)', *TEBS*, 5.5 (1988), 32–40.

43. See Phillips, 'George Buchanan' (note 13 above); and Stern, pp. 204–5.

44. See Priscilla Bawcutt, *Gavin Douglas* (Edinburgh, 1976), pp. 201–6.

45. Cf. Florence Ridley, 'Surrey's Debt to Gawin Douglas', *PMLA*, 76 (1961), 25–33.

46. For documentation, see Introduction to Denton Fox's edition of *The Poems of Robert Henryson* (Oxford, 1981). On Kinaston, see also Richard Beadle, 'The Virtuoso's *Troilus*', in *Chaucer Traditions*, ed. Ruth Morse and B. Windeatt (Cambridge, 1990), pp. 213–33.

47. Fox, p. lvi.

48. See Geddie, p. 176.

49. See Gabriel Harvey's *Marginalia*, ed. G. C. Moore Smith (Stratford upon Avon, 1913), p. 159.

50. See Fox, p. xiv.

51. See, for instance, Denton Fox and William Ringler's introduction to the Scolar Press Facsimile of the Bannatyne Manuscript (1980).

52. Aberdeen Diet Book 1503–1511 (SRO, SC 1/2/1), f. 77^r. The verses are a later addition. For a transcript, see *The Miscellany of the Spalding Club*, vol. II (Aberdeen, 1842), p. xxix.

53. Cf. N. Blake, 'Wynkyn de Worde and the *Quatrefoil of Love*', *Archiv*, 206 (1969), 189–200 (199).

54. Preface to 1568 *Warkis*; printed in Hamer, I, pp. 397–403.

55. See *The Shorter Poems of Gavin Douglas*, ed. P. Bawcutt, STS (Edinburgh and London, 1967), pp. xxii–xxvii; and *The Palis of Honoure*, ed. David Parkinson (Kalamazoo, Mich., 1992).

56. A. J. Aitken, 'The Language of Older Scots Poetry', in *Scotland and the Lowland Tongue*, ed. J. D. McClure (Aberdeen, 1983), p. 39.

57. See Bennett, pp. 261–5; and *Pieces from the Makculloch and Gray Manuscripts*, ed. G. Stevenson, STS (Edinburgh and London, 1918), pp. 33–7 (treated, unfortunately, as three separate poems). For the English witnesses, which have a northern provenance or northern linguistic features, see *IMEV*, 1119.

58. Aberdeen University Library, MS 28, ff. 27^r–29^v. This MS was compiled by Andrew Melville and his family.

59. Cf. B. J. Whiting, 'Proverbs and Proverbial Sayings from Scottish Writings before 1600', *Mediaeval Studies*, 11 (1949), 125. On the manuscript, see Thomas (Fortescue) Lord Clermont, *A History of the Family of Fortescue* (1880), pp. 250–311; and A. Middleton, 'The Audience and Public of "Piers Plowman"', in *Middle English Alliterative Poetry and its Literary Background*, ed. D. Lawton (Woodbridge, 1982) p. 108.

60. On Sir John Fortescue's presence in Scotland, see *The Governance of England*, ed. Charles Plummer (Oxford, 1885; rept. 1926), pp. 56–62. I owe this reference to Sally Mapstone; see her 'The Advice to Princes Tradition in Scottish Literature 1450–1500' (D.Phil. thesis, Oxford Univ. 1986), p. 110.

4

EARLY MODERN SCOTTISH LITERATURE AND THE PARAMETERS OF CULTURE

A. A. MacDonald

In the following pages an attempt is made to indicate some of the more important parameters bearing upon the culture of Scotland within the period stretching from the end of the Middle Ages through the Renaissance and into the Baroque. Although individual writers and their works are reviewed, the discussion tries to avoid flitting from poet to poet in a merely chronological fashion. The objective, rather, is to shed some light on the relation between, on the one hand, qualities immanent within literary works themselves and, on the other, general factors of cultural history which impinged upon the production and reception of those same works.

Various factors can present obstacles in the modern critical assessment of early literary works. Not surprisingly, perhaps, one of the most familiar problems is that of periodisation. Where this is too rigidly applied, the resulting literary history may seem constricted; but equally, where periodisation is treated in a capricious way, the contours become blurred. An example of the latter is afforded by C. S. Lewis's classic study of the English literature of the late Middle Ages and the Renaissance; this well-known book divides the period into three parts, labelled 'late medieval', 'drab' and 'golden' respectively.[1] Faced with the problem of what to do with Middle Scots literature, Lewis packs all of it into the first of his critical-historical categories. This produces oddities: in Lewis's book the comments on Alexander Hume (d. 1609) precede the discussion of either John Skelton (d. 1529) or Alexander Barclay (d. 1552), and one may feel that the critic has stretched the term 'late medieval' to breaking point. Lewis's arrangement, of course, has a practical advantage for the English reader, who is thereby enabled rapidly to traverse the rugged and unfamiliar terrain of Middle Scots literature, *en route* to more familiar and agreeable country. Yet it is at least debatable whether this is a desirable effect, since Lewis's arrangement produces many unfortunate wrenches of critical perspective. Such an approach, furthermore, also obstructs the comparative discussion of works from different but related literatures, where these underwent similar and synchronous cultural influences. For example: the Reformation was undoubtedly responsible for much 'drabness' in sixteenth-century poetry, but it is wrong to imply that England had a monopoly on that drabness.

More insidious for the modern critic is the danger of making apparently innocent assumptions concerning earlier poets and writers – such as that of their 'personality'. As a consequence of the emphases of the humanists, the writers of the Renaissance, as compared with their medieval forebears, laid an increased value upon the subjective element in literary production. Sir Philip Sidney, one will recall, was enjoined by his muse simply to look into his heart and write.[2] This tendency was eventually to lead to the subjectivity and emotionalism of the Romantics, and to modern conceptions of the artist as a quasi-autonomous entity. The study of most medieval and much early modern literature, however, is not facilitated by such a recourse to the concept of poetic individuality. While it is obviously and absolutely true that there can never be any poetry without a thinking mind to create it, the process of artistic composition, both today and in earlier periods, is likely to involve a complex of actions and reactions. In a period of culture in which the deliberate projection of the artistic self was not fashionable (and might indeed rather be deprecated as a manifestation of pride), the reactions may be more significant than the actions. In the absence of external biographical accounts of the earlier Scottish poets, one is constrained to discover their personalities in, and through, the poetry alone. While the bland proposition that each of the makars has his own personality is perhaps unlikely to meet with much resistance, it lacks a solid foundation. It is not likely that these late-medieval and Renaissance Scottish poets wrote in order to let their powerful feelings overflow; they may even have been deliberately concealing, or at least subordinating, their own personalities; their productions, therefore, probably depend more upon generic and stylistic conventions than upon the promptings of the muse.[3] A further complicating factor is afforded by literary patronage; as the adage has it, he who pays the piper calls the tune. This means that the expression of personality, often taken as the starting-point of modern verse and the analysis thereof, can be of slight importance in the study of the early Scottish poets to be discussed here, most of whom wrote to commission.

The point may be illustrated from William Dunbar's works. Dunbar has frequently been praised for his stylistic versatility, but the compliment is two-edged, and comes close to saying that Dunbar's personality, if he has one, is at best protean.[4] In Kinsley's edition, the poems are arranged in the following categories: divine poems; poems of love; poems of court life; visions and nightmares; and moralities.[5] The poems of court life and the moralities are the largest groups, and this fact colours one's impression of the poet. On the basis of Kinsley's categories, however, one might wonder whether Dunbar was peculiarly prone to nightmares, something which might make him a Romantic *avant la lettre*. Although it is not very likely, perhaps, that many readers of Dunbar, *pace* Kinsley, will draw this perverse conclusion, what is one to make of the prominence given by the editor to the so-called poems of love? This supposed 'group' contains one of the most celebrated pieces of anti-romantic satire in all English literature (*The Tretis of the Twa Mariit Wemen and the Wedo*), one of the most scurrilous and hilarious parodies of courtly *chanson d'aventure* ('In secreit place this hindir nycht'), one of the most rhetorically accomplished and most intellectually vapid allegories of love (*The Goldyn Targe*), as well as one of the most frigidly decorative lyrics ('Sweit rois of vertew and of gentilnes'). Dunbar's poetic practice suggests that his attitude to love is normally one of humorous detachment, if not of clerkly disdain. As has recently been said: 'his most frequent role is neither as participant nor critic, but rather as the amused and ironic observer of the game of love'.[6] It would therefore be preposterous to claim that his poetry is the expression of anything within his erotic soul. In considering Dunbar's poems on this topic, one should rather look to the way that, as a poet of the court, Dunbar was expected to provide poems which would appeal to the taste of James IV and his entourage.

The same problem presents itself in relation to Alexander Scott, whose poems evince, according to one editor, a 'bewildering'[7] variety of attitudes to love, ranging from the traditional and adoring sort ('Hence, hairt, with her that must depart', 'Richt as the glass bene thirlit throuch with beams'), through poems providing intellectual commentary on love ('Love preysis but comparison', 'It comes you lovers to be laill') to poems full of cynical-sounding advice ('Lovers, lat be the frennesy of love', 'Ye lusty ladeis look'). The editor himself is uncomfortable with this seeming inconsistency, and takes refuge in a biographical hypothesis, according to which Scott would have written his poems over some twenty years, during which period his attitudes to love would have had time to develop.[8] The power of the biographical theory is truly great: another critic, who begins by saying that 'Scott's development as an individual corresponds to the general national pattern', puts flesh on the skeleton of historical fact:

> It is easy to read Scott's lyrics as recording the effect on a tempera-
> ment naturally inclined to detachment and cynicism of an unhappy
> experience of passionate love, an experience which ultimately
> impelled him towards total rejection and a position from which it
> was easy for him to adopt some, perhaps all, of the more rigorous
> beliefs and attitudes of the Reformers.[9]

In this view, Scott commences as a writer of subtle erotic poetry, only
to end as a dour paraphraser of psalms. The difficulty is, that with only
a few exceptions, it is quite possible that all Scott's poems were composed
during the personal reign of Mary Stewart in Scotland (a period of five
or six years). In such a brief span, profound psychological developments
of the sort proposed for Scott do not seem plausible. Pseudo-biographical
hypotheses, of course, gain their force from the fact that it is not easy
to find an alternative theory with equally facile explanatory power; but
this lacuna, perhaps needless to say, has no necessary implications for
the truth-value of the biographical hypothesis.[10] The poetry of Dunbar
and Scott is the product not only of individual genius but also of
historical circumstance, and the latter would dictate that such poetry
be at least as much governed by what the audience wished to hear as
by what the poets themselves wished to say. At any rate there is no
reason to think that post-Romantic simplifications will be of much help
in general characterisations of the work of either Dunbar or Scott.

The modern reader might therefore wonder whether anything at all
can be certainly known about how or when medieval Scottish poets
give voice to their own personalities, since these poets' own views (like
those of medieval poets in general) can seldom be disentangled from
the surrounding ethos. A perceptible change begins to affect Scotland
in the sixteenth century, when some poets clearly began to speak for
themselves, recording their feelings as individuals, or taking a stand
against the prevailing culture.

Gavin Douglas provides us with a first example. Whereas in his early
work, *The Palice of Honour*, he writes in the first person singular, and
one recognises that this is essentially in accordance with the conventions
of Chaucerian dream-vision poetry, by the time he comes to the *magnum
opus* of his poetic maturity, the *Eneados* translation, his praise of Chaucer,
though still loyally expressed, is not devoid of personal nuance, and
Douglas has the confidence to challenge his great English predecessor:

> I say no*ch*t this of Chauser for offens,
> Bot till excus my lewyt insufficie*n*s,
> For as he stand*is* beneth Virgill in gre,

> Vndir hym alsfer I grant my self to be.
> And netheles into sum place, quha kend it,
> My mastir Chauser gretly Virgill offendit.[11]

Another place in which we see Douglas display a new and individual attitude is in the opening sentence of his first prologue – a sentence which *nota bene* is exactly the same length as that more familiar specimen which opens the General Prologue of the *Canterbury Tales*:

> Lawd, honour, praysyng*is*, thank*is* infynyte
> To the and thy dulce ornat fresch endyte,
> Maist reuerend Virgill, of Latyn poet*is* prynce,
> Gem of engyne and flude of eloquens,
> Thow peirles perle, patroun of poetry,
> Roys, regester, palm, lawrer and glory,
> Chosyn charbukkill, cheif flour *and* cedyr tre,
> Lantarn, laid stern, myrro*ur* and A per se,
> Maister of master*is*, sweit sours and spryngand well
> Wyde quhar our all rung is thyne hevynly bell –
> I meyn thy crafty wark*is* curyus
> Sa quyk, lusty and maist sentencyus,
> Plesand, perfyte and feilabill in all degre,
> As quha *the* mater beheld tofor *th*ar e,
> In every volume quhilk the lyst do wryte
> Surmontyng fer all other maner endyte,
> Lyke as *the* roys in Iune with hir sweit smell
> *The* maryguld or dasy doith excell.
>
> ('Proloug', ll. 1–18)

Among the many interests of this passage is Douglas's demonstration that as an artist he is free to break away from the medieval English tradition of poetic influences (such as one sees duly recorded in the conclusion of Dunbar's *Goldyn Targe*), in which, for example, Chaucer was praised for rhetoric, Gower for morality.[12] Douglas rather ostentatiously transcends all of this, and recurs to sources which are, in different ways, both more ancient and more modern. Douglas goes on to criticise William Caxton's version of the story of Aeneas, which, based as it was on a French prose retelling of the *Roman de Troie*, was perforce immeasurably inferior to Virgil.[13] He also compliments Lorenzo Valla, the great torchbearer of the new movement of humanism. Such details reveal the Scottish translator's notable literary self-awareness as a poet in tune with the latest scholarly trends. Although it is true that Douglas is also fully cognisant of the vernacular poetic models available to him, it is evident that a sub-text of this prologue is the promulgation of the poet's independence of sources which up to and including his day were regarded as canonic. Douglas's achievement is thus an example of poetic originality striking out on a new path.

The case of Sir Richard Maitland of Lethington presents an interesting paradox: whereas on the one hand Maitland deplores the destructive factionalism of the mid-sixteenth century, this same political trouble provides him with a new theme and may thus be said to be artistically stimulating. There is much in Maitland which is a direct continuation of the moral attitudes of the Middle Ages, especially of those views conspicuous in 'advice to princes' literature,[14] yet his historical claim upon our attention is that he is the first Scottish lyric poet to treat contemporary politics from the perspective of the individual experience of someone not dependent on any position at court; in so doing he raised political awareness into a novel theme of art. In a New Year poem, which presumably refers to the conflicts of January 1560, Maitland exclaims:

> I can not sing for the vexatioun
> Of Frenchemen and the Congregatioun,
> That hes maid trowbill in this natioun,
> And monye bair biging:
> In this New Yeir I sie bot weir,
> Na caus to sing;
> In this New Yeir I sie bot weir,
> Na caus thair is to sing.[15]

In this and in other poems Maitland makes himself the barometer of national events, and the poet's emotional state is imbued with unprecedented significance. His comments on the deleterious effects of the Reformation are familiar, and have often been cited:

> Quhair is the blyithnes that hes beine,
> Baith in burgh and landwart sene,
> Amang lordis and ladyis schene,
> Daunsing, singing, game and play?
> Bot now I wait not quhat thay meine,
> All merines is worne away.
>
> (*MQ*, p. 15)

Within the context of Scottish verse, the novelty of such a passage is the idea that it is natural for the poet to see his role as the spokesman of and for his age, whereby his perceptions have a claim upon the attention of all right-thinking men. One might even go so far as to say that Maitland slips into the modern role of poet as the one who, as recorder and critic of social and political events, almost inevitably assumes a certain artistic distance *vis-à-vis* the common pursuits and shared assumptions of his contemporaries.

The factor responsible for this aspect of Maitland's poetry was undoubtedly the Reformation. This phenomenon, the most significant of all the upheavals to affect sixteenth-century Scotland, forced this traditionally-minded poet to a reassessment of his position within the society of his time. By contrast, the poetry of Maitland composed before the Reformation had given expression to collective national sentiments: examples are his congratulation of Henry II on the latter's capture of Calais from Mary Tudor (*MQ*, pp. 30–2), or of Mary Queen of Scots on her marriage to the Dauphin (*MQ*, pp. 19–23). After the deposition of the queen, Maitland was personally to suffer – for example, by the (temporary) loss of his estate at Blyth.[16] This economic deprivation, coupled with the elderly poet's growing sense of alienation from the culture and attitudes of a new age, lends the poetry of Maitland a distinctive tone. Maitland's individuality is thus quite different from that of Dunbar, who tends rather to emerge, by comparison, as someone trying, through his habit of prince-pleasing, to justify his continuing existence within the charmed circle of the royal court. Dunbar's 'individuality' is thus a result of a deliberate process of self-fashioning in the mould imposed by court circumstances. Maitland may also be contrasted with Sir David Lindsay. Lindsay certainly allowed himself to be inspired by contemporary events (such as, in 1537, the death of Madeleine of France, wife of James V, and, in 1546, the murder of Cardinal David Beaton). In such poems, and in his pungent allegorical depiction of the state of Scotland in his *Satyre of the Thrie Estaitis*, Lindsay is typically the spokesman of the majority view in society – whether in his role of poet at court, or, later, as a supporter of the movement for religious reform. In this respect, Lindsay's verse has a public function which leaves little room for the expression of the poet's own, individual thoughts. Though Maitland is a minor writer, when compared with either Dunbar or Lindsay, he yet makes a surprising appeal to certain modern expectations of the poet.

The middle of the sixteenth century was an age of intense factionalism. This not infrequently also took literary form, as witness the efflorescence of works of religious controversy, including satirical and propagandistic ballads; the fairly regular enactments against such ballads and pasquils imply, however, that such works were once much more abundant than the surviving evidence might suggest. As a specimen we may take the most notorious item in the *Gude and Godlie Ballatis*:

> The Paip, that Pagane full of pryde,
> He hes vs blindit lang,
> For quhair the blind the blind dois gyde.
> Na wounder baith ga wrang;
> Lyke Prince and King, he led the Regne,
> Of all Iniquitie:
> Hay trix, tryme go trix, vnder the grene wod tre.[17]

Such pieces would have commended themselves to a wide readership, through their unbeatable combination of simplistic thought and triumphalist language. In the light of this, it is interesting to observe Sir Richard Maitland impugning the practitioners of such bad art:

> Sum of the poetis and makeris that ar now,
> Of greit dispyite and malice ar sa fow
> Sa that all lesingis that can be inventit
> Thay put in writ, and garris thame be prentit,
> To gar the peopill euill opinioun tak
> Of thame quhome of that they thair balladis mak.
> With sclanderous wordes thay doe all thing thay can
> For to defame monye gud honest man,
> In setting furth thair buikis and thair rymis,
> Accusand sum of improbabill crymis.
>
> *(MQ, p. 173)*

Alexander Arbuthnot, a lawyer who in 1569 became principal of Aberdeen University,[18] and whose poems are preserved in manuscript alongside those of Maitland, says rather similar things, in his moral poem, 'O wratched waird, I fals fein3it fortoun':

> In poetrie I pleis to pas the tyme,
> Quhen cairfull thochtis with sorrow fain3eis me,
> Bot gif I mell with meter or with ryme,
> With rascall rymouris I sall reknit be;
> Thay sall me als burding with monye lie,
> In chairging me with that quhilk neuer I ment:
> Quhat mervell is thocht I murne and lament!
>
> *(MQ, p. 124)*

Both Maitland and Arbuthnot distance themselves from the rascal multitude of rhymers, towards whom they are distinctly supercilious. Such attitudes seem to indicate a bifurcation of literature into high and low sorts, with Maitland and Arbuthnot locating their achievements clearly in the former category. A critical opposition between superior

Figure 1: The arrival of Helen at the gates of Troy, from the fifteenth-century *Chronique Universelle*, c.1460 (New York, Pierpoint Morgan Library, MS M. 214, fol. 84ʳ)

Figure 2: Gate for entry at Bruges, 1515 (Rémi du Puys, *La Tryomphante et solem-nelle entree ... de Charles ... en sa ville de Bruges*, Paris, 1515; reproduced from G.R. Kernodle, *From Art to Theatre: Form and Convention in the Renaissance*, Chicago, 1944, fig. 24, p. 79).

Figure 3: Double pageant, Bruges, 1515 (du Puys, reproduced from Kernodle, as fig.2, fig. 26, p.79).

Figure 4: Judgment of Paris, Brussels, 1496 (Staatliche Museen Berlin, Kupferstichkabinett MS 78 D5, fol. 57ʳ).

Figure 5: Annunciation, from the Book of Hours of James IV and Margaret Tudor (Vienna, Österreichische Nationalbibliothek, MS 1897, fol. 59ᵛ).

Figure 6: Justice crushing Nero, Force crushing Holofernes (Hours of Simon Vostre; reproduced from Emile Mâle, *L'art religieux de la fin du moyen âge en France*, 5th edn. 1949, fig. 187, p. 335).

Figure 7: Dragon of the Apocalypse, from M. Luther (trans.), *Biblia Deutsch*, Wittenberg, 1534, p. cxci (British Library, 1b. 10).

Figure 8: The Beast of the Apocalypse, from M. Luther (trans.), *Biblia Deutsch*, Wittenberg, 1534, p. cxcv[v] (British Library, 1b. 10).

and inferior art is, needless to say, almost a universal feature within literature, though this is not the same thing as the conventional medieval distinctions of high, middle and low styles. In the remarks of Maitland and Arbuthnot, however, we see the adumbration of a contrast in contemporary Scottish poetry between an elevated sort of poetry, appropriate to the articulation of the refined awarenesses of 'true' poets, and another kind of verse, of an essentially 'applied' sort, which serves as the voice of faction.

Sir Richard Maitland (1496–1596) enjoyed a long life; the first seventeen years of his life were passed in the reign of James IV, and he lived through the reigns of the latter's son and granddaughter, into the personal reign of James VI. When Maitland's son, William, was at the peak of his career, under Mary Queen of Scots, Sir Richard was able to withdraw somewhat from the scene; this was even more the case after the downfall of the Secretary, along with the Marian party, in the civil war of 1570–3. Toward the end of his life, Maitland would seem to have retreated to his family home, at Lethington, and it was presumably there that the Maitland Folio and the handsome Maitland Quarto manuscripts were compiled. In the latter collection there is a poem (*MQ*, pp. 216–22) in praise of the poet's residence, which ends with lines on the honour of the Maitland family:

> Quha dois not knaw the Maitland bliud,
> The best in all this land,
> In quhilk sumtyme the honour stuid
> And worship of Scotland?
> Of auld Sir Richard of that name
> We have hard sing and say,
> Of his triumphant nobill fame,
> And of his auld baird gray;
> And of his nobill sonnis thrie,
> Quhilk that tyme had no maik,
> Quhilk maid Scotland renoumit be,
> And all England to quaik.
>
> (*MQ*, p. 222)

The poem is not deficient in hyperbole. Although the Sir Richard mentioned here is not the poet, but the latter's legendary medieval ancestor, the attractiveness of the comparison is irresistible for the unknown author, and in the conclusion of the poem the link is drawn between the two patriarchal figures of the same name, each with his trio of famous sons. This poem, however, is more than just a piece of versified family history and myth; as has been pointed out elsewhere, it is in all likelihood the first country house poem in Scotland.[19] As such, it is evidence of another new cultural phenomenon of the age, the evocation of the life of the happy man, far from the cares of the city. The political intrigues of his son forced Sir Richard Maitland into his rustic retreat, but he had sufficient culture to make a virtue out of necessity, and to appreciate the comparison of the landscape of East Lothian to the Vale of Tempe:

> To speik of the, O Lethingtoun,
> Quhilk standis fair on Tyne,
> Quhais worthie praysis and renoun
> Transcendis my ingyne.
> Thow meritis Homer or Virgill
> Thy worschip till advance,
> And put thy name, digne and nobill,
> In dew rememberance.
>
> (*MQ*, p. 218)

This significant poem thus allows one to antedate by a quarter of a century a pattern of cultural life in country houses usually held to date from the period after the departure of James VI for London.[20]

One of the most crucial parameters of culture is the social and economic relationship which binds poets to sources of patronage. There were very few Scottish writers indeed, during the Middle Ages and the Renaissance, whose artistic production was not in some way dependent thereupon. Sir Richard Maitland of Lethington, as has been observed, did enjoy such privileged freedom, but he was an exception among contemporary poets. Maitland belonged not only to the gentry but also to the class of public servants and administrators (he was a judge), and could therefore stand aloof from the madding crowd. In the early seventeenth century one might point to another such independent person as Elizabeth Melville, Lady Culross, author of the *Godlie Dreame*, printed by Robert Charteris in 1603; this lady's sex would have precluded her from seeking patronage, even had she wished it.[21] By contrast, gentleman-courtiers such as Sir David Lindsay, Alexander Montgomerie, and John Stewart of Baldynneis were not free to write just as they pleased: Lindsay had several crown appointments, both under James V and under the regency of Mary of Guise;[22] Montgomerie and Baldynneis, for their part, had to ingratiate the youthful James VI, and indeed the only surviving copy of the poems of Baldynneis consists of the manuscript volume in which they were presented to his sovereign.[23] Even Gavin Douglas, who came from the noble family of the earls of Douglas, had to think about patronage, as one sees from the fulsome dedication

of the *Palice of Honour* to James IV, and also from his direct address
to Henry, Lord Sinclair, in the opening prologue of the *Eneados*.[24] And
this is to say nothing of William Dunbar, who, though he may have
been connected in some way with the family of the earls of Dunbar
and March, was a notable practitioner of the topos of the quest for
patronage.[25]

The trouble with patronage, at least in Scotland, is that it was
intermittent; this was especially true where it involved the court. During
the sixteenth century the number of years of regency is approximately
equal to the number in which there was a monarch capable of dispensing
patronage in his or her own name. Furthermore, during the same
century that other great institutional source of funding, the church,
underwent – in modern idiom – radical restructuring. Though there is
no room here to review the far-reaching ideological innovations of the
Reformation, certain specific factors relating to church-inspired literary
culture must be mentioned. The lavish patronage exercised by certain
members of the hierarchy was removed almost immediately. When,
for example, one thinks of what was done at Aberdeen by William
Elphinstone, by way of establishing the new college and organising the
liturgical and hagiographical researches connected with the Aberdeen
Breviary,[26] of what was done at Glasgow by Gavin Dunbar, who *inter
alia* fostered the career of John Bellenden,[27] and of what was done at
St Andrews by Archbishops James and David (Cardinal) Beaton and
John Hamilton, whose college of St Mary became an important centre
of counter-Reformation theology,[28] then the profound consequences for
literary culture may at once be appreciated. Not many bishops were
themselves poets, though that was the case with Gavin Douglas, bishop
of Dunkeld, and Andrew Durie, former abbot of Melrose before becoming bishop of Galloway (and *ipso facto* of the Chapel Royal). The
religious orders – such as the Augustinian canons, the Dominicans and
the Observant Franciscans, which all had a significant impact upon
literary culture – were likewise casualties of the Reformation. It has
been pointed out, in connection with the vernacular *speculum principis*
of William of Touris, just how great was the influence which his order,
for example, could bring to bear upon late-medieval Scottish sovereigns,
who chose their confessors from among the Observant Franciscans.[29]
Another important loss was that of the non-academic secular collegiate
kirks: among the pre-Reformation poets who were attached to such
institutions might be noted Gavin Douglas (at St Giles, Edinburgh),
George Clapperton (at Trinity College, Edinburgh, and at the Chapel
Royal), John Roull (at Corstorphine), John Fethy and Alexander Scott
(both at the Chapel Royal, Stirling).[30]

In the second half of the sixteenth century there is little record of literary activity by those members of the Catholic hierarchy who still lingered on for a while, or by the superintendents and Protestant bishops who succeeded them. Certain dignities of the medieval church continued to exist only in theory, in the etiolated conditions of commendatorship. Quintin Kennedy, for example, the abbot of Crossraguell and the opponent of John Knox in a celebrated debate (Maybole, 1562) about the efficacy of the mass, had as his successor none other than the humanist scholar and poet, George Buchanan, who, at that stage in his career, was a declared Protestant. At Crossraguell the post of abbot survived until 1645: the last abbot was one Peter Hewatt, minister of St Giles, Edinburgh, who was presented to the post by James VI; at the Restoration of Charles II the abbey was finally annexed to the bishopric of Dunblane.[31] So great had been the changes in doctrine and the disturbances to patterns of public and private devotion that nearly all the literary activity in the immediate post-Reformation period was directed at doctrinal and/or polemical ends: a plethora of catechisms, psalm-books and other works of religious instruction was complemented by historiographical works of varying degrees of tendentiousness. By the end of the century, however, the dust of theological battle had begun to clear, and through the encircling Calvinistic gloom one begins once again to encounter a few productions which are discernibly works of the literary imagination. Pride of place here must go to Alexander Hume, whose *Hymnes Or Sacred Songs* was published by Robert Waldegrave in 1599, complete with a dedication to Elizabeth Melville, whose own *Godlie Dreame* has been mentioned above.[32]

The most celebrated work in Hume's collection is without a doubt *The Day Estivall*, a poem which deserves the place which it holds in all anthologies of earlier Scottish poetry. The subject of Hume's poem, the description of a day of preternatural warmth and tranquillity in the middle of summer, is couched in simple language, reminiscent, as a recent editor as remarked, of the diction of the psalms.[33] The following will suffice for an illustration of the quality of Hume's writing:

> The brethles flocks drawes to the shade
> And frechure of their fald,
> The startling nolt, as they were made,
> Runnes to the rivers cald.

> The heards beneath some leaffie trie,
> Amids the flowers they lie,
> The stabill ships upon the sey
> Tends up their sails to drie. (117–24)

It is almost certainly not the case that it was Hume's intention to provide a naturalistic account of that evanescent phenomenon, the Scottish summer, or of any particular landscape.[34] Rather, the poet gives an idealised picture of the beauty and orderliness of God's creation, and the 'message' emerges with discretion, only becoming explicit at the very end:

> All labourere drawes hame at even,
> And can till other say,
> Thankes to the gracious God of heaven,
> Quhilk send this summer day. (229–32)

The Day Estivall belongs, in spirit, with the poetry of retreat, and as such may be associated with certain of the productions of Sir Richard Maitland of Lethington, and, later, with those of William Drummond of Hawthornden and Sir William Mure of Rowallan.[35] Alexander Hume became the minister of Logie, near Stirling,[36] and was himself of gentle blood, being the younger brother of the Patrick Hume of Polwarth who conducted a flyting with Alexander Montgomerie; the works of such poets are suffused with deep piety combined with a wide literary culture.

After the departure of James VI for the greater pleasures of London, poetic culture in Scotland exhibits a threefold division. As we have seen, there was a rural culture typical of the landed gentry, which kept alive much of the tradition of Castalian court verse. In the country houses collections of poetry and song were preserved, and there these compositions, one presumes, retained something of their original appeal. The Bannatyne Manuscript, compiled by George Bannatyne between 1565 and 1568, was in the seventeenth century passed down in the family of Foulis of Ravelston and Woodhall (several of whom left their signatures upon the folios), until the scribe's great-great-grandson presented it in 1712 to William Carmichael, father of the fourth Earl of Hyndford; the latter, in turn, after lending out the manuscript to Allan Ramsay and others, presented it to the Faculty of Advocates in 1772.[37] The Maitland family also maintained an interest in poetry: Sir Richard's second son, John, Lord Thirlestane, was a close associate of the poet-king James VI, and is the author of several poems preserved in the Maitland Quarto Manuscript. John Maitland's poems, together with those of his father and others, were transcribed by his sister Mary. The latter's own son, George Lauder (of Haltoun, in East Lothian), inherited a respectable talent for poetry, and was the author of, among other works, *The Scottish Souldier* (1629), *Tweeds Teares of joy, to Charles great Brittains King* (1639), and the *Hecatombe Christiana* (1661).[38] In the years 1622–3, moreover, a selection from the Maitland Folio Manuscript was copied into the Reidpeth MS (CUL, MS Moore LL. v. 10); this enterprise also argues a continuing interest in the older poetry of Scotland. Such a climate of scholarly retreat and discreet literary pursuits may well have been the precondition for one of the most surprising publications of early seventeenth-century Scotland: this was *Granados Spiritual And heuenly Exercises*, printed by Robert Waldegrave, at Edinburgh, in 1600. This work consisted of 'seuen celestiall meditations', for each day of the week (the topics dealt with are: The misery in which man is created; Of sin and what discommodities come by it; How dangerous it is to delay repentance; Of the content of the world and with what hatred and diligence it is to be eschewed; Of the vanity of the glory and magnificence of the world; How death is to be feared, and that a Christian ought so to live that death may never find him unprepared; Of the joys of the blessed in heaven and of the pains of the damned in hell), followed by an exposition of Psalm 51 (Vulgate 50), and a prayer to the Name of Jesus. The publication by the King's Printer of this work by the great Spanish Dominican, Luis de Granada (it was a reprint of an earlier English edition), may intrigue the modern student of cultural history. The pietistic tone of the book, however, was well suited to appeal to an élite of aristocratic and cultured readers, whose devotional proclivities could be served by such an intrinsically old-fashioned work. De Granada's writings, as it happens, had the ability to exert a profound influence even on Presbyterian readers, as is demonstrated in the references to him in the diary of the perfervid Archibald Johnston of Warriston.[39]

A second phenomenon was the proliferation of academic and literary works in Latin. This was a continuation of the humanistic tradition of the previous century, as represented by such scholars as Florence Wilson, Henry Scrimgeour, Patrick Cockburn, John Lesley and George Buchanan.[40] Among the many notable productions of the early seventeenth century one might mention the collection of Scottish-Latin verse, *Delitiae Poetarum Scotorum*, published at Amsterdam in 1637, and the Latin novels of John Barclay.[41] This academic compartment of post-Reformation Scottish culture was not really vitiated by the departure of the Court to London; James VI had been favourably disposed towards the Latin scholars of his kingdom – unless extreme Presbyterianism rendered them obnoxious – but they could survive away from his proximity; and Catholic intellectuals would in any case tend to move to the Continent. One example of the latter was William Barclay, the father of the Latin novelist; in 1577 William Barclay became professor of Law at the new Jesuit university of Pont-à-Mousson, in Lorraine, where the first rector was Edmund Hay, his brother-in-law. Latin culture was a Europe-wide phenomenon, and could overcome barriers of time or language. This was the period during which the Englishman, Sir Francis Kinaston, translated Chaucer's *Troilus and Criseyde* into classical Latin, together with its Scottish appendix, Robert Henryson's *Testament of Cresseid*.[42] The period, which saw the composition of much excellent Neolatin verse and which was also that of the 'Aberdeen Doctors', shows that literary culture of an academic sort, especially when nourished by professionals such as lawyers, ministers and university teachers, could have a dynamic of its own.[43] Nonetheless, though Latin was available as a natural international language for a section of society, the use of the learned tongue inevitably implied that the resulting cultural productions were at some remove from more quotidian occupations.

The third area of interest here is that which concerns satirical, religious and political productions in the vernacular, as distinguished from the dignified and refined compositions of the country houses. If the two aspects of literary culture just sketched have not received their due critical attention, then this is still more true of this third category. A glance at Aldis's list of books published in Scotland before 1700 shows that the total number of books dating from before 1600 is tiny in comparison with what appeared after the turn of the seventeenth century.[44] Despite this, the latter century is the great unknown period in the literary history of Scotland. The poetry of the Presbyterians and other contemporary religious parties has not proved popular with the modern reader, and although the field is not altogether unsurveyed, there is great scope here for research.[45] Zachary Boyd, for one, has recently been rediscovered to be a writer of interest.[46] Much of this mass of literature consists of paraphrase or explication of the Bible, but this in itself is no disqualification. Poetry of this sort is not unknown even from before the Reformation; an example is George Makeson's paraphrase of Genesis (dated 1554).[47] As a specimen of the moral and pietistic literature of the age – once so enthusiastically received but which has now almost disappeared into a collective unconscious – one might mention *The Christian's Great Interest* of William Guthrie (1620–65), first published in 1658, and translated into Dutch, German, French and Gaelic. This book of Protestant devotion was almost constantly in print, with some eighty editions between the first appearance and the beginning of the twentieth century; it is therefore likely that the influence of this sort of book was greater than the works which are usually reckoned to belong to 'literature' proper.[48] Awareness of such things helps to put certain other aspects of reception history into a truer perspective. When he died (1602), the printer Robert Smyth had in his stock 1034 copies of the 'Dundee Psalms', the collection of religious poems more familiar under the title of *The Gude and Godlie Ballatis*.[49] Since the book had by that time reached at least its fourth edition (the first, as far as we know, dates from 1565), one may surmise that interest in it had not yet begun to wane; this conclusion, moreover, is confirmed by the existence of a still later edition, in 1621. A case could be made out for regarding the book also as a seventeenth-century collection, since it remained influential during that period. One recalls that the *Gude and Godlie Ballatis*, in the words of the prologue, was designed to provide basic and pleasant religious instruction for the benefit of young people, with the express intention of spreading the word of the Gospel in the country at large.[50] It is clear that this kind of literature, unlike the less strident products of the country house or the Latin compositions of the learned, was well attuned to popular taste, which it would simultaneously help to form and instruct.

A constant factor determining the fate of culture is commercial opportunity. While in the Middle Ages the economics of manuscript production acted as a constraint in the diffusion of literature,[51] in the sixteenth century the new medium of print offered untold possibilities. In this period there is a fascinating interaction between the two written media.[52] Perhaps paradoxically, this is also the great century for Scottish literary manuscripts, as seen in the following large collections of medieval and Renaissance verse: the Asloan MS; Arundel MS 285; the Bannatyne MS; the Maitland Quarto MS; the Maitland Folio MS. It is remarkable that none of these anthologies, and only a mere fraction of the poetry which they contain, was to appear in print until modern times – although the Bannatyne MS, it has been argued, may have been compiled with a view to being printed.[53] This abundance of manuscript anthologies (rather than of printed books) may have something to do with the Catholicism underlying much of the poetry which these manuscripts contain, but it may also be connected with changes in fashion – involving changing conceptions of the nature and function of poetry. Whatever the reason, it is a fact that the medieval literature of Scotland continued to be copied and studied even well into the seventeenth century. The taste for this kind of literature was never quite extinguished, but its social base contracted until, as has already been noted, it became more or less coterminous with country-house culture.

An examination of the printed books of the later sixteenth century also sheds some light upon several points connecting with the foregoing, as, for example: which medieval works continued to be available? What proportion of the total output of printed books was taken up by works of imaginative literature, prose or poetry? What were the characteristics of literary taste, in the age of the printed book? In this enquiry we can draw upon the evidence provided by lists of books published, and also upon the inventories of the stock of publishers and booksellers, which were compiled in connection with the financial settlement of estates after their death.[54]

The third of these questions is perhaps the one most easily answered. By far the largest category of literature is that of religious books; this includes books of psalms, catechisms, assorted works of religious instruction, sermons, and (even) Bibles. The Bible, despite the fact of its having been printed by Alexander Arbuthnet (not the poet Arbuthnot) in 1576–9, is not at all so common in these lists as one might perhaps presume. This was because a complete text of the Bible was not yet a standard possession in every household, and also because of the high price required for such a book. In the inventory of Henry Charteris, who died in 1599, we find one folio Bible, valued at £7, one octavo Bible, gilt, at £4.13.4, two quarto Bibles, at £5, and twenty-two New Testaments, valued at 12s. each. These modest holdings contrast with Charteris's stock of 6204 catechisms (of various sorts), 3345 Psalms (of various sorts), 1880 books of assorted religious literature, and 1516 works of secular literature (of which fully one half (788) consists of works by Sir David Lindsay, writings which display a marked concern with religious topics). Secular literature thus accounts for little more than one-tenth of the total stock of this printer-publisher. Even so, this is the man of whom Dickson and Edmond speak so fondly:

> There is perhaps no Scottish printer whose name is more honoured
> by those who love the vernacular poetry of the country than that of
> the worthy burgess of Edinburgh, Henry Charteris. It was through
> his enterprise that several of the works of our old writers first ap-
> peared in print; and, but for the editions issued at his expense, our
> knowledge of these early poets would be very limited.[55]

This *laudatio* deserves to be tempered somewhat. The vernacular literary productions of Charteris consist, according to Dickson and Edmond, of: Lindsay, *Works* (1582, 1592 and 1597); Lindsay, *Squyer Meldrum* (1594); Lindsay, *Satyre of the Thrie Estaitis* (1594); Henryson, *Testament of Cresseid* (1593); and Hary, *Wallace* (1594). This list of seven works is not imposing, and, in reality, the quoted comments on the enterprise of Charteris deserve only to apply to his publication of Lindsay. Yet even in this latter regard Charteris was no innovator: an edition of Lindsay's *Works* had been published by John Scot in 1568, and another by Thomas Bassandyne in 1574 (to say nothing of lost prints by Thomas Davidson, and of editions published in France and England).[56] Moreover, the alleged Charteris edition of Lindsay's *Satyre* of 1594 is a ghost, and the very real edition of the *Satyre* of 1602 was actually the work of Henry Charteris's son, Robert. As far as the *Wallace* is concerned, an earlier edition had been published by Lekpreuik in 1570, and fragments of an edition from early in the century survive, in the types used by Chepman and Myllar. The earliest known print of the *Testament of Cresseid* is the London one of William Thynne, in 1532. Even if literature in Latin be included for consideration, the praise of Charteris still needs to be given greater nuance. It is true that Charteris did print George Buchanan's *Baptistes* in 1578, but Thomas Vautrollier had printed the same work in 1577 and again in 1578, and in the latter year there were also editions at London and at Frankfurt.[57] From this evidence one can draw more than one conclusion: first, the evident prestige of Sir David Lindsay is so overwhelming, that even modern bibliographers are tempted to be carried away by it in their estimations of the contribution to culture made by printers and publishers in late sixteenth-century Scotland; second, the survival rate of pre-Reformation works of literature is regrettably slight; third, purely secular works are but a tiny proportion of the total contemporary output.

Would the situation appear different were one to choose different publishers? Yes and no, is the answer. The publishers Thomas Vautrollier and Robert Waldegrave clearly had a bias towards literary works emanating from the circle of King James VI. If one were to consider their output jointly one would list: James, *Essayes of a Prentise*, *His Majesty's Poetical Exercises*, *Demonology* and *Basilikon Doron*; Thomas Hudson, *The Historie of Judith*; Alexander Hume, *A Treatise of the Felicitie of the life to come* and *Hymnes Or Sacred Songs*; Alexander Montgomerie, *The Cherrie and the Slae*; Sir William Alexander, *A Short Discourse* and *The Tragedy of Darius*; Walter Quin, *Sertum Poeticum*; together with the interesting reprints of: Sidney, *Arcadia*; Southwell, *Saint Peter's Complaint*; Granada, *Devotional Exercises*. These titles provide unambiguous evidence of a deliberate cultural programme, centering on the king. If, on the other hand, one were to examine the stock of Robert Smyth, in 1602, one would find much the same pattern of evidence as that indicated by that of Henry Charteris. Here too psalms, catechisms, religious and grammatical works abound, and the only other works are Aesop's *Fables*; the romance of *Gray Steill*; Henryson's *Testament of Cresseid*; and John Rolland's *Sevin Seages*. The books in Smyth's stock numbering more than one thousand speak eloquently of his commercial expectations: *First Part of Latin Grammar* (2060); *Prayers before the Psalms*

(2000); *Second Part of Latin Grammar* (1820); *Testament of Cresseid* (1638); *Select Epistles of Cicero* (1275); *Colloquia Corderii* (1258); *Ane Godlie Treatise* of James Anderson (1134); *Gude and Godlie Ballatis* (1034). Such abundance argues a literary culture sustained by a numerically larger group than merely the small circle at the court. The evidence from both Charteris and Smyth, therefore, provides a guide to the cultural interests and priorities associated with the worlds of school, moral edification and Presbyterianism.

While it may be a truism to say that a society gets the literary culture which it deserves, late sixteenth-century Scotland is no exception to the rule. Contrasting with the organic unity of court-centred and church-inspired culture of the period before the Reformation,[58] one finds in the later century fissiparousness. In the decades ensuing upon the chaotic end of the reign of Mary Queen of Scots there comes to be a division of culture into the following components: *first*, a court culture (mainly in the vernacular) for the élite, seen in the frenchified and italianate productions of the 'Castalian Band' patronised by James VI; after the king's departure for the fleshpots of London, this became reduced to the efforts of the gentry in the country houses; *second*, a learned, clerical and academic culture which participated in the wider intellectual horizons provided by Latin; *third*, a more popular strain of vernacular culture, connected with the education and evangelisation programmes of the established Protestant church. These three cultural developments should not, however, be assumed to coincide with the denominational trichotomy of Catholic, Episcopalian and Presbyterian, since various overlappings and combinations were possible. In the days of James IV and James V, vernacular literature was a natural concomitant of religious and moral instruction and the cultivation of Latin letters, all in the context of a royal court with European horizons; after the Reformation, however, cultural initiatives must reckon with the parameters just indicated. The comprehensive integration of medieval culture was gone for good, and each of the three successor traditions is marked in some way by a sense of attenuation.

One final example may be given, in the attempt to throw into dramatic relief the changed cultural situation of the early seventeenth century. In 1629 John Wreittoun published at Edinburgh an interesting little book, which, despite the existence of a modern reprint, has been largely neglected. This was *The Confession and Conversion of the Right Honorable, Most Illustrious, and Elect Lady, My Lady C. of L.*[59] The lady of the title was Helen Hay, who in 1583–4 became the wife of Alexander, seventh Lord Livingston; in 1600 Livingston was raised by James VI to the title of earl of Linlithgow. The countess enjoyed wealth and high social status, and she was appointed governess to the king's daughter, the princess Elizabeth, the future queen of Bohemia. Unfortunately for the countess, however, she would not abandon her Catholic faith (which her husband did not share), and, from as early as the 1580s she was frequently denounced by the Kirk as a 'most malicious Papist', was summonsed to explain her contumacy, and eventually excommunicated. Towards the end of her life (she died in 1627) her spirit was at last broken, and she submitted to the Presbyterian Church. In connection herewith she was encouraged, or was forced, to write a confession of the errors of her former ways. This document, issued as a piece of Protestant propaganda, is quite a challenge to the modern, liberal reader. The following articles are representative:

2. I renounce and condemne all worshipping, or praying to Angels, hee or she Saints, not now excepting the blessed Virgin Marie, and conforme to the expresse direction of the Angell to Iohn *Revel.* I take me to worship GOD; and as CHRIST, *Math.* 4.10 commandeth him only to serue, and to pray to my father. *Math.* 8.9. who is in Heaven, to whom only belongeth religious worship, both of prayer and praise.

3. I renounce and condemne all prayers in Latin, or any vnknowne tongue to mee, taking mee heereafter, by the grace of GOD to pray with the Spirit, and with vnderstanding also, 1 *Cor.* 14.15. and not to mumble and number my prayers according to the order and distinction of beads, which I haue caused breake and destroy, with present and perpetuall thanksgiving to GOD therefore.

4. I acknowledge with *Ieremie* 10.14 that a molten image is falshood, thay are vanitie and the workes of errors: and therefore casting away all those abominations of images, pictures, medalles, and pretended reliques: I take me whollie to the pure and plaine Gospell of IESUS CHRIST, and his holie Sacraments, wherein the lyuelie picture of CHRIST is, and the most hallowed Crucifixe that I can set before mine eyes, handle with mine hands, and carry vpon my breast; wherein I rejoice, and ever shall doe, by Gods helpe and assistance, and finds great comfort in the conference and prayers of GODS Ministers, who now resort vnto me frequently: resolving by the grace of GOD never thereafter to craue, nor admit the company of Priests, and other teachers of lyes, guides of idolatrie; which all now I haue forsaken by the light and force of GODS Spirit: and woes mee that I hearkned so long to these seducers.[60]

Such a text shows how in the post-Reformation period it was possible to set a jingling padlock on the mind, even for one of the most privileged in society. Not even a country house could protect against the inquisition of an irate Kirk. It is ironic that just in the period when, by moving from Edinburgh to London, from Scotland to Great Britain, James VI had enormously expanded his own possibilities, his subjects at home were drawing the noose ever tighter. In such circumstances, culture could be no laughing matter.

1. C. S. Lewis, *English Literature in the Sixteenth Century, excluding Drama* (Oxford, 1954).

2. *The Poems of Sir Philip Sidney*, ed. William A. Ringler (Oxford, 1962), p. 165 ('Astrophil and Stella', poem 1).

3. For a recent discussion of the absence of a fully constructed authorial personality within Scottish Renaissance verse see: Theo van Heijnsbergen, 'The Bannatyne Manuscript: Literary Convention and Authorial Voice', in *The European Sun*, ed. G. D. Caie, R. J. Lyall and K. G. Simpson (forthcoming).

4. As Priscilla Bawcutt has aptly put it, ' "the self" and "the personality" are slippery concepts': Priscilla Bawcutt, *Dunbar the Makar* (Oxford, 1992), p. 5.

5. *The Poems of William Dunbar*, ed. James Kinsley (Oxford, 1979).

6. Bawcutt, p. 297.

7. *The Poems of Alexander Scott*, ed. Alexander Scott (Edinburgh, 1952), p. 7.

8. Ibid., pp. 8–9.

9. *Ballattis of Luve*, ed. John MacQueen (Edinburgh, 1970), pp. xli, liv.

10. For further discussion of this problem see: Theo van Heijnsbergen, 'The Love Lyrics of Alexander Scott', *SSL*, 26 (1991), 366–79.

11. Gavin Douglas, *Virgil's 'Aeneid' translated into Scottish Verse*, ed. David F. C. Coldwell, STS, 4 vols (Edinburgh and London, 1957–64), II, 14: 'Proloug', ll. 405–10.

12. Kinsley, pp. 29–38.

13. See: A. A. MacDonald, 'Vergilius in de Engelse literatuur van de Middeleeuwen', in *Dwergen op de Schouders van Reuzen*, ed. H. van Dijk and E. R. Smits (Groningen, 1990), pp. 117–26.

14. On which see: Sally Mapstone, *The Wisdom of Princes* (forthcoming).

15. *The Maitland Quarto Manuscript*, ed. W. A. Craigie, STS (Edinburgh and London, 1920). p. 26. All Maitland quotations, unless otherwise specified, are taken from this edition.

16. cf. the poem: 'Blind man, be blythe, thocht *that thow* be wrangit': *The Maitland Folio Manuscript*, ed. W. A. Craigie, STS, 2 vols (Edinburgh and London, 1919–27), I, 43–4. Further on Maitland see: Maurice Lee Jr., 'Sir Richard Maitland of Lethington: A Christian Laird in the Age of Reformation', in *Action and Conviction in Early Modern Europe*, ed. T. K. Rabb and J. E. Seigel (Princeton, 1969), pp. 117–32; A. A. MacDonald, 'The Poetry of Sir Richard Maitland of Lethington', *Transactions of the East Lothian Antiquarian and Field Naturalists' Society*, 13 (1972), 7–19.

17. *The Gude and Godlie Ballatis*, ed. A. F. Mitchell, STS (Edinburgh and London, 1897), pp. 204–7.

18. On whom see David Stevenson, *King's College, Aberdeen, 1560–1641: From Protestant Reformation to Covenanting Revolution* (Aberdeen, 1990), pp. 25–30.

19. A. A. MacDonald, 'The Sense of Place in Early Scottish Verse: Rhetoric and Reality', *English Studies*, 72 (1991), 12–27 (25).

20. See Helena M. Shire, *Song, Dance and Poetry of the Court of Scotland under King James VI* (Cambridge, 1969), pp. 207–14.

21. For a text of the *Godlie Dreme* see *Early Scottish Metrical Tales*, ed. David Laing (London and Glasgow, 1889), pp. 179–96. The first ten stanzas are reproduced in: *An Anthology of Scottish Women Poets*, ed. Catherine Kerrigan (Edinburgh, 1991), pp. 154–6. For another selection see: *Kissing the Rod: An Anthology of Seventeenth-Century Women's Verse*, ed. Germaine Greer, Susan Hastings, Jeslyn Medoff and Melinda Sansone (1988), pp. 32–8.

22. On Lindsay see Hamer's introduction: *The Works of Sir David Lindsay of the Mount 1490–1555*, ed. Douglas Hamer, STS, 4 vols (Edinburgh and London, 1931–6), IV, ix–xlvi. For the fullest consideration see: Carol Edington, *Court and Culture in Renaissance Scotland* (Amherst, 1994).

23. On Montgomerie and Stewart see: Shire, *passim*; R. D. S. Jack, *Alexander Montgomerie* (Edinburgh, 1985).

24. See Priscilla Bawcutt, *Gavin Douglas* (Edinburgh, 1976), pp. 47–50.

25. Bawcutt, *Dunbar the Makar*, pp. 1–8.

26. Leslie J. Macfarlane, *William Elphinstone and the Kingdom of Scotland 1431–1514* (Aberdeen, 1985), pp. 290–402, 231–46.

27. D. E. Easson, *Gavin Dunbar: Chancellor of Scotland, Archbishop of Glasgow* (Edinburgh and London, 1947); John Durkan and James Kirk, *The University of Glasgow 1451–1577* (Glasgow, 1977), pp. 206–13.

28. Margaret H. B. Sanderson, *Cardinal of Scotland: David Beaton, c. 1494–1546* (Edinburgh, 1986, pp. 122–3; James K. Cameron, 'Humanism and Religious Life', in *Humanism in Renaissance Scotland*, ed. John MacQueen (Edinburgh, 1990), pp. 161–77 (166–8).

29. A. A. MacDonald, 'Catholic Devotion into Protestant Lyric: the case of the *Contemplacioun of Synnaris*', *IR*, 35 (1984), 58–87. See also: Anthony Ross, 'Some Notes on the Religious Orders in Pre-Reformation Scotland', in *Essays on the Scottish Reformation 1513–1625*, ed. David McRoberts (Glasgow, 1962), pp. 185–244.

30. Cf. *Fasti Ecclesiae Scoticanae Medii Aevi ad annum 1638*, ed. D. E. R. Watt, second draft (St Andrews, 1969), *passim*. On the latter institution see: Theo van Heijnsbergen, 'The Scottish Chapel Royal as Cultural Intermediary between Town and Court', in *Centres of Learning: Learning and Location in Pre-modern Europe and the Near East*, ed. J. W. Drijvers and A. A. MacDonald (Leiden, 1995), pp. 299–313. On poets and their official connections see: A. A. MacDonald, 'William Stewart and the Court Poetry of the Reign of James V', in *Stewart Style 1513–1542: Essays on the Court of James V*, ed. Janet Hadley Williams (East Linton, 1996), pp. 179–200 (185–7).

31. Ian B. Cowan, 'Ayrshire Abbeys: Crossraguell and Kilwinning', in *Ayrshire Collections*, 14 (1986), 279, 286–7. Also *Quintin Kennedy (1520–1564): Two Eucharistic Tracts*, ed. C. H. Kuipers (Nijmegen, 1964).

32. *The Poems of Alexander Hume*, ed. Alexander Lawson, STS (Edinburgh and London, 1902).

33. Priscilla Bawcutt, in *Longer Scottish Poems Volume One: 1375–1650*, ed. Priscilla Bawcutt and Felicity Riddy (Edinburgh, 1987), p. 291 (the poem appears on pp. 293–302).

34. Cf. MacDonald, 'The Sense of Place in Early Scottish Verse'.

35. See Michael Spiller, 'Poetry after the Union 1603–1660', in *The History of Scottish Literature vol. I*, ed. R. D. S. Jack (Aberdeen, 1988), pp. 141–62.

36. R. Menzies Fergusson, *Alexander Hume: an Early Poet-Pastor of Logie and his Intimates* (Paisley, 1899).

37. *The Bannatyne Manuscript*, ed. W. Tod Ritchie, STS, 4 vols (Edinburgh and London, 1928–34), I, xx. See also: Theo van Heijnsbergen, 'The Interaction between Literature and History in Queen Mary's Edinburgh: the Bannatyne Manuscript and its Prosopographical Context', in *The Renaissance in Scotland*, ed. A. A. MacDonald, Michael Lynch and Ian B. Cowan (Leiden, 1994), pp. 183–225.

38. Lauder's poems are most easily consulted in *Various Pieces of Fugitive Scotish Poetry; principally of the seventeenth century*, ed. David Laing (Edinburgh 1825).

39. *Diary of Sir Archibald Johnston of Warriston 1632–1639*, ed. George Morison Paul, SHS (Edinburgh, 1911), pp. 197–200, 228. For a recent discussion, see David Stevenson, *King or Covenant? Voices from Civil War* (East Linton, 1996), pp. 150–73, 'Depression and Salvation: Sir Archibald Johnston of Warriston'.

40. John Durkan, 'The Cultural Background in Sixteenth-Century Scotland', in McRoberts, pp. 274–331; John MacQueen, 'Aspects of Humanism in Sixteenth and Seventeenth Century Literature', in *Humanism in Renaissance Scotland*, ed. MacQueen, pp. 10–31, *et passim*.

41. James Macqueen, 'Scottish Latin Poetry', in *History of Scottish Literature*, ed. Jack, pp. 213–25; John Barclay, *Euphormionis Lusinini Satyricon*, ed. David A. Fleming (Nieuwkoop, 1973); Marc Fumaroli, 'A Scottish Voltaire: John Barclay and the character of nations', *TLS*, 19 January 1996, pp. 16–17.

42. Oxford, Bodleian MS Addit. C. 287 (dated 1639). See: *The Poems of Robert Henryson*, ed. G. Gregory Smith, STS, 3 vols (Edinburgh and London, 1906–14), I, xcvii–clxii. On Kynaston see also: Richard Beadle, 'The Virtuoso's *Troilus?*', in *Chaucer Traditions: Studies in Honour of Derek Brewer*, ed. Ruth Morse and Barry Windeatt (Cambridge, 1990), pp. 213–33.

43. D. Macmillan, *The Aberdeen Doctors: A Notable Group of Scottish Theologians of the First Episcopal Period* (1909); Stevenson, pp. 61–93. See also: Macqueen, 'Scottish Latin Poetry', pp. 221–5; James W. L Adams, 'The Renaissance Poets: Latin', in *Scottish Poetry: A Critical Survey*, ed. James Kinsley (1955), pp. 68–98.

44. Harry G. Aldis, *A List of Books Printed in Scotland before 1700*, EBS (Edinburgh 1904; corrected reprint 1970).

45. For an introductory overview see Duncan Anderson, *The Bible in Seventeenth-Century Scottish Life and Literature* (1936).

46. David W. Atkinson, 'Zachary Boyd: A Reassessment', in *Proceedings of the Third International Conference on Scottish Language and Literature (Medieval and Renaissance)*, ed. R. J. Lyall and Felicity Riddy (Stirling and Glasgow, 1981), pp. 438–56; *Selected Sermons of Zachary Boyd*, ed. David W. Atkinson, STS (Edinburgh and London, 1989); David W. Atkinson, 'Zachary Boyd as Minister of the Barony Parish: a Commentator on the late Reformation Church', *Scottish Church History Society Records*, 24 (1990), 19–32.

47. Hans H. Meier, 'A Pre-Reformation Biblical Paraphrase', *IR*, 17 (1966), 11–23.

48. On Guthrie and other such works see Adam Philip, *The Devotional Literature of Scotland* (1922), pp. 37–9. *The Christian's Great Interest* was most recently reprinted at Edinburgh, in 1994.

49. Robert Dickson and J. P. Edmond, *Annals of Scottish Printing* (Cambridge, 1890; reprint Amsterdam, 1975), p. 483.

50. Mitchell, p. 1.

51. Cf. *Book Production and Publishing in Britain 1375–1475*, ed. Jeremy Griffiths and Derek Pearsall (Cambridge, 1989), especially R. J. Lyall, 'Books and Book Owners in Fifteenth-century Scotland', pp. 239–56.

52. Denton Fox, 'Manuscripts and Prints of Scots Poetry in the Sixteenth Century',

in *Bards and Makars*, ed. A. J. Aitken, M. P. McDiarmid and D. S. Thomson (Glasgow, 1977), pp. 156–71.

53.   A. A. MacDonald, 'The Printed Book that never was: George Bannatyne's Poetic Anthology (1568)', in *Boeken in de late Middeleeuwen*, ed. Jos M. M. Hermans and Klaas van der Hoek (Groningen, 1994), pp. 101–10; this article also provides bibliographical details concerning editions of the MSS mentioned in the previous sentence.

54.   The details presented here are taken from Dickson and Edmond.

55.   Ibid., p. 348.

56.   For a full bibliography see: Hamer, IV, 15–122.

57.   See the check-list of Buchanan's works in: I. D. McFarlane, *Buchanan* (1981), pp. 490–518. See also: John Durkan, *Bibliography of George Buchanan* (Glasgow, 1994).

58.   See: A. A. MacDonald, 'Religious Poetry in Middle Scots', in *History of Scottish Literature*, ed. Jack, pp. 91–104 (94).

59.   *The Confession and Conversion of my Lady C. of L.*, ed. George P. Johnston (Edinburgh, 1924).

60.   Ibid., pp. 7–9.

5

THE SCOTTISH COURT AND THE SCOTTISH SONNET AT THE UNION OF THE CROWNS

Michael R. G. Spiller

The vogue for writing sonnets, and particularly sonnet sequences, which swept across Europe in the sixteenth century, reached Britain late, but, as so often happened in matters of culture and the intellect, Scottish court circles responded more promptly than the English. Though the very first British sonnet sequence was published in 1560 by a Londoner, Anne Locke (whose circumstances and mind were heavily influenced by John Knox),[1] the introduction of the sonnet in Britain by Sir Thomas Wyatt had not been followed by any sustained interest south of the Border, and when James VI published his own sequence of twelve sonnets, with prefatory sonnets from his 'Castalian Band', only Spenser, with his juvenile 1569 translation of Du Bellay, and the lamentable John Soowthern had preceded him. Sidney had completed, but not issued, *Astrophil and Stella*, and it was not until the posthumous publication of that great sequence, in 1591, that the sonneteering vogue began in earnest in England.

However, although Scotland produced a very respectable number of sonneteers during this period – eight of note, including Drummond of Hawthornden, among some forty in Britain as a whole – the early promise of James's venture was not fulfilled. Stewart of Baldynneis, Montgomerie and Fowler did not have their sonnets published in their lifetimes; in fact, not until the Scottish Text Society editions of the nineteenth and twentieth centuries.[2] Craig of Rosscraig, Sir David Murray and Sir William Alexander published much that was written in the vogue years of the 1590s, but only after the Union of the Crowns;[3] and Drummond, the greatest of them all, published only when by any calculation the sonnet vogue was past.

Of the three Castalians who might have followed their prentice prince into print, and added an early Scottish voice to the European sonnet chorus, Stewart of Baldynneis seems in some ways the most promising:[4] his interest in Italian literature was keen, and his thirty-three surviving sonnets, in the Stewart MS, are lively and inventive; but they are miscellaneous, and show no signs of a sonnet sequence in the making. After that manuscript (in which his major but equally unprinted works, *Roland Furious* and *Ane Schersing Out of Trew Felicitie*, are of course also present), we have no more poetry from him. Alexander Montgomerie, James's laureate poet in the 1580s, was a devotee of Ronsard, and clearly interested in the dramatic possibilities of the sonnet. Like Sidney he was quick-witted, ironic and passionate; but like Sidney too, he was fatally attracted to the world of Parolles rather than Petrarch, and after his imprisonment and quarrel with James, his Catholic sympathies drove him into plotting, exile and outlawry, and early death in 1598. His fame was established by *The Cherrie and the Slae*, which went through numerous editions before 1700, but that poem seems to have eclipsed his sonnets, of which there are seventy. They are, however, occasional sonnets, very varied in style and occasion, and would not obviously form publishable work on their own.

Sir William Fowler's case is harder to explain: about ten years younger than Montgomerie, he lived from 1560 to 1612, and was a rich and moderately influential courtier of King James and Queen Anne for thirty years, with ample power and opportunity to publish. When in the latter half of his life he made a list of his works, he included three books of sonnets,[5] so he clearly still reckoned them among his literary works; but even though one of these books was his Petrarchan sequence *The Tarantula of Love*, containing seventy-five sonnets, he apparently made no attempt to print it.

Its non-appearance is even odder when one considers that during Fowler's lifetime, two of his friends, Sir William Alexander and Sir David Murray, published their youthful sequences. Alexander's *Aurora* appeared in 1604, a huge Petrarchan sequence of 106 sonnets and other poems; and David Murray published his sequence, *Caelia*, of twenty-one sonnets with other verses, in 1611, so there can be no question that sonneteering was a permissible, indeed an admirable, courtierly activity. Indeed, as late as 1616, we have a record of King James and Sir William Alexander passing a freezing February day at Newmarket talking poetic theory and writing sonnets.[6] If we ask what might have stopped Fowler, for all his literary ambitions, from publishing a sonnet sequence which had certainly cost him a lot of labour, when his contemporaries were publishing theirs, the answer is certainly not Petrarchan structure or themes. Petrarchan themes continued to be fashionable even after the decline of the sonnet sequence, in lute songs and madrigal books, right into the 1620s, and the Petrarchan structure, that is, the long sonnet sequence with inserted madrigals and songs, was actually what Sir William Alexander and Drummond of Hawthornden used themselves. No: one might guess that what he feared, looking back at sonnets written in the late 1580s, was ridicule – ridicule for a style that had now, in a different court and country, become obsolete and clumsy.

In considering the problem of the two styles we have one interesting, but problematic, piece of evidence from the very centre of Castalia: a sonnet written by James to Sir William Alexander concerning his 'harshe vearses after the Inglishe fasone':

> Hould hould your hand, hould, mercy, mercy spare
> Those sacred nine that nurst you many a yeare
> Full oft alas with comfort and with care
> Wee bath'd you in Castalias fountaine cleare
> Then on our winges aloft wee did you beare
> And set you on our stately forked hill
> Where you our heauenly harmonyes did heare
> The rockes resoundinge with there Echoes still
> Although your neighbours haue conspir'd to spill
> That art which did the Laurel crowne obtaine
> And borowing from the raven there ragged quill
> Bewray there harsh hard trotting tumbling wayne
>> Such hamringe hard the mettalls hard require
>> Our songs ar fil'd with smoothly flowing fire

This title, and this version of the sonnet, comes from Additional MS 24195, the manuscript collected by Prince Charles and corrected by James himself about 1617. One correction ('spill' for 'kill') is in the King's hand in this sonnet. Another version is found in the Denmilne MSS, with two interesting variants: 'Who borowing' for 'And borowing' (l. 11) and 'youre mettles' for 'the mettalls' (l. 13).[7]

The question of which verse, and what occasion, prompted this criticism of English verse is not easily settled. James Craigie, who prints both versions in his edition of James's poems, assigns the sonnet to 1607 or after, on the grounds that the pun on 'metals/mettle' in l. 13 would only have had point after the grant to Alexander in 1607 of mining and mineral rights within his barony of Menstrie (the point is made in the title which the Denmilne version supplies for the sonnet). But the version which the King corrected has 'the mettalls', that is 'the metals of your neighbours', and although a mining joke is still possible, that much weakens Craigie's point. R. D. S. Jack, who very oddly finds this humorous and exaggerated sonnet 'curtly admonishing' and 'blunt', assigns it to the court in Edinburgh, prior to 1603.[8] He offers no evidence, but the phrase 'your neighbours' obviously makes the assumption of an Edinburgh utterance a reasonable one. The difficulty which remains for that conjecture is that the first eight lines of the poem imply by periphrasis that Alexander had already produced poetry of the Castalian kind, and there is nothing to correspond to that before 1603, when his first drama, *Darius*, was published in Edinburgh. Significantly, however, it was in the Preface to *Darius* that Alexander proclaimed

> the English phrase ... worthie to be preferred before our owne for elegance and perfection thereof[9]

– a challenge to which James might well have responded, using the same opposition of 'us' to 'English' and 'neighbours'. T. H. McGrail, in his biography of Alexander, noted that when in the following year Alexander published his sonnet cycle, *Aurora*, in London, there was 'a marked lack of Scottish provincialisms'[10] in comparison with *Darius*, suggesting that in preparing *Aurora* for the press Alexander had acted upon what he said in his Preface the year before.

I propose, then, in exploring now the issues raised by James's sonnet, to suppose that it was written in 1604, occasioned by the publication of *Aurora* along with the reissued *Darius* and the new tragedy of *Croesus*. When James referred to 'vearses' (assuming the MS title to be his), I take it that he meant by it what he meant in his *Reulis and Cautelis ... in Scottis Poesie* of 1584, namely, short poems ('songs') or stanzas, of which 'Sonet verse' was one, and not continuous narrative rhymes, which he declared 'yit are nocht verse.'[11]

It is not surprising that someone who was a very competent technical critic of verse should have registered, upon the Union of the Crowns, that there was an 'Inglishe fasone' different from the Scots; what is odd is that he should have described it in precisely opposite terms from Alexander's. Where Alexander found the English phrase elegant and polished, James, speaking through the Nine Muses, finds it – as Alexander had apparently practised it – 'a harsh hard trotting tumbling wayne', as against Scottish poetry 'fil'd with smoothly flowing fire'. From what James said in his *Reulis and Cautelis ... in Scottis Poesie* of 1584, we know what he meant by these two words, 'tumbling' and 'flowing', and as they are technical terms, not just words of praise and dispraise, it is reasonable to assume that the sense holds good in 1604. By 'flowing', he meant verse that has a regular metre; by 'tumbling', he meant what we would call alliterative verse, that is verse with a fixed number of stresses but a variable number of syllables – the verse of *Gawain* or *Kynd Kyttok*, which was still used in flyting and comic poetry in James's youth, as by Montgomerie in his flyting with Polwarth.

But in 1604, of course, nobody – and certainly nobody in poetic circles in England – was writing this kind of alliterative verse. Nor was Sir William Alexander, so what could James have been referring to as verse after the 'Inglishe fasone'? There is, perhaps, a further clue in the Aesopian allusion about borrowing from the raven: the point about ravens is that they don't sing, but they do mimic human speech, or, if we want to be precise, they disjointedly mimic human words, but not human sentences. Now a sentence, which a raven can't manage, as distinguished from a mere series of words, which it can, exhibits the flowing of human rationality. A sentence is the locus of *sententiae*, the considered reasoned human verdict upon experience, and it is noticeable that it is in this period, the period from about 1580 to about 1650, that 'sentence' begins to lose its sense of 'a wise and rational human observation' and remain with only its modern sense of 'a grammatical unit making a complete utterance'. I am going to suggest that one of the reasons why 'sentence' shifts its meaning is that there is a shift in the notion of what eloquence involves, and that it was as a result of this shift that James recorded his half-humorous disapproval of Alexander's style, and that Fowler felt disinclined to publish his sonnets.

The shift from the flowing style of the Muses to the tumbling speech of the raven, from the Castalian to the Corvine, if I might put it pithily, is one which anyone who reads the literature of the period will come across evidence of, but it does not always look like what James says it is. For example, Sir Philip Sidney, whom James much admired, and thought a true servant of Castalia, had himself distinguished two 'fasones' of writing in the XVth sonnet of *Astrophil and Stella*, 'You that do search for everie purling spring'.[12] Those who sang poor Petrarch's long deceased woes, who used all the flowers of Castalia, and ran their rhymes in rattling rows, were of course the Petrarchan poets of the 1580s, among whom, even if Sidney had not read their works in particular, were the Scots Castalian band around the young King James; James's sonnets appeared in 1585, three years after Sidney wrote *Astrophil and Stella*. Sidney's point is not so much that these 'dictionary' writers are old-fashioned, but rather that they are clumsy and inadequate to describe the essence of love. Now of course Sidney himself uses Petrarchan conceits and alliteration and exotic vocabulary just as much as James or Fowler, but, with the benefit of critical hindsight, we can see that what he did do, and what they didn't, was to get the subtlety of the rhythms of dramatic speech into his verse, most strikingly by the use of enjambment and caesural pauses. Sidney's sonnets give the feeling of a mind speaking immediately, not recording what has been composed. With this goes irony, mockery and that greatly admired courtierly quality of *sprezzatura*, the avoidance of heavy learning and pedantry. Had Sidney known the sonnets of Montgomerie, he might have recognised a kindred spirit – though he would have been put off by Montgomerie's fondness for *vers enchainés* and other French patternings.

But we, of course, trained to think of lyric poetry as responsive to the movement of the mind, the interior voice, find Sidney's voice *more* flowing than that of his contemporaries. When *Astrophil and Stella* was published in 1591, the new, lighter style of ironic or whimsical Petrarchanism became the dominant mode of the sonnet, and it seems very strange to us that anyone should not find this a poetic improvement, or call this 'Inglishe fasone' harsh. But the pressure towards dramatic speech, and away from sententious speech, could produce effects that for someone trained as James or Montgomerie or Fowler had been, would seem disordered. For example, let us consider the following three sonnets, one by James (which is actually a free translation of a sonnet by Mélin de Saint-Gelais) and two by Alexander, from his sequence *Aurora*:

> [T]he Cheuiott hills doe with my state agree
> In euerie point excepting onelie one
> For as there toppes in cloudes are mounted hie
> So all my thoughts in skies be higher gone
> There foote is fast, my faithe a stedfast stone
> From them discends the christall fontains cleare
> And from mine eyes butt fained force and mone
> Hoppes trickling teares with sadd and murnefull cheare
> From them great windes do hurle with hiddeous beir
> From me deepe sighs, greate flocks of sheepe they feede
> I flockes of loue, no fruicts on them appeare
> My houpe to me no grace can bring or breede
>   In these alike, in this we disagree
>   That snowe on them, and flames remaines in me.
>   [Add. MS 24195 fol. 7ʳ]¹³

> The most refreshing waters come from rockes,
> Some bitter rootes oft send forth daintie flowres,
> The growing greenes are cherished with showres,
> And pleasant stemmes spring from deformed stockes:
> The hardest hils do feed the fairest flockes:
> All greatest sweetes were sugred first with sowres,
> The headlesse course of vncontrolled houres,

To all difficulties a way vnlockes.
I hope to haue a heauen within thine armes,
And quiet calmes when all these stormes are past,
Which coming vnexpected at the last,
May burie in Obliuion by-gone harmes.
    To suffer first, to sorrow, sigh, and smart,
    Endeeres the conquest of a cruell hart.

                                      [*Aurora* 79]

Hvge hosts of thoughts imbattled in my brest,
Are euer busied with intestine warres,
And like to Cadmus earth-borne troupes at iarres,
Haue spoil'd my soule of peace, themselues of rest.
Thus forc'd to reape such seed as I haue sowne,
I (hauing interest in this doubtfull strife),
Hope much, feare more, doubt most, vnhappie life.
What euer side preuaile, I'm still orethrowne:
O neither life nor death! o both, but bad
Imparadiz'd, whiles in mine owne conceit,
My fancies straight again imbroyle my state,
And in a moment make me glad and sad.
    Thus neither yeelding quite to this nor that,
    I liue, I die, I do I wot not what.

                                        [*Aurora* 6]

James's sonnet is an excellent example of the flowing style applied to love, with all the effects that James recommends in his *Reulis and Cautelis*, including alliteration and what he called 'wilful reasonis, proceeding rather from passioun nor reasoun'.[14] Nearly all the tropes and schemes are directed towards intensification, and the poem is a steady accumulation of points smoothly following on one after another. What keeps it within the realm of *sentence* is the overall structure of rational analysis, which provides the beginning and end of the sonnet. This is a very deliberate performance of developed passion, very sober extravagance, bespeaking an analytic or rational mind. And attention is directed outward from the speaker to the external world – specifically, the Cheviot Hills.

Alexander can write like this, and often does, because he seems naturally to have been a rather pompous and pedantic man; but because he was younger, and published his sonnets in 1604, he had read verses of the 'Inglishe fasone', and every so often one notices the change. In his sonnet 79, 'The most refreshing waters', the octave is certainly in the flowing sententious style, which develops one simple point by intensifying it through a series of tropes – in this case the apophthegm, reinforced with alliteration. But at the sestet, the style changes to something apparently simpler and (as we should think) actually more melodious and flowing, an accent borrowed or imitated most probably from Samuel Daniel. However, there is an element of speech complexity here in the use of hyperbaton, or disruption of normal word order: 'quiet calmes' is a postponed object parallel with 'a heauen'; 'coming vnexpected at the last' is an embedded phrase, and 'in Obliuion by-gone harmes' is a slight inversion of object and predicate. The syntax of these four lines is actually more complicated and disruptive than that of the first eight, though the effect is still, as we should say, flowing. But there is much more of a sense of someone talking in these lines, rather than, as in the first eight, addressing a public meeting or reciting his home-work in class.

The last sonnet, *Aurora* 6, is getting nearer to the corvine. It is much more hyperbolic, but Alexander does what Sidney had taught his age to do: he lets the excitement or passion affect the syntax, so that we get parentheses, ellipses, exclamations, enjambments, runs of very short sentences – the impression of a mind thrown about by its own passion. Obviously this is just as much a rhetorical contrivance as the repetitive antitheses in the earlier sonnet, but the impression made is of disorder proceeding from immediate excitement. This sonnet directs attention inward, as James's and *Aurora* 79 do not, and might be thought to show much more clearly the 'inward touch' that Sidney had desired.

To develop this difference, let us contrast *Aurora* 79 with a sonnet by William Fowler which uses the same Petrarchan topos as a producer of confusion – one of 'poor Petrarch's long deceased woes':

> I burne by hope, I freise agayne by feare;
> I fredome searche, yet spoyles me of the same;
> I peace embrace, from rest I doe reteire;
> I am in hel, and yet the heavens I clayme;
> I see far off, yet vayles to eyes I frame;
> as I me yeild, so bakward I withdrawe;
> I her extoll quhome I agane doe blame,
> And puft with pryde I prostrat me more lawe;
> yea, dombe I cry, and smyling sadnes schawe;
> I walk with light, and taks a blynd for guyde;
> yea, not attentiue, I bothe heare and knawe;
> the more I crave, the more I am denyde:
> > thus love me binds and drawes by double rope,
> > and maks me fondlye perrish be my hope.
>
> [*Tarantula* 59]

The contrast between the Castalian sonneteer and the Anglified one lies not so much in a difference of lexis or tropes or schemes – they are both using Petrarchan conceits and vocabulary, both use alliteration and antithesis, and either of them could have written the other's first line – as in a kind of unconscious strategy, if one can have that. The Castalian speaker is as one might say using a forensic persona, exposing a case to the view and judgment of an audience by settling into a position which he then intensifies by repetition. Just as one knows that an advocate in court is not going to deviate from his line, however he may embroider it, so here one has a sense that this speaker has prepared his case in advance, in a tradition of humanistic eloquence in which the sign of wisdom is the sentence, the summation of experience that closes off, rather than opens up further speech. Adequacy, or success, for this speaker lies in defining himself successfully, that is rhetorically, as a locus of conflict; and the rhetoric which he inhabits works, as James himself put it,

> ... with summaire raisons suddainlie applied,
> For euerie purpose vsing raisons fitt
> With skillfulness where learning may be spied,
> With pitthie wordes for to expresse yow by it ...[15]

Alexander, who starts the sonnet with an alliterative line very much in Fowler's manner, takes a different stance. His speaker is not reporting on an experience which is neatly understood, but is ironically distanced from a state of affairs which puzzles him. There are two indications of this, one learnt from Sidney, and the other from Donne, perhaps: Sidney showed his age what could be done with parenthesis, the device that shifts a speaker aside from or above what he is talking about: here 'hauing interest in this doubtfull strife' takes both speaker and hearer a little bit aside from what is going on. The moment that happens the apparently inert piece of learning in the third line acquires point: one recalls that in the story of the dragon's teeth, Cadmus sowed the magic teeth, and when the 'earth-borne troupes' arose, he, having interest in that doubtful strife, subdued them by standing aside and throwing a stone among them, so that they all fought and killed one another. This he did by the advice of Pallas Athena, who rescued him from his perplexity and danger. This witty analogy, which Alexander gives us by implication, ironises the speaker's position, and locates him, like Cadmus, on the side of the field wondering what on earth to do, until Athena – perhaps in the next sonnet – solves the problem for him.

The second device is what we might now after Donne recognise as metaphysical compression: having offered us the conventional

Petrarchan antithesis, 'O neither life nor death!', just as Fowler might have done, he rejects the possibility of giving another parallel antithesis, e.g.

> O neither life nor death, not ice nor fire,
> Nor heaven yet nor hell, not peace nor ire.

and gives us instead the more complicated idea of a life which contains death, 'but bad Imparadiz'd', like Satan at the ear of Eve. This complication and ironisation produces a conclusion which is the opposite of a *sententia*: 'I do I wot not what' – the *sententia* is the place where very clearly one *does* wot what is what. Sidney's legacy to his age was partly the confidence to employ mockery and doubt, and leave a sonnet questioning or undercut. Both poets come to the final couplet with 'thus', but whereas Fowler's 'thus' really is conclusive, enforced by the rhyme, the intensification of 'drawes by double rope' and the recurrent antithesis, the fourteenth of the poem, Alexander's is undercut by the negatives, the slightly defective rhyme of 'that/what' and the phonic silliness (borrowed from Sidney) of 'wot not what'.[16] There is only one enjambment in Alexander's sonnet, at 'bad/Imparadiz'd', but it is a very telling one, offering the reader a shock both conceptual and metrical; and finally, the line 'Hope much, feare more, doubt most, unhappie life' introduces a kind of off-balance rhythm into the sonnet that is quite alien to Fowler's very diligent medial caesuras, rocking their way steadily through the sonnet.

Now it would certainly be possible to find very Castalian sonnets by Alexander, and more dramatic ones by Fowler – for example, *Aurora* 25, compared with *Tarantula* 57. Fowler was a very able poet, and Alexander's grip on his 'Inglishe fasone' was not uniformly steady. But the stylistic shift that I am trying to point to is not easily identified with any particular trope or scheme or kind of conceit: though heavy alliteration, antithesis, iteration of figures and parallelism tend to mark the sententious style, while hyperbaton, ellipsis, irony and parenthesis tend to mark the corvine or dramatic style, neither has the monopoly of particular schemes or tropes. But when Alexander takes his cue from Sidney (or perhaps from Drayton) and begins a sonnet, as they often do, dramatically, as if in the middle of a conversation, one can see that the result might have seemed harsh to James:

> I cannot comprehend how this doth come,
> Thou whose affections never yet were warme,
> Which cold disdaine with leaden thoughts doth arme:
> Though in thy self still cold, yet burn'st thou some.
> Even as the Sunne (as th'Astrologian dreames)

In th'airie region where it selfe doth move,
Is neuer hote, yet darting from aboue,
Doth parch all things that repercusse his beames:
So thou that in thy selfe from fires art free,
Who eye's indifferent still, as Titan's stayes,
Whilst I am th'obiect that reflect thy rayes:
That which thou neuer hadst, thou workst in me.
   Since but below thou shew'st that power of thine,
   I would the Zodiack be whence thou dost shine.

                        [*Aurora* 37][17]

Apart from a disastrous rhyme in l. 4, and a doubtful reading in l. 10 ('Whose eye' seems neatest), this is an extremely competent sonnet in the manner of the mature English writers of the late 1590s, Drayton, Shakespeare and Donne. After the dramatic opening, there is one trace of Castalian style in the third line, which is a mere expansion of l. 2; but then the sonnet moves very swiftly forwards, with multiple elisions, very little alliteration, no iteration (consider the deft economy of 'from fires art free'), and a kind of metaphysical quizzicality that reminds of Donne, but in its bareness ('That which thou neuer hadst, thou workst in me') is really more reminiscent of Shakespeare – though he would have made something much more corrosive out of that 'indifferent eye'. The false congruence of the first quatrain (the first 'thou' has no verb) and the third (the third 'thou' likewise has no verb) mimics the stops and starts of a mind perplexed. The harshness of clogged sibilants throughout is dramatically effective, and enforces the ferocity of the speaker's resentment.

But the rejection of Castalian sententiousness did not inevitably propel the Anglophile poet into harshness. James has left no record of his opinions of Sir Robert Ayton's poetry, but it seems unlikely that he would have thought this sonnet 'trotting' or 'tumbling' – yet it is certainly not Castalian in style:

I bid farewell unto the world and thee,
To the[e], because thou art Extreame vnkinde,
Vnto the world, because the world to me
Is nothing, since I cannott move thy minde.
Were any mercy in thy soule inshrin'd,
Could sighes or teares make soft thy flinty heart,
I could perhaps more easily be inclin'd
To spend my dayes with the[e] then to depart.
But since thou knowes not Cupid's golden dart,
But hath been wounded with a shaft of lead,

> It is but folly to pretend his Art
> To sue for favour, when I find but feade.   [i.e. *feud*]
>   So farewell, Nimph, farewell for aye as now,
>   And welcome death more mercifull than thou.[18]

This has none of the roughness of Alexander's sonnet above, but it has instead a lightness of manner which one might call *galante*, and which Ayton picked up quickly at court – as Fowler, one may suppose, did not. If we set alongside Ayton's sonnet an apparently similar one from *The Tarantula of Love*, the novelty of Ayton's stance may be clearer:

> I hope to see, sueit soule, at my returne
> the heunlye couleur of your angel face,
> which is the fyre and flame quhairby I burne,
> and never is empaird by time nor place;
> quhair ye sal als behald in me this space
> no other chainge bot that of haire and hewe;
> as for my hart, which liues in payne but peace,
> euen as it was, so sal yow find it trewe:
> bot quhat sal I in yow agayne revewe
> bot rigours, frost, denyells and disdaynes,
> and in that face (through which dois ay ensewe
> the streaming course of my vnceasent paynes)
> a farder fairnes with a farder pryde,
> which til my deathe so long with the must byde.
>
> [*Tarantula* 28]

Allowing for the Scotticisms, both Fowler and Ayton write 'flowingly', without hyperbaton or inversions (except for l. 9 of Fowler); neither uses much learning, and the lexis of both is straightforward, drawn from the repertoire of European Petrarchanism. What is distinctively Castalian, I suggest, is the absolutism of the speaker of Fowler's sonnet: he consistently clarifies and intensifies his position, as James says of the perfect poet,

> ... for to expresse yow by it
> His full intention in his propre leide,
> the propertie whereof well hes he tryit ...[19]

The rhetoric of humanism, based upon the 'sentence', creates an 'I' with authority, who uses rhetorical devices to decorate a world plainly seen and decisively displayed, in which the individual 'I' is subject to general laws of behaviour. To use rhetoric so as to dislocate or fragment this 'I' is to go against humanist moral rhetoric, and the roughness of the sonnets of Donne or Shakespeare, or Alexander at times, is to that extent counter-humanist. Ayton's rhetoric tends towards the colloquial, not in the sportive vein of Montgomerie, but in the service of a more relaxed or uncommitted 'I', whose hyperboles can be read as comic gestures, not intense statements, and who affects disengagement rather than commitment. If the dominant trope of Castalian rhetoric is intensification, the dominant one of Ayton's 'galante' rhetoric is litotes:

> I could perhaps more easily be inclin'd
> To spend my dayes with the[e] then to depart'

This wariness, the hedging of emotional bets, is discernable in Wyatt, and is a component in the make-up of the experienced courtier: it does not, however, sit easily with any kind of idealism, Petrarchan, moral or religious. In the early days of James's court, and the 1590s in England, it was suppressed, except in satire; it returns to English poetry in the early years of the seventeenth century, and remains a dominant note until the Enlightenment. It is possible that what James was reacting to, in his humorous expostulation to Alexander, was not crudeness, but sophistication, the kind of Jacobean restless impatience with older idealism that made Fowler and others either suppress their poetry or apologise for it as juvenilia. And it is probably because of the 'Inglishe fasone' at court after 1603 or 1604 that the best sonneteers of the period are those whose passions were directed elsewhere than at the objects of a courtier's desire: Drummond of Hawthornden, John Donne, and George Herbert.[20]

1. Michael R. G. Spiller, 'A Literary "First": the Sonnet Sequence of Anne Locke (1560)', *Renaissance Studies*, 11 (1997), 41–55.

2. William Fowler, *The Works of William Fowler*, ed. H. W. Meikle, 2 vols, STS (Edinburgh and London, 1914, 1936); vol. 3, ed. H. W. Meikle, J. Craigie, J. Purves (Edinburgh and London, 1940). Alexander Montgomerie, *The Poems*, ed. James Cranstoun, STS (Edinburgh and London, 1885–7); *Poems ... Supplementary Volume*, ed. George Stevenson, STS (Edinburgh, 1910). John Stewart of Baldynneis, *Poems*, ed. Thomas Crockett, STS (Edinburgh and London, 1913).

3. William Alexander of Menstrie's *Aurora. Containing the first fancies of the Authors youth* was published in London in 1604. David Murray's *Caelia. Containing certaine Sonets* was published in 1611, and was described on its first page as the work of 'my infant Muse'. The volumes of Murray and Alexander are reproduced in facsimile in *English and Scottish Sonnet Sequences of the Renaissance*, ed. Holger M. Klein, 2 vols (New York, 1984), and Alexander's *Aurora* was edited by L. E. Kastner and H. B. Charlton in their two-volume edition of *The Poetical Works of Sir William Alexander*, STS (Edinburgh and London, 1921 and 1929), vol. II, pp. 439–521 and notes. Alexander Craig of Rosscraig published his *Poeticall Essayes* in 1604, his *Amorose Songs, Sonets and*

Elegies in 1606, and his *Poetical Recreations* in 1609. Though an extremely prolific sonneteer, he did not produce a sonnet sequence. His *Poetical Works* were edited by J. Laing, Hunterian Club (Glasgow, 1872–3).

4. There is a very brief notice of Stewart by R. D. S. Jack, 'Imitation in the Scottish Sonnet', *Comparative Literature*, 10 (1968), 316–18.

5. Fowler, *Works* II, p. 3.

6. *The Works of William Drummond of Hawthornden* (Edinburgh, 1711), p. 149.

7. The sonnet is reproduced in parallel texts in vol. II of *The Poems of King James VI of Scotland*, ed. James Craigie, 2 vols, STS (Edinburgh, 1955, 1958), pp. 114–15. The Additional MS version has the title 'A Sonett: on Sr William Alexanders harshe vearses after the Inglishe fasone'; and the Denmilne MS has 'The complainte of the Muses to Alexander vpon him selfe for his ingratitude towardes them by hurting them with his hard hammerd wordes fitter to be vsed vpon his mineralles.' The Denmilne version spells 'fil'd' in the last line as 'filld', but the antithesis between the verse of 'your neighbours' and 'our songs' (i.e. the Muses and Alexander as he formerly was) is strengthened if the former are 'hammered' and the latter are 'filed'.

8. 'Imitation in the Scottish Sonnet', 325; *Alexander Montgomerie* (Edinburgh, 1985), pp. 7–8.

9. Kastner and Charlton, I, p. cxcvi.

10. Thomas McGrail, *Sir William Alexander: a Biographical Study* (Edinburgh, 1940), p. 26.

11. James VI, *The Reulis and Cautelis … in Scottis Poesie*, printed in *The Essayes of a Prentise, in the Divine Art of Poesie* (Edinburgh, 1585), ed. Edward Arber, English Reprints Series (1869), p. 66. The first edition was, as stated above, in 1584.

12. References to Sidney's works here and elsewhere are to the standard edition of the poems, *The Poems of Sir Philip Sidney*, ed. William A. Ringler (Oxford, 1962).

13. James VI, *Poems*, II, pp. 70–1, and see note on p. 227.

14. James VI, *The Reulis and Cautelis …*, p. 63.

15. James VI, *Poems*, II, p. 112. This sonnet ('Ane rype ingyne, ane quick and walkned witt'), entitled 'Sonnet decifring the perfyte poete' had appeared as a prefatory sonnet to the *Reulis and Cautelis … in Scottis Poesie* of 1584. It is interesting that the Additional MS version of *c.* 1617, overseen by James, assembled this sonnet with four others on the subject of writing poetry, and placed all five immediately before the sonnet to Alexander.

16. *Astrophil and Stella*, 74: 'Some do I heare of Poets' furie tell,/ But (God wot), wot not what they meane by it'.

17. Kastner and Charlton suggest the emendation 'Whose eye's' II, p. 637.

18. Sir Robert Ayton, *The English and Latin Poems*, ed. C. B. Gullans, STS (Edinburgh, 1963), p. 166.

19. 'Sonnet decifring the perfyte poete' – see n. 15.

20. Donne certainly would have been a courtier, given a less savage reaction to his marriage, but all his sonnet writing belongs to the clerical side of his life. Herbert absorbed courtly rhetoric – mainly of the *galante* kind – very thoroughly, but uses it ironically to disparage secular concerns. As early as 1610 he reacted in a sonnet sent to his mother:

> Doth Poetry
> Wear venus livery? Only serve her turn?
> Why are not Sonnets made of Thee? and layes
> Upon Thine altar burnt?

(*The Works of George Herbert*, ed. F. E. Hutchinson (Oxford, 1941), p. 206.) Shakespeare, who is the best of the best, was certainly involved with a courtier, but it is uncertain whether his 1609 *Sonnets* do actually belong to this period, in whole, or in part, or were written in the decade before, despite their 'late' mannerisms.

6

FOLKLORIC PATTERNS IN SCOTTISH CHRONICLES

Juliette Wood

An early editor of the Scottish chronicles complained that one of the problems in dealing with chronicle material was the difficulty of sorting out the fragments of 'true history' from the fables.[1] If true history is taken to mean factual history, then much of the fabulous material may indeed seem tangential if not actually intrusive or illogical. Fortunately, attitudes have altered considerably on this point and modern editors are willing to consider that some at least of these episodes are rooted in a folk cultural register. Once such material is designated as folklore, it becomes an aspect of the chronicle which must be accounted for rather than an intrusion which needs to be 'sorted out'. This change in attitude has consequences for the treatment of chronicle material, not least of which is the definition of folklore within the context of historical writing. The folklore connections of certain obvious items are comparatively easy to identify. For example beliefs about the supernatural underpin the confrontation between Macbeth and the weird sisters,[2] which first appears in Wyntoun.[3] Some chronicle commentaries even provide the apparatus of folklore analysis, such as motif numbers and speculations about possible sources.[4] There have been a number of perceptive studies of individual episodes in the chronicles. Nora Chadwick considered the implications of *compert* tales, narratives which deal with the birth and childhood stories of heroes, in relation to Scottish kingship.[5] Susan Kelly examined the use of Arthurian material in Scottish sources,[6] and more recently John McGavin has analysed an episode of 'rough music' in Bower's *Scotichronicon*.[7] Such studies, however, still maintain a fundamental distinction between history and 'folk' (i.e. non-historical) material. While they contribute to our appreciation of the range of subject matter which was incorporated into the chronicles, the folklore material is still treated as item rather than as process and is ultimately regarded as extraneous to the larger framework of the chronicle. However, there have been moves to see this material not simply as occasional and interesting items of legendary lore but as a functional part of the narration, as for example in Edward Cowan's wide-ranging study of the link between national myth and ethnic identity in Scottish chronicle writing[8] and W. F. H. Nicolaisen's study of narrative pattern in Barbour's *Bruce*.[9]

The study of folkloristics can perhaps offer a wider understanding of the function of traditional elements in chronicles. Many of the older studies equated folklore with exclusively oral sources. However oral and written material have a long history of interaction, and while the concept of transmission by word of mouth is still a prominent element in modern definitions of folklore, it is no longer considered the central criterion for definition. Many contemporary studies focus on the nature of culture and are therefore concerned with folklore as a range of complex expressive behaviour which can convey aspects of cultural identity.[10] This study uses the term, 'traditional', to describe such material in the chronicles. This broader definition does not eliminate all the problems connected with folklore in historical sources, but it does widen the discussion from narrow considerations of oral sources to include function and meaning.[11] The chronicles used in this study were written for different audiences and the various compilers undoubtedly had different aims. The context for folklore in the chronicles is affected by these factors which makes it more difficult to determine how widely traditions may have varied or to corroborate material since the chronicle is often the only source. Despite these limitations, folklore methodology can provide a useful means for widening our understanding of the function of this material in the context of a chronicle. The folklorist Richard Dorson considered some of the ramifications of folklore as a source for history in his survey of oral sources for Highland history.[12] Dorson was concerned with sifting historical fact from folk tradition. Nevertheless, he began with the premise that orally preserved versions of history have value for revealing what episodes of the past endure and what forms they take in memory unaided by printed sources,[13] and he suggested a number of criteria for evaluating the historical validity of oral tradition. These included identifying folklore themes which had been grafted onto historical events, the importance of the personal or emotional bias of oral accounts, and the need for independent corroboration by checking oral accounts against printed records, local geography and available material culture.[14] Subsequent work by Alan Bruford and John MacInnes[15] suggests that Dorson was perhaps too simplistic in his approach, but he is to be commended for attempting to put the matter on a rigorous footing. Perhaps his most important contribution in terms of this study is his insight that oral accounts are not merely inadequate versions of written accounts but contribute actively to the construction and interpretation of an event.

For example, folk traditions can function as rhetorical and symbolic strategies that create a sense of linkage between the past and the present. W. F. H. Nicolaisen characterises the process of storytelling as a series of rhetorical and narrative strategies which create an illusion of 'continuous self' by narrating a past which provides the basis for a shared identity.[16] The present study focuses on three aspects of chronicle writing in which the strategies for narrating the past can be said to have resonances in folklore. The most powerful and varied of these is the effect which genres of all types exert on the development of an extended narrative. In addition, this study will examine the function of legend and anecdote as a technique of characterisation, and the use of portents and prophecies as commentary on action. The material is drawn from a range of chronicles, mainly those of Fordun, Wyntoun, Bower and Bellenden. Although these chronicles were intended for different audiences and cover a time span of at least two centuries, they were popular and widely circulated works. As such they can provide a synchronic dimension for traditional material which together with recent folklore research can extend our understanding of the relationship between tradition and historical content.

Differing approaches to the relationship between history and folklore have been presented by two past presidents of the Folklore Society. Margaret Murray believed that the techniques of folklore could reveal the distant origins of historical documents. This provided the theoretical framework which underpinned her suggestion that records of Scottish witchcraft trials contained distorted accounts of an ancient fertility cult.[17] Hilda Davidson, on the other hand, suggests that legend and fact are part of a syncretic process in historical writing,[18] a position which is supported by historians such as Benjamin Hudson, who suggests that the confusion and conflation of history and legend are part of the synthesising approach to Scottish history.[19] Recent interest in less formal genres of narrative provides additional perspectives on the traditional aspects of chronicle material. A productive field of modern storytelling research centres on personal-experience narratives. Although these narratives, usually in anecdotal form, are rooted in actual experiences about real people, the sequencing of events and the depiction of character resemble the structure of more fictive narratives such as wonder tales and legends.[20] In a study of life stories of contemporary neo-pagan witches, Elisabeth Tucker noted that personal-experience narratives played an important role in communication. The ways in which her informants presented themselves mimicked their understanding of the heroic behaviour of characters in folk narratives. These contemporary witches usually characterised themselves as initially unpromising, and their life stories often turned on some dramatic event which transformed their outlook and attitude to life. This turning-point usually occurred in dramatic circumstances and was initiated by a helper figure. The sequence of events in their narratives paralleled an intensely personal process of self-discovery. By using the structures of folktales, the narrators could signpost critical emotional changes in a manner which conveyed the importance of the event and yet maintained some emotional distance between narrator and listener.[21] Other folklorists have examined various aspects of the interrelation between traditional tale structure and personal experience. Such research suggests that resemblances between traditional and literary narrative,[22] the increase of conventional elements as history becomes legend,[23] and the use of legend structures in narrating life stories[24] are indicators that shared cultural values, as well as personal meaning, can be communicated through traditional narrative structures.

While the application of such techniques to historical material is subject to the constraints outlined above, many of the rhetorical strategies expressed through these narrative patterns are identifiable in chronicle accounts. The most recent edition of the *Scotichronicon* suggests that Bower had access to traditions about a meeting between Wallace and Bruce at Falkirk in 1298 which he included in book 6 of the chronicle.[25] The reference to 'plebis et populares' in particular suggests that the sources here are traditional tales.[26] While the commentary appears to equate traditional with oral material, the suggestion is a persuasive one. The origins of the traditions and the circumstances by which they reached the chronicle writer will probably remain unknown, but the chronicle itself provides a context for the episode. The two men face each other across a valley and Wallace exhorts Bruce to be loyal to Scotland. The text describes Bruce's conversion as waking from a deep sleep. There is no proof that such a meeting occurred, and one might question the credibility of so sudden a change. However, the incident shares certain features with the dramatic events in folktales which direct unpromising young heroes on a life of adventure, and in so far as these events happen to real people, rather than folktale heroes, there are similarities with the epiphany experiences described in life-stories of contemporary witches. Looked at in terms of the structure of personal-experience narratives, Wallace acts as a catalyst who helps the vacillating (i.e. unpromising) Bruce find his true Scottish identity. Whether Bower had heard these traditions as a developed oral tale or not can never be more than speculation. However the chronicle seems to be drawing on a register of traditional narrative patterns in which a particular sequencing of events reveals something about the nature of the action. The similarities between the epiphanies described in personal narratives and the dramatic development of Bruce's character in this passage suggest that chronicle writers such as Bower did not merely recount history but helped to structure it. The figures of Wallace and Bruce have been intertwined in Scottish tradition from the beginning. Narrative has played as important a part as history in this process. It has helped shape the accounts of Wallace's life and structured the heroic roles of both figures.[27]

The dynamics of a chronicle episode and the constructive role of the chronicle writer are clearly illustrated when the same event is treated in different chronicles. The dramatic death of Kenneth II at Fettercain occurs in both Bower's *Scotichronicon* and Bellenden's translation of Boece. Both chronicles give an account of the king's death at the hands of a woman, Finella. They tell essentially the same story about Kenneth's attempts to reform the laws of royal succession, his repentance after Malcolm's death and the events leading to his murder. There are however striking differences both in detail and in emphasis. In Bower,[28] Kenneth's reasons for killing Finella's son are unknown. Finella joins a conspiracy and lays a trap at a cottage (*domuncolo*) which consists of a statue booby-trapped with crossbows. When the king goes hunting, she invites him to her house promising to reveal a plot against his life. She shows him the statue, claiming it will provide good sport and Kenneth, heretofore characterised as an astute and cunning man, walks tamely into the trap. The disjunction between the canny ruler and the gullible victim is even more marked in Bellenden's translation.[29] Kenneth governs 'in grete iustice' but the poisoning of Malcolm preys on his mind and precipitates a warning dream vision. As a penance he makes a pilgrimage which brings him to the domain of Finella. Bellenden's account claims that Finella was 'cousinace' to Malcolm and that her son was slain by the king's justice. Finella's trap is considerably more elaborate here. The statue, made in Kenneth's likeness holding a jewelled apple, is housed in an opulently decorated tower with bows and arrows hidden behind the tapestries. When the victim touches the apple, a mechanism causes the tapestries to rise and discharge the arrows. The account also stresses Kenneth's competence as a ruler until this episode when he becomes the gullible victim of an intricate and bizarre murder plot.

Bower's version is less dense, although the devices of the hunt, the remote cottage and the scheming woman arguably reflect the kind of patterning common in traditional tales. In the Bellenden version traditional themes are rationalised. Kenneth is warned through a dream, a common supernatural experience, but this one is couched in rhetoric appropriate for advice to princes and conforms to medieval dream theory.[30] The figure of Finella is more complex here. The fact that her son was executed for some unspecified crime undermines the justification for vengeance. However she is linked to her eventual victim in a way that would explain her desire for revenge, even though such a code may have been obsolete by the time the chronicle was written. One commentator has suggested that Finella may be a mythological figure,[31] although the motif of the treacherous woman is common enough in its own right. The opulent tower is certainly not the otherworld, but it does contain the elements of beauty and danger often associated with traditional descriptions of this environment. In so far as touching an apple causes the death of the male character, there may even be a hint of the Adam and Eve story.

Clearly in passages as dense as these two, identifying the 'folk register' becomes more complex than simply finding occasional items which have strayed in from oral tradition. The identification of traditional structures and analysis of their function helps to understand their complexity and the different cultural registers available to writers. For example, warning dreams are common in personal-experience narratives, but seldom do they use the rhetoric found here. Mechanical devices are featured in medieval narratives, although usually as protective talismans (D1268. Magic statue) rather than instruments of murder. This highlights the difficulty in merely identifying material as folklore without a consideration of context and function. The hunt as a setting for adventure (N771. King lost on hunt has adventures), the scheming woman (K910. Scheming relatives/associates), the beautiful but dangerous environment (F171. Extraordinary sights in Otherworld), the warning dream (D1813.1. King gets advice in dream) are recognisable as folk motifs with many parallels elsewhere, while features such as the rhetoric of the dream and, if one accepts the Adam and Eve reference, the symbolism of the apple, indicate that there are non-traditional elements as well. What allows us to identify these episodes as traditional is not their connection with oral sources, but the way they are filtered through patterns which themselves reflect cultural attitudes.

One of the most striking features of these accounts is the seeming discrepancy between Kenneth as a realistically portrayed and competent ruler and as the gullible victim of Finella. The tradition of treacherous powerful females is well-established in both literary and folk registers. Figures such as Circe and Medea came to epitomise such negative aspects of femininity as vengefulness, duplicity and eventually diabolic power,[32] and there is considerable common ground between these figures and the witches, supernatural females and wicked queens of popular belief and folk narrative. Finella embodies a number of these negative female attributes,[33] and Bower, copying Fordun, uses the term 'malifica' to describe her.[34] Finella's assurances to the king are heavy-handed and the audience can foresee the ending even if the intended victim does not. When Kenneth enters her sphere, he becomes an innocent male victimised by a treacherous female, rather than a real king accustomed to the machinations of court life. There is a shared narrative expectation on the part of the audience at least, that Kenneth has been caught in a net of his own actions[35] and that both characters embody ideas about male and female behaviour. The two are brought together by the dynamics of the narrative and it is almost a compliment to his character that a king who deals in law and justice should not suspect the existence of such a fiendish plot.

The dramatic irony inherent in the situation is all the more striking since the accounts move with such naturalness from the world of historic Scottish politics to the unreal world of sinister mechanical devices and devious women. The folklorist Tristram Coffin suggested that folk narratives contain codes that audiences can interpret and used the term 'folk logic' to account for the apparent logical disruptions which happen when conflicting views of the same figure occur in the same narrative.[36] Although the terminology implies a somewhat artificial distinction between folklore and history, it allows us to view Kenneth's apparently inconsistent behaviour as appropriate to the narration of his life story. Narratives such as these of bizarre or alternative death-stories in chronicles reveal the king's character in a manner which is different, but just as important, as the other events of his life. Unusual and supernatural features signpost the character's importance,[37] and criteria of truth and falsehood become less relevant in these narratives than attitudes to authority and power.

Another way to understand the dynamics of the narrative is to view it as a process by which action and character become progressively conventionalised.[38] The emphasis then shifts to the balance between individuation and stereotyping, rather than the accuracy of the account. It has been suggested that an important function of personal narratives is to 'present arenas in which types strongly identified with a group can play out their roles in non-fictional yet supra-individual situations'.[39] In the context of the chronicles, narrative is an important medium for conveying character and what is interesting is the selection of incidents which illustrate this and the way those incidents are structured. Kings are depicted as having kingly characters, but there is more to royal biography than recounting the events of a life and reign. The two protagonists in the narrative of Kenneth's death are clearly a mixture of real individuals and conventionalised types. Finella, a sub-plot figure in this kingly biography, is more easily stereotyped in both character and action while Kenneth's character develops in several phases reflecting his wider and more complex role. Both Kenneth and Finella embody gender ideals to some degree. Overall Kenneth fulfils expectations on a social and narrative level of a king maintaining the order and balance of the kingdom through his actions, while Finella embodies the destructive force of the vengeful female. In his comparison of supernatural and historical legends in Scottish tradition, Alan Bruford noted that reported historical information tended to be exaggerated to highlight events and could be stretched to the point of fiction in regard to death.[40] Both these features characterise the treatment of Kenneth's life in the Bower and Bellenden accounts.

Legendary material of various types forms the basis for numerous episodes in the chronicles. Bower's account of a revenant [41] exemplifies the type of material most easily recognised as folklore since it often contains supernatural and unusual elements associated with traditional views. Bower recounts how a man, excommunicated because he refused to pay tithes, returns from the grave, together with the priest who excommunicated him. The excommunicant makes restitution and both revenants rest peacefully. Underpinning the narrative is a common and widespread belief that the dead cannot rest if they have unfinished business on earth.[42] Such beliefs about the fate of the dead provided a kind of popular and unofficial purgatorial system. Implicit in this narrative are an admonition to a particular form of behaviour and sanctions for non-compliance. The links between traditional beliefs, narrative pattern and social constraints are extremely close, but the narrative expresses these beliefs without actually articulating the moral consequences.[43]

In book 8 of Wyntoun's *Chronicle*[44] the Lady Godiva legend has become attached to Malcolm Canmore's daughter. The protagonist of this well-known legend outwits her opponents and preserves her modesty.[45] Amours notes that Godric and Godiva were nicknames applied to Malcolm and his daughter elsewhere, thus suggesting another factor that might have affected the presence of this legend in the chronicle.[46] Whatever the reason for its inclusion, it implies a view of Malcolm's daughter as clever within accepted parameters of feminine modesty. The actors in narratives with an historical dimension such as these need to be more individuated than in, say, wonder tales, but they can still remain type-centred.[47] Both Malcolm Canmore's daughter and Finella embody views of women which were widely recognised and accepted in society. Stereotyped characterisation presents a positive view of this particular figure, while the same technique of characterisation elsewhere presents a negative view of Finella.

Both Wyntoun and Bower mention Robin Hood.[48] Wyntoun does not give any narrative detail, but in his account of the year 1283 says that Robin Hood was praised as an outlaw (*waytheman*). A recent study points out that the reference occurs in a context in which Wyntoun 'stresses the violence used by Edward I against the Scots'.[49] As an anti-authority figure pitted against an anti-Scottish king, Robin Hood is, by implication, someone a Scottish chronicle writer would regard favourably. Bower's reference is more elaborate, although it too seems to be exploiting the anti-authoritarian aspect of the outlaw figure. The account includes a pious anecdote, possibly based on an early ballad, that Robin Hood was discovered by the sheriff's men attending a woodland mass. The outlaw refused to flee out of respect for the sacrament and always treated churchmen with respect. Both Wyntoun and Bower suggest a figure of legitimate rebelliousness against tyranny. Bower adds the pious element which is not usually part of the outlaw's life, but may have been directed at a clerical audience.[50] Both chronicles seem aware of traditions about a particular, and from their point of view historical, outlaw but adapt them to specific contexts in the chronicle.[51]

Wyntoun's account of the death of David I's son in 1136 draws on a different kind of legend material.[52] His version contains somewhat vague details of a rather sensational murder. The story, which appears more fully in another chronicle,[53] recounts how David I befriends a maimed priest with artificial iron fingers. The ungrateful cleric pretends to caress the king's son, but stabs him with his iron fingers instead. There is no obvious motive for the murder and the atrocity is made all the more frightful because the boy is apparently safe in his nurse's arms. The rather macabre character of the narrative is obvious even in Wyntoun's fragmented version, and similarities between this narrative and the contemporary legend genre are marked. Characteristically these legends, to paraphrase David Buchan, contain both ancient and modern elements and exhibit traditional variation. They are rooted in a context contemporary with the events, but demand belief in something unlikely or, as here, fantastically horrific.[54]

The foregoing examples indicate both the range of legendary material which is included in the chronicles and how it functions in revealing character or adding a new dimension to the interpretation of events.[55]

However this does not exhaust the ways in which the power of traditional narrative can be moderated by the aims of chronicle writers. As a type of folk narrative genre, anecdotes recount the activities and accomplishments of real persons, often with some degree of exaggeration or irony. Anecdote is an important element in the creation of historical narrative and one whose traditional links are often overlooked. A number of the anecdotes used in Scottish chronicles may be rooted in folkloric tradition. In his description of Robert III, Bower includes an anecdote about a canon of Scone Abbey who uses unorthodox but recognisably traditional methods to obtain satisfaction from the king. It has been suggested that this episode must have substance since Bower was writing only a short time after the event [56] which might be told of any king, but as Bower localises it and was writing within twenty years of the event it must have some substance. However, other studies have noted the speed with which traditional patterns impress themselves on historical events,[57] and the episode is just as likely to be a traditional anecdote as a real event. The link between written sources and oral tradition can sometimes be illusive, and it may be better to focus on the way anecdotes such as these with their characteristically exaggerated or ironic recounting of an event can add an extra dimension to the understanding of human action.

In his account of the reign of king Robert III Bower incorporates several anecdotes which illustrate the king's judgment. One occurs on the day of the king's coronation,[58] when an aggrieved canon granger whose field had been trampled appears with a crowd of commoners carrying basins, sticks and a corn-dolly. Bower says that the sound of the trumpet awoke the king who listened sympathetically to the granger's plea. Bower is specific as to the purpose of this anecdote, stating that he included this incident to show the king's love of justice. Underlying the episode is the tradition of 'rough music', a widely practised form of public censure for a whole range of anti-social activities. Bower claims to give the details exactly, but it is not entirely clear against whom the 'rough music' was directed. Bower suggests, for example, that the sound of a trumpet, rather than the noise of the basins and sticks, woke the king. However, it is the king who recognises the justness of the protest and arranges compensation.[59]

Bower includes another anecdote about an English knight 'altiloquus satis et verbosus' who claims that the conquering English lords fathered children on Scottish women and therefore the vigour of current Scots aristocrats is the result of English breeding. A Scottish knight agrees, but adds that while the English were in Scotland, their wives took lovers from among churls, serfs, villains, friars and confessors and therefore the present generation of Englishmen are not suited for warfare.[60] Bower amalgamates this story to his depiction of kingship, by having Robert reward the Scot and demand repetition of the tale. The same Scottish knight engages in a joust with an Englishman who complains about the inequality of arms. The Scot acquiesces but claims that since he has lost an eye, the English knight should do so too. As a result the English knight forfeits the joust.[61] Here too the king is linked to the episode since he stops further quarrelling and claims the Scottish knight has bested the Englishman in both word and deed. In both these anecdotes the antagonist is made to look inadequate, and the protagonist wins by cleverness rather than strength.

The figure of the ruler provides a framework for dynastic narrative. Indeed the genealogical framework for dynastic succession is itself a narrative device.[62] Within this framework anecdotal patterns can provide a narrative alternative to explicit and detailed analysis. Anecdotes give the appearance of impartiality, implying that the audiences can draw their own conclusions and judge for themselves. The figure of the king provides a frame for the anecdotes in the chronicle by offering occasions for characterisation in connection with important events in his life, such as his coronation or an appearance at a public gathering. Anecdotes which are recounted in contexts such as these become *ipso facto* narratives about the king, even though he may not be the actual protagonist. The justice of the granger's case and the verbal success of the Scottish knight against his English counterpart reflect qualities of justice and wit in the king himself. The king is presented as a ruler interested in justice for all his subjects and, by association at least, is a fine example of Scottish manhood in contrast to the cowardly cuckolded English. As an alternative to complex character analysis in Bower's chronicle, anecdotes reveal the king's character indirectly by means of narration rather than encomium. In regards to Robert III, these dramatic anecdotes furnish an image of kingship which is all the more interesting for being applied to a monarch whom even the chronicler feels compelled to admit was 'the worst of kings'.[63]

Kingly biographies frequently focus on particular times in the ruler's life-cycle: birth, the approach of maturity, the accomplishments or failures of his life and the circumstances surrounding his death. Narrative episodes which reveal aspects of character are particularly prominent in the life-cycles of kings, and their life stories are in turn an important part of the chronicle narrative.[64] This is undoubtedly how any biography might be structured, and biographical pattern shapes the construction of many personal narratives,[65] and other types of folktale as well.[66] While kingly biography reflects the same pattern as the 'rites

of passage' in ordinary human lives, biographical pattern has an additional function in the life-stories of historical and pseudo-historical
heroes since their experiences and the events of their lives embody
qualities which are relevant on a national or cultural scale.[67] Childhood
actions and adventures are seen to foreshadow adult character, seemingly
random events precipitate critical choices, and birth and death are often
surrounded by unusual circumstances.

An unusual birth tale is attached to Malcolm Canmore in Wyntoun's
Original Chronicle which suggests that he was the illegitimate child of
the king and a miller's daughter. Nora K. Chadwick has compared
certain features of this tale with the structures of heroic narrative. Her
suggestion that kingly biography may have had a function other than
a simple account of actual events is still worth considering. Chadwick
notes that certain events in the Malcolm Canmore tale are very unlike
'ecclesiastical narrative' and that Wyntoun, or his immediate source,
might have used oral narratives still current in the locality.[68] Amours
may also suggest this indirectly when he says of Wyntoun's account of
the life of Duncan that Wyntoun 'must bear the whole responsibility
for this story. No other chronicler knows anything about the fair
daughter of the miller of Forteviot'.[69] Chadwick puts a more positive
construction on this and sees Wyntoun acting as 'a raconteur'.[70] According to Chadwick, the story of Duncan and the Miller's daughter at
Forteviot which results in the birth of Malcolm Canmore has the
appearance of 'one of the fosterage stories involving human princes
fostered by supernatural beings which were current in both Norse and
Celtic oral literature about this time'.[71] A number of similarities between
Norse/Celtic fosterage tales and chronicle accounts such as this one are
identified by Chadwick. Duncan loses his way while hunting, and, after
dark, he finds himself at the home of the Miller of Forteviot who
entertains him lavishly. The miller's beautiful daughter bears him a son
destined for greatness, namely Malcolm Canmore. The elements which
Chadwick suggests have links with an oral saga tradition include the
hunt as a setting for adventure, the separation of the young prince from
his companions, the darkness, the wealthy man and his daughter, and
the lavish hospitality followed by a temporary 'marriage' to the
daughter. She suggests that this material may ultimately derive from an
early saga about Scottish kings, but the existence of an early, but now
untraceable, saga is problematic. Many of the elements which Chadwick
identifies are recognisable and well-known folktale motifs, but this does
not necessarily mean, that there is an oral saga source behind the episode.
There is nothing supernatural about the tale, and the text may indicate
that the daughter was already the king's mistress. Nevertheless, the

similarity between tale and history remains an interesting suggestion, although Chadwick perhaps interprets their origin rather too strictly in terms of oral sagas giving way to written chronicles.[72] Current narrative research indicates that imaginative motifs can become attached to historical events.[73] If one focuses the story on Malcolm Canmore rather than his father, the circumstances of unusual birth are a common way to mark the specialness of a hero, whether fictional or historical. That the structures of traditional tales, such as legends and anecdotes furnish an added dimension to historical narration, and not just in relation to kings, is clearly indicated in the foregoing examples,

Comments about the purpose and function of chronicles from the writers themselves are rare, however one medieval chronicler claimed that they should tell of the deeds of kings and princes and record any portents, miracles or other events.[74] Portents, the final aspect of this consideration of folkloric patterns in Scottish chronicles, bridge the gap between traditional sources and popular culture. As an aspect of narrative structure portents are a type of belief legend. Much of the portent material existed and circulated in manuscript or printed form, and the perception of folklore as an essentially oral register is not readily applicable to them. In so far as this material overlaps with the related genre of prophecy the links between folk and élite culture are even more complex.[75] Although prophecy as such is uncommon in traditional narratives[76] it was certainly part of the 'arsenal of power' available to ruling élites.[77] Portents and prophecies were frequently symptomatic of political unrest,[78] but this may be too simplistic a way to explain their appearance in chronicles.

Portents have much in common with a broad area of folk belief which encompasses traditional omens of death and disaster, and their formal structure often resembles the types of legends which express such beliefs. Narratives involving portents come closest to the register of folk culture in the mechanism which links the omen to the event. Like legends about death omens, portents often take the form of a short narrative, sometimes little more than a statement, in which the ominous sign is identified and linked to some specific event. The mechanism is common to numerous and highly conventionalised omens in folklore. The appearance of animals, weather events and supernatural phenomena of various kinds often precede important life events in a community. The description of an omen is usually followed by the foreshadowed event and an 'independent' witness, either the narrator or a third party, validates the truth of the experience. In the context of chronicles, the portents' function is not unlike atmospheric background music in an epic film. They anticipate events, but not by enough to spoil the suspense and provide an implicit and conventionalised commentary on the course of action. Like film music, portents and prophecies use a common fund of experiences and what makes then appealing is not their originality but their familiarity.[79] Many of the images draw heavily on printed and written ephemera such as chapbooks and broadsheets, or even ballads and the legends which depended on them. The occurrence of portents in chronicles anticipates some of the characteristics of modern mass culture. This may be an area where it would be useful to consider the aims of the compilers and translators of these chronicles and their intended audiences. At present however such research is hampered by the absence of complete listings of folklore in Scottish chronicles and the present consideration is limited to more general concerns.

For illustration I have selected passages in Bellenden's *Chronicles*. Book 10 opens with the description of two comets which appeared in spring and in autumn and describes a mysterious battle. At night armed men were seen in the air rushing together with spears, while during the day only the sound of the battle was heard near the town. These signs were interpreted as both good and bad, as the diviner pleased.[80] At the beginning of book 11 Bellenden lists another series of marvels. Two natural monstrosities were born and blood flowed from a hill in Galloway which turned the rivers and streams a purple colour. The meaning of these events was interpreted by the Spaymen as foreshadowing disaster and indeed the rest of the section shows how this disaster came about.[81] Chapter 4 of the same book describes how horses devoured their own flesh, a woman gave birth to a natural monstrosity, a sparrowhawk and an owl were strangled and perpetual darkness obscured the light of both the sun and the moon.[82] The aftermath of Kenneth II's death is described at the end of book 6. Fish were found dead on the sand and people died from eating the poisoned fish. A bloody moon appeared, crops failed and priests warned the people to amend their lives.[83] The death of King David was also followed by 'sindry merwellis'. Ravens, crows and magpies nested in winter. The crops were infested by mice and rats and there were floods.[84] After the assassination of James I, a deformed sow was born, comets were seen, the frost was so severe that wine and ale were sold by the pound and had to be melted before the fire. Finally a sword appeared in the sky to the fear and admiration of the people.[85]

The kinds of portents which appear in these passages are a fairly typical selection of natural monstrosities, disruptions of nature, and supernatural visions. With the exception of the visions of the battle and the appearance of the sword, all the events could have been real.

The severe frost which affected the wine and ale, the contaminated fish, crop failures and unusual weather conditions are realistic enough. So too are comets and defective births. What transforms them into portents is that they are designated as the cause of subsequent events, and the interpretation is made by an authority figure, such as Spaymen, diviners and priests. That certain signs anticipated events was a widespread and powerful mechanism in systems of traditional folk belief.[86] Within the system of folk belief, the ominous sign is more likely to be a supernatural event, however disruptions to the course of nature do occur. The natural monstrosities became increasingly popular in the later Middle Ages and were the subject of numerous pamphlets and manuscripts descriptions. A growing interest in classical culture and humanistic interest in interconnecting systems undoubtedly fostered an increased interest in portents.[87]

Two visionary signs occur in this sample, a battle in the sky and a sword, both of which are connected to disturbing events. The visual battle is seen at night, but during the day the same portent manifests itself as the noise of battle heard near the town. Visions are an interesting feature of portent lore because visions provide an outward manifestation of the traditional grammar of images and meanings.[88] These two supernatural visions have much in common with a traditional phenomenon known as the Wild Hunt. The title is somewhat misleading since the phenomenon is just as likely to be a battle, as it is here. Whatever the manifestations, many of the pre-modern references occur in chronicles,[89] and nearly all of these indicate that the phenomenon was always accompanied by clamorous noise.[90]

Portent and prophecy have overlapping functions and use some of the same rhetorical devices. Like the anecdote, portents underline the importance of events in a compressed and dramatic manner, and like the omen they exploit the belief in the congruence between the natural and supernatural world. What emerges is not so much a picture of clear lines of influence as a mixture of folk, popular and élite cultural registers in which all these registers have access to a traditional grammar of image and to the belief structure which support them. The portent is another means for the chronicle writer to signpost an important action indirectly by exploiting traditional realms of authority associated with the supernatural and the bizarre.

Much work remains to be done in identifying folkloristic resonances in chronicle material in Scotland. At present there is no checklist of folklore in these chronicles or even clear criteria for identifying such material. However this study has attempted to demonstrate that folkloric patterns are an integral part of the chronicle form and not merely extraneous material. This raises the question as to how conscious the writers were of using folklore and whether different chronicles use folklore materials in different ways. Phrases such as Bower's reference to 'plebis et populares' are indicators that imply some understanding of source, but it is equally possible that the use of legends and anecdotes in characterisation was simply part of their discourse. Peter Burke has suggested that élite culture accepted and freely manipulated materials from folklore.[91] McGavin follows this in his study of 'rough music' in which he suggests that Bower understood the language of festival as appropriate to the popular realm of discourse.[92] This still implies an essentially one-way direction of influence with the demands of high culture predominating. There are indications that popular and élite culture intermix more freely and that borrowing is not so conscious nor so controlled as Burke's model implies.[93]

However further detailed study is needed in order to clarify how far this is the case in Scottish chronicles. The chronicle material collected here under the heading 'traditional' includes anecdote, legend, personal-experience narrative and accounts of portents. Some of the content is based on actual events, some drawn from a wider story telling register but localised in space and time, some of it has widely recognised legend characteristics of the miraculous or the supernatural, while some can be linked to legend types only recently identified. Its cohesiveness lies in the way it is used in the chronicles. The personal anecdotes whether they derive from historical events or legends or life-experience narratives have a strongly stereotyped quality. They reveal characters as good or bad kings, loyal or disloyal subjects, saintly or immoral men and women. For the folklorist this material provides information about the cultural context for early traditions which is in itself reason enough for further study. For Scottish chronicles it provides an under-appreci-ated means for understanding the formal construction of these complex documents and the construction of their meaning for audiences whose lives and reading must inevitably have involved the coming together of material both popular and learned.

1. W. F. Skene, ed. *Johannis de Fordun Chronica Gentis Scotorum* (Edinburgh, 1871) vol. I, p. 18.

2. K. Wentersdorf, 'Witchcraft and Politics in Macbeth', in *Folklore Studies in the Twentieth Century Proceedings of the Centenary Conference of the Folklore Society*, ed. V. Newall (Woodbridge, Suffolk, 1980) pp. 431–7.

3. K. Farrow, 'The Historiographical Evolution of the Macbeth Narrative', *SLJ*, 21 (1994), 5–23.

4. *Walter Bower, Scotichronicon*, vol. 2, ed. J. MacQueen and W. MacQueen (Aberdeen, 1989), hereafter *Scotichronicon*. Much of the editorial comment on *Scotichronicon* shows an awareness of the folklore dimensions. See for example vol. 2 p. 488 n. to ch. 31 and p. 507 n. to ch. 52.

5. N. K. Chadwick, 'The Story of Macbeth, A study in Gaelic and Norse Tradition', *SGS* 6 pt 2 (1949), 198–211. 'The Story of Macbeth (continued)', *SGS* 7, pt 1 (1951), 1–25, 199–198.

6. S. Kelly, 'The Arthurian Material in the *Scotichronicon* of Walter Bower', *Anglia*, 97 (1979), 431–8.

7. J. J. McGavin, 'Robert III's "Rough Music": Charivari and Diplomacy in a Medieval Scottish Court', *SHR*, 74 (1995), 144–58.

8. E. J. Cowan, 'Myth and Identity in Early Medieval Scotland' *SHR*, 63 (1984), 111–35.

9. W. H. F. Nicolaisen, 'Stories and Storytelling in Barbour's *Brus*' in *Bryght Lanternis: Essays on the Language and Literature of Medieval Scotland*, ed. D. McClure and M. Spiller (Aberdeen, 1989) pp. 55–66.

10. R. A. Georges and M. Owen Jones, *Folkloristics: An Introduction* (Bloomington, 1995) pp. 159–61.

11. D. E. Bynum, 'Oral Evidence and the Historians: Problems and Methods', *JFI*, 8 (1971), pp. 82–92; J. Wood, 'Walter Map: The Contents and Context of *De Nugis Curialium*' *Transactions of the Cymmrodorion Society* (1985), 91–103.

12. R. Dorson, 'Introduction: Folklore and Traditional History', 'Sources for the Traditional History of the Scottish Highlands and Western Islands', *JFI*, 8 (1971–2), 79–81, 145–84.

13. Ibid., 147.

14. Ibid., 79–81; 182–3.

15. A. J. Bruford, 'Problems in Cataloguing Scottish Supernatural and Historical Legends' *JFI*, 16 (1979), 155–55; J. MacInnes, 'Clan Sagas and Historical Legends' *TGSI*, 57 (1990–1), 377–94.

16. Nicolaisen considers the similarities between storytelling and historical narration in a number of contexts, for example, in relation to folktales, contemporary Scottish fiction and personal-experience narratives. See W. F. H. Nicolaisen, 'Time in Folk-Narrative', in Newall, *Folklore Studies in the Twentieth Century*, pp. 314–19; 'The Past as Place: Names, Stories, and the Remembered Self' *Folklore*, 102 (1991) 3–15; 'Why Tell Stories' *Fabula* 31 (1990), 5–10.

17. M. Murray, 'Folklore in History', *Folklore*, 56 (1954), 57–66; *The Witchcult in Western Europe* (Oxford 1921, rept. 1962).

18. H. Davidson, 'Folklore and History', *Folklore*, 85 (1974), 73–92. The view that folkloric elements are not merely ancient survivals, but are an integral part of the historicising process has provided an important theoretical model in recent folklore studies and is the one adopted here. Questions as to the origin or distribution of particular elements have not been considered. However, references to these elements, known as motifs, based on the standard listing in *Motif Index of Folk Literature*, 6 vols (Bloomington 1955–8) by Stith Thompson, have occasionally been included.

19. B. Hudson, 'Historical Literature of Early Scotland', *SSL*, 26 (1991), 141–55.

20. S. Stahl, 'Introduction', 'The Personal Narrative as Folklore', *JFI*, 14 (1977) 5–8; 9–30.

21. E. Tucker, 'I Saw the Trees Had Souls: Personal Experience Narratives of Contemporary Witches', in *Creativity and Tradition in Folklore: New Directions*, ed. S. Bronner (Logan, Utah, 1992) pp. 141–52.

22. M. Lüthi, 'Parallel Themes in Folk Narrative and in Art Literature', *JFI*, 4 (1967), 3–16; A. Taylor, 'Biographical Pattern in Traditional Narrative', *JFI*, 1 (1964), 114–29.

23. Nicolaisen, 'Stories and Storytelling in Barbour's *Brus*' in *Bryght Lanternis*, pp. 56–60; Bruford, 155–66; MacInnes, 377–81.

24. Gábor Klaniczay, 'Legends as Life Strategies for Aspirant Saints in the Later Middle Ages', *Journal of Folklore Research*, 26 (1989), 151–71.

25. *Scotichronicon*, ed. D. E. R. Watt *et al.*, vol. 6 (Aberdeen, 1991), pp. 88–93, 94–7.

26. Ibid., p. 241.

27. T. Milligan, 'Images of William Wallace, Robin Hood, King Arthur and Don Quixote' *Cencrastus*, 43 (1992), 11–12.

28. *Scotichronicon*, vol. 2, pp. 368–81. The traditional elements of the narrative are virtually the same in both Bower and Fordun. Cf. *Chronica Gentis Scotorum*, vol. 2 pp. 165–7.

29. John Bellenden, *The Chronicles of Scotland*, ed. R. W. Chambers, E. C. Batho and H. W. Husbands, 2 vols, STS (Edinburgh and London, 1938–41), hereafter Bellenden *Chronicles* (STS), II, pp. 114–17. In the examples cited in this study, Bellenden follows Boece closely at least in regards to the traditional elements in his account. However, for the purposes of this discussion, the issues of the relation between Boece's *Scotorum Historia* and Bellenden's translation of it, considered elsewhere in this volume by Nicola Royan and Sally Mapstone, are of less immediate relevance, although they would certainly be worth pursuing.

30. S. F. Kruger, *Dreaming in the Middle Ages* (Cambridge, 1992) pp. 5–17, 21–32.

31. *Scotichronicon*, vol. 2, p. 484.

32. G. Roberts, 'The Descendents of Circe: Witchcraft and Renaissance Fictions', in *Witchcraft in Early Modern Europe*, ed. G. Roberts, J. Barry, M. Hester (Cambridge, 1996), pp. 183–206.

33. Jesse Patrick Findley, *Tales of the Scots* (Inverness, 1914), pp. 67–79.

34. *Scotichronicon*, vol. 2, p. 378. Bellenden calls her '*abhominabill weche*', vol. 2 pp. 165–7.

35. Lüthi, 3–8.

36. T. P. Coffin, 'Folk Logic and the Bard: Act I of Macbeth', in *Medieval Literature and Folklore Studies Essays in Honor of Francis Lee Utley*, ed. J. Mandel and B. A. Rosenberg (New Jersey, 1970) pp. 323–31.

37. A. J. Bruford, 'Supernatural Accretions to Scottish Accounts of Local Tragedies', in *Papers III: 8th Congress for the International Society for Folk Narrative Research*, ed. R. Kvideland and T. Selberg (Bergen, 1985), pp. 167–76.

38. J. Fentress and C. Wickham, *Social Memory: New Perspectives on the Past* (Oxford, 1992) p. 57.

39. Stahl, 'Introduction', 3–8.

40. Bruford, 'Problems in Cataloguing', 163–4.

41. *Scotichronicon*, vol. 2, pp. 94–9.

42. T. Brown, *The Fate of the Dead: A Study of Folk-Eschatology in the West Country After the Reformation*, Mistletoe Series (Cambridge, 1969) pp. 24–34.

43. L. Dégh, 'The Theory of Personal Experience Narrative', in Kvideland and Selberg (as n. 37), pp. 233–42; W. F. H. Nicolaisen, 'Legends as Narrative Response' in *Perspectives on Contemporary Legend*, ed. P. Smith, CECTAL Conference Paper Series no. 4. (Sheffield, 1984) pp. 167–78.

44. *Andrew of Wyntoun, Original Chronicle*, ed. F. J. Amours, 6 vols, STS (Edinburgh and London, 1914), V, pp. 228–31.

45. H. Davidson, 'The Legend of Lady Godiva', *Folklore*, 80 (1969), 107–21.

46. *Original Chronicle*, I, p. 97, 1.1017 n.

47. Stahl, 7.

48. *Original Chronicle*, V, p. 137; *Scotichronicon* vol. 5, ed. D. E. R. Watt, S. Taylor and B. Scott (Aberdeen, 1990), pp. 354–5, 356–7.

49. S. Knight, *Robin Hood, A Complete Study of the English Outlaw* (Oxford, 1994) pp. 31–4.

50. Knight, p. 36; *Scotichronicon* vol. 5, p. 470 n.

51. Knight, pp. 34–7.

52. *Original Chronicle*, IV, pp. 228–33.

53. *Original Chronicle*, I, p. 76.

54. David Buchan, 'The Modern Legend', in *Language, Culture and Tradition* ed. A. E. Green and J. D. A. Widdowson, CECTAL Conference Papers Series, no. 2 (Leeds and Sheffield, 1981), pp. 1–15.

55. Dégh, p. 235; O. Blehr, 'The Analysis of Folk Belief Stories and the Implications for Researches on Folk Belief and Folk Prose', *Fabula*, 9 (1967), 259–63.

56. McGavin, 147.

57. B. A. Rosenberg, 'Custer, the Legend of the Martyred Hero in America', *JFI*, 9 (1972), 110–32. See especially pp. 129–30 for a discussion of the close proximity between legend and event.

58. *Scotichronicon*, vol. 8, pp. 2–5.

59. See D. Gray, 'Rough Music: Some Early Invectives and Flytings', in *English Satire and the Satiric Tradition*, ed. C. Rawson (Oxford, 1984) pp. 1–39 (21–3).

60. *Scotichronicon*, vol. 8, pp. 14–17.

61. Ibid., vol. 8, pp. 16–18.

62. J. Fentress and C. Wickham, *Social Memory: New Perspectives on the Past* (Oxford, 1992), pp. 150–3.

63. *Scotichronicon*, vol. 8, pp. 64–5.

64. Fentress and Wickham, p. 150.

65. Stahl, 6; Tucker, pp. 141–5.

66. A. Taylor, 'Biographical Pattern', *JFI*, 1 (1964), 116–20.

67. T. Ó Cathasaigh, 'The Heroic Biography of Cormac Mac Airt', *Eriú*, 28 (1977), 107–11; A. Taylor, 116.

68. Chadwick, 201.

69. Amours in *Original Chronicle* I, p. 63.

70. Chadwick, 199.

71. Ibid., 200.

72. See B. T. Hudson, 'From Senchus to Histoire: Traditions of King Duncan I' *SSL*, 25 (1990), 100–20.

73. Bruford, 'Supernatural Accretions', pp. 167–70; MacInnes, 377–82.

74. A. Grandsen, 'The Chronicles of Medieval England and Scotland', in *Legend, Tradition and History of Medieval England* (1992), pp. 199–238. Gransden is here quoting Gervase of Canterbury.

75. E. B. Lyle. 'Thomas of Erceldoune, The Prophet and the Prophesied' *Folklore*, 79 (1968) 111–21; 'The Relationship Between "Thomas the Rymer" and "Thomas of Erceldoune"', *Leeds Studies in English*, 4 (1970), 23–30.

76. David Buchan, 'Hogg and Folktales', *Studies in Hogg and His World*, 4 (1993), 91–3. There are of course references to well-known prophecies in the Scottish chronicles. Bower, for example, refers to the prophecies of Merlin in Books 9 and 15 of *Scotichronicon*. These are more specific references with clear political messages than are usually the case with portents.

77. S. L. Jansen, *Political Protest and Political Prophecy Under Henry VIII* (Suffolk, 1991) pp. 149–56.

78. O. Niccoli, *Prophecy and People in Renaissance Italy*, trans. L. G. Cochran (Princeton, 1990) pp. 99–100, 104–6; Jansen, pp. 16–19, 22–3.

79. Jansen, p. 147.

80. Bellenden *Chronicles* (STS) II, p. 50.

81. Ibid., II, pp. 88–9.

82. Ibid., II, pp. 97–9.

83. Ibid., II, p. 118.

84. Ibid., II, p. 335.

85. Ibid., II, p. 402.

86. L. Dégh and A. Vazony, 'Legend and Belief Genre', *Genre*, 4:2 (1971), 281–304.

87. Niccoli, pp. xiii–xiv, 68–69; Jansen, pp. 10–19.

88. Niccoli looks at a specific cluster of apparitions in Italy during the sixteenth century and examines both their links to political events and their use as propaganda. pp. 61–88.

89. O. Dreisen, *Der Ursprung des Harlekin* (Berlin 1904) is still the most comprehensive listing of early occurances of the Wild Hunt. Bower describes two visions, both involving apparitions of armed men on the night before a battle and linked to important events political events in Scotland. *Scotichronicon*, vol. 5, p. 339; vol. 6, p. 335.

90. H. Newstead, 'Some Observations of King Herla and the Herlething', in. Mandel and Rosenberg (as n. 36), pp. 105–11.

91. P. Burke, *Popular Culture in Early Modern Europe* (New York, 1978).

92. McGavin, 144–58.

93. J-C. Schmitt, 'Les Traditions folkloriques dans la culture médiévale; Quelques reflections de méthode', *Archives de Sciences des Religions* 52, no. 1 (1981), 5–20.

7

THE RELATIONSHIP BETWEEN THE *SCOTORUM HISTORIA* OF HECTOR BOECE AND JOHN BELLENDEN'S *CHRONICLES OF SCOTLAND*

Nicola Royan

> The editors of this text leave to historians the question of
> Bellenden's handling of his original, sometimes remarkably free, and
> the more important question of Hector Boece's view of the duties of
> an historian.[1]

So say the most recent editors of John Bellenden's translation of the
Scotorum Historia of Hector Boece. Neither of these questions can be
answered fully in so brief a space as this essay, and the 'more important'
one requires a large-scale study, but it is hoped to make here some
preliminary points on the other, 'Bellenden's handling of his original,
sometimes remarkably free'. There is a tendency in discussions of the
Scotorum Historia and Bellenden's translations to treat the original Latin
text and the translations as interchangeable. This depends on the un-
warranted assumption that Bellenden was a reliable translator, whose
sole purpose was to render the *Scotorum Historia* accurately into Scots.
While such an assumption may be made of a twentieth-century translator, it is not necessarily appropriate for Bellenden, heir to a tradition
which included Gilbert Hay and John Ireland, both at one level creative
translators.

The plural 'translations' best describes Bellenden's work, suggesting
another reason why his versions should not be used as reliable witnesses
for Boece's own words. The Bellenden translation exists in two discrete
forms: there is a manuscript text, which is most accessible in the Scottish
Text Society edition, and the printed text, which is available both in
facsimile and in an edition of the nineteenth century.[2] The manuscript
used as the base text of the Scottish Text Society edition was that
presented to James V himself, and is the one for which Bellenden was

paid.[3] While it is the most handsome manuscript and the one with the most obvious claim to be definitive, it is most certainly not the only one.[4] Bellenden seems to have begun his work in 1530 and finally presented the finished manuscript to the king in July 1533, about six years after the king had received the *Scotorum Historia* from Boece's hands. Thereafter he reworked his translation thoroughly several times, as is evident from the different manuscripts, before submitting the work to print. There is no agreement as to when the first edition of the *Chronicles* was printed, nor indeed whether there was more than one edition, since the surviving copies are undated, but the period suggested for publication is somewhere between 1536 and 1540.

Even the relationship between the printed text and the manuscripts has been the subject of muted controversy for some time, particularly over the assertion in the printed text that 'the History and Croniklis of Scotland' were 'compilit and newly correckit be ... Maister Hector Boece'.[5] If this is the case, it is surprising that Bellenden did not include a translation of the two further, unprinted, books of the *Scotorum Historia*, which Boece left incomplete on his death in 1536.[6] Had Boece and Bellenden been in regular contact over the translation, it might be expected that Bellenden would have taken responsibility for the accounts of James II and James III, half-finished as they are. Furthermore, while Boece may have contributed to the corrections of factual error for the printed version of Bellenden's text, other revisions of the translation are not in character with the Latin text or its author, for they demonstrate an authorial self-consciousness much more typical of Bellenden's writing. While it is possible that Boece saw the translation and even made corrections to the text, it is also possible that Bellenden made his own corrections in line with his own alterations in content and presentation.[7]

However, it is not the object of this essay to discuss Bellenden's development of his translation, but rather to identify where Bellenden diverges from his original text. Suffice to say that the two versions differ quite considerably in places, and their differences reflect the same sort of changes in audience which probably contributed to Bellenden's divergence from the *Scotorum Historia* in the first place. In order to demonstrate that even in his first translation, Bellenden made alterations to the text, the version commonly cited in this essay is the STS edition; the text of the *Scotorum Historia* cited is that of 1527, the one which Bellenden would have used.[8]

It is clear that the editors of the manuscript translation shared doubts as to its reliability.[9] The differing circumstances of productions of the Latin and Scots versions suggest that there might be variation in the material they contain. Hector Boece, graduate of Montaigu College and an acquaintance of Erasmus, wrote his history in Latin and had it printed in Paris by one of the leading humanist printers, Josse Bade Ascensius. From the present distribution of extant copies, it would seem that it was read all over north-west Europe.[10] Its very composition in the best humanist Latin suggests that it was written as much for a European audience as for a purely Scottish one, and a scholarly one at that.[11] Bellenden was commissioned by James V, the dedicatee of the original, or by someone close to him, to translate the *Scotorum Historia* into the rising vernacular of Scots, in effect to produce a text for an audience who could not read Latin. This probably included the king himself, whose education had been patchy, as well as some of the lay courtiers, the nobility and perhaps even the merchant class.[12] While the two audiences overlapped and would continue to do so, they were also recognisably different. Apart from the difficulties inherent in any act of translation especially into a literary language perhaps not yet fully developed for such a project, such a difference in audience might easily have led to some tailoring of material.[13] Such tailoring might be structural to make the text easier to read, or explanatory, or might involve the omission and inclusion of material appropriate to the audience. All these feature in Bellenden's translation, although the passages of omission and insertion are those responsible for the greatest divergence.

Before embarking on close textual analysis, it is important to note the most obvious and immediate differences between the *Scotorum Historia* and its translations. Firstly the titles: Boece called his work the *Scotorum Historia*, 'a history of the Scottish people from their first origins', while Bellenden produced the *Chronicles of Scotland*. While this may appear to be a minor discrepancy, it raises interesting questions. Boece recognises the Scots to be of an Irish race and therefore Gaelic in origin; as a result, he has much more sympathy for the people whom Mair calls in his history the 'wild Scots'.[14] Boece therefore acknowledges the foundation of the Scottish people to be Gaelic, and the Picts, the Saxons and the Normans who settle in the Scottish sphere of influence become subsumed in the Scottish identity and antiquity. Bellenden, on the other hand, refers to a geographical definition which had existed for less than four hundred years and gives a sense of permanency to the history missing from Boece's account. When a people are under attack from an invader, they may be driven out, overrun or conquered, but a geographical entity is permanent and its inhabitants, if not irrelevant, are replaceable. Bellenden's usage also implies that the king of Scots had power over the whole of Scotland from the beginning, rather than being king of a people who inhabited only a part, and thus it serves as a glorification of the monarch. It also loosens the claim of the despised Gael to be superior to the Lowlander, quite important for those whose lives centred on the court.

The other discrepancy between these titles is Bellenden's substitution of *Chronicles* for *Historia*. 'Chronicles' suggests a much less finished work, which may be supplemented with impunity by others as time goes on; 'History' or 'historia' has the sense of a complete work covering a clearly defined period, such as Bede's *Ecclesiastical History of the English People*. Of course, these are only the connotations of the words, for Bower in his *Scotichronicon* is no less in control of what he includes than Boece. In the *Scotorum Historia*, Boece supplemented and rewrote the *Scotichronicon*, the Scottish chronicle, to make it suitable for a humanist readership; despite Boece's assertion of his work's status, Bellenden saw it, from the evidence of his title, as Boece saw *Scotichronicon*, which does not promise too much respect for the text he translates. When a translator breaks from his original in his rendition of the very title, it does not bode well for the accuracy of the rest.

There is also the matter of Bellenden's chapter divisions. One of the features that makes the *Scotorum Historia* so very awkward to read is that it has no division within it smaller than the book, neither chapters nor paragraphs. This method of presentation must have been a conscious decision on Boece's part, and it is, as far as it is possible to tell, without parallel among his contemporary historiographers. Both John Mair and Robert Gaguin use chapter divisions, while Boece disdains even running titles.[15] Bellenden divides his translation into chapters and even provides chapter summaries.[16] The other prose translator of the *Scotorum Historia*, the near-contemporary but probably independent writer of the Mar Lodge version, does likewise, so Bellenden was presumably making an appropriate and acceptable decision on behalf of his audience in his divisions of the *Scotorum Historia*.[17] Generally, the divisions which Bellenden makes are based on narrative breaks, when such phrases as *eodem tempore* occur, but occasionally Bellenden inserts such a phrase to make the transition. This can be seen here:

> Sed Joannes Cumein Red cognomento, a facie rubicunda dictus, ac
> Robertus Brusius questi inter se de misera Scotiae servitute et oppress-
> ione, tandem ubi uterque animum gemitibus ac suspiriis alteri
> indicasset, Robertus Brusius Joanni regnum, si vellet, obtulit.[18]

> (But after John Comyn, called by the nickname 'Red' from his
> ruddy face, and Robert Bruce complained to each other of the
> wretched servitude and oppression of Scotland, when at last they had

revealed their mind to each other with groans and sighs, Robert
Bruce offered John the kingdom, should he wish it.)

> In the menetyme Robert Bruse and Johnne Cwmyn Rede convenit
> to gidder, quhair thai lamentabilly regratit the calamite fallin to
> Scottis be tyranny of King Edward.[19]

Whereas by not using a transitional Boece emphasises the rolling effect
of Edward's rule and implies that the alliance between Bruce and Comyn
was almost accidental, Bellenden's insertion of 'in the menetyme' obviously aids the transition, but gives the impression that the alliance
between the two men is slightly divorced from what is happening
elsewhere in the realm. Such a change only marginally alters the account
of the episode, but it reveals Bellenden's different perspective on events.[20]
The same is true of Bellenden's division of the murder of Comyn from
the betrayal of Wallace.[21] These events occur in juxtaposition in Walter
Bower's *Scotichronicon*, which was certainly Boece's major source for
the period, but Boece moves from Comyn's murder to Wallace's betrayal without a break, setting up a strong and unavoidable contrast
between the two events.[22] In separating these two episodes into different
chapters, thus returning to Bower's original pattern, Bellenden weakens
the contrast between the characters of Bruce and Wallace. By no means
could this be said to change the course of the narrative, but it does
indicate that Bellenden did not feel constrained to reproduce exactly
the organisation of the author he was translating, but rather arranged
his narrative from his own perspective.

Such is true of the entire translation: often the discrepancies between
the translation and its original do not affect the content of the text,
but simply put a particular interpretation upon it, whether by the
specific translation of a word, or by the omission of some minor detail.
However, even such minor alterations demonstrate that Bellenden did
not consider the *Scotorum Historia* to be above reworking, but rather
that it was a text open to paraphrase as well as translation. There are,
however, occasions when the word used gives a false interpretation,
when the translation is incorrect, when the omission of phrases distorts
the passage or when material is added which changes the outlook of
its context, and these sometimes alter something vital to Boece's text.
Then Bellenden can no longer be considered a translator, but rather a
writer of his own version of events.

To turn to textual comparison: one of the blessings of Bellenden is
that he translates the various Latin names for Scottish places. For
example, once Corbredus has returned from his wars with the Roman
invaders,

Eo ubi deventum, Moravis qui stragem evaserunt, expertam ob belli-
cam virtutem, agros quos Torna et Speia flumina claudunt, regia pro
magnificentia tradidit incolendos, quibus Moraviam quum antea
Vararis dicerentur a nova gente nomen dedit ad posteros, pulsis inde
Vararis (de quibus supra affatim) atque in diversas dispersis regiones
quod plus domi in sui vicinarumque gentium perniciem quam foris
pro publica salute bellum gerere consueverant.[23]

(When he arrived there, such was his royal generosity, he awarded
to the Moravians who had escaped the slaughter, on account of their
tested courage in war, the fields to inhabit which the rivers Torna
and Spey enclose. To them he gave from the new people the name
Moravia for posterity, though previously they were called Varari;
once the Varari (of whom I have spoken earlier) had been defeated
and scattered into different regions because they were more accustomed to wage war at home to the ruin of their neighbours and
their race than to wage it outside for the public good.)

Corbreid ... gaif to the Murrayis quhilkis wer eschapit oute of the
feild, for thair manhede provin in this last bataill, all the landis liand
betuix Speye and Inuernes, quhilk landis wer callit eftir thame Mur-
raye Land.[24]

Here Bellenden identifies the land given to the Moravians as that which
lies between the Spey and Inverness. This is something of a paraphrase,
since Boece quite clearly states that the land lies between two rivers,
but Bellenden goes for clarity rather than accuracy. Here it is helpful,
but on occasions such intervention only adds to the confusion. One
such example is Bellenden's consistent translation of *Mona* as 'Man'.
Boece himself is not always clear as to whether he means 'Anglesey'
or 'Man', and it is usually only the context which can differentiate
between them. Bellenden makes no attempt to differentiate the two
islands even though the sense of the narrative depends on it.

Personal names are treated more erratically. Bellenden fails to identify
the Earl of Gloucester from Boece's use of 'Glomere' and he also fails
either to correct the reference to Bruce's brother as 'David' or to rectify
the confusion between the Black Prince and Richard II, which Boece
makes in book 15.[25] At the very opening of book 14, there is a scribal
correction of 'Jacobus Wernis' to 'Michel Wemis', the only correction
to a personal name made in the manuscript translation.[26] Quite what
the last example suggests about scribal intervention is open to question:
it may simply be that the scribe took a second look at the minims on
his page. It can be seen therefore that Bellenden's editorial policy is

erratic in these matters of nomenclature and detail, and while these are easily recognised, more subtle variations may be missed and give a false impression of the text.

This is particularly true in places where Bellenden is simply wrong in his translation, without there being any evidence of a conscious decision. Errors are of course almost unavoidable in translations, especially where the work in question is as vast as the *Scotorum Historia*, and to be fair to Bellenden, they seem remarkably rare in the *Chronicles of Scotland*. Yet to realise fully Bellenden's achievement, it is necessary to recognise also his deficiencies, even if they are few. For example, when Corbredus Galdus' *cognomen* is under discussion, Bellenden interprets it wrongly: what Boece says is that 'Galdus' is the name given to a man with foreign habits, *quem sui sanguinis virorum alieni mores et instituta ornaverint* ('whom customs and practices alien to men of his own blood adorned'). Bellenden opts for something familiar to him: men who are 'componit and honest' are 'callit galyeart'.[27] The Mar Lodge Translation has a more correct interpretation of what Boece says:

> Herefore the vulgar pepil gaif him Gald to surname; ffor Scottis yit
> in oure dayis, quhare ane man of thare blude is instructit in maneris
> of alienis, thai vse to name him Gald.[28]

Neither 'Galdus' nor 'Gald' appear in either of the major Scottish dictionaries and it looks like Bellenden opted for the nearest he knew in his own speech, since 'gailyeart' and its variants are quite common.[29] However, even allowing for his difficulties in finding a word to match the meaning which Boece had given, Bellenden has neglected his duty as translator in changing the definition, to fit what seemed to him most likely. This changes the attribute which made Galdus different, that he had received a foreign education. Although it does not matter much in the terms of the narrative, since Galdus' foreign education has less bearing on his actions than his foreign relatives, it demonstrates that Bellenden was not as committed to producing a close translation of his original as has been assumed.

Sometimes the translation errs in a word: in book 4, Bellenden uses 'reprevit' where Boece has *infestus*, again closer to the Mar Lodge 'favourit nocht'.[30] In book 9, Bellenden uses 'reprevit' again, this time to translate *acriter eum est obiurgatus*, which is a much stronger phrase.[31] There is also a literary point to this, for in book 4, the man who 'reprevit' the king is murdered, and the rebellion of the nobility is in part caused because the victim did nothing more than disapprove of the king's way of life. In book 9, on the other hand, Boece uses *obiurgatus* to describe Columba's response to Aidan's unnecessary

declaration of war on the Picts, where the saint goes on to excommuni-
cate the king. In using 'reprevit' in both places, Bellenden obliterates
the difference Boece saw between the two episodes. While it is often
difficult to render fully the connotations of another language, here the
difference is so marked as to make it essential for that difference to be
brought out. If such an error is possible in one word, the likelihood
of greater errors is equally large.

Discrepancies between translation and original, however, more often
result from conscious alteration. For example, Bellenden does not show
nearly the same respect towards the names of the great classical writers
as Boece does. This can be seen with ease in book 4, where Bellenden
greatly abbreviates the summaries of great men contained in the original:

> Florente Corbredo in Scotia, claruerunt in Italia Stathius Papinus
> poeta melicus, Persius poeta satyricus, Lucanus poeta item melicus,
> Cordubensis genere, Plutarchus Cheronaeus historiae scriptor, et
> morum praeceptor insignis.[32]

> (While Corbredus was flourishing in Scotland, in Italy Stathius
> Papinus, a lyric poet, Persius, a satirical poet, Lucan, also a lyric
> poet from Cordoba, and Plutarch of Cherenaea, a writer of history
> and a distinguished teacher of morals were all famous.)

> In the tyme of Corbreid flurist in Italy nobill poeittis and histori-
> cianis, as Statius, Persius, Lucianius and Plutarcus.[33]

The impression given by Bellenden is that he has not read any of the
writers, since he makes a mistake in Lucan's name, turning him into
another Renaissance favourite, and fails to appreciate Plutarch's wider
talents. It is true that these lists appear with almost monotonous regu-
larity in the earlier books of the *Scotorum Historia*, where they provide
the most helpful means of dating the events Boece describes. Even so,
and even allowing for the fact that Bellenden appears to date his
narrative more regularly than does Boece, he still takes a fairly free
approach to the translation of Boece's descriptions of famous men.
Quite possibly, Bellenden felt that his audience would have found
Boece's enthusiasm unappealing, since many of the writers cited,
whether classical or scholastic, were inaccessible to them and largely
irrelevant to the progress of Scottish history. In contrast, Boece, as a
humanist with European credentials, was steeped in the new learning.
Moreover, as a Scot writing as much for a European audience as for a
Scottish one, he may well have wanted to emphasise that Scotland was
fit to take her place in the wider world and to imply by the juxtaposition
of a Scottish king and the great minds of the Roman Empire that the

inhabitants of Scotland were not savages, even at that early time. Something of this is expressed when he is discussing the wars between the Scots and the Romans:

ut dignoscant qui nostram simul atque Romanam legerint historiam, quam utraque quadret alteri.[34]

(so that those who read our history at the same time as Roman history should realise how one squares with the other.)

The influence of Bellenden's audience can be detected also in the abbreviation in the manuscript version of Boece's account of the martyrdoms of Peter and Paul.[35] This was not its final state, however, since it was expanded again for the printed edition. It is possible that this alteration may have been at the request of Bellenden's printer, Thomas Davidson, in order to appeal to an audience of burgesses perhaps in sympathy with the Reforming cause.[36] It is tempting to speculate that neither church history nor classical learning were of much interest to the court of James V.

Other enthusiasms of Boece receive similarly short shrift: his hero-worship of Elphinstone is omitted in book 12, where the creation of the diocese of Aberdeen is mentioned, and his insistence on the naming of the land-mass of Scotland, England and Wales as 'Albion', not 'Britannia' is drastically abbreviated.[37] While the former can be explained in terms of Boece's devotion to his patron, which Bellenden did not inherit, the latter is in fact very important for the history as a whole. 'Albion' was a name used by earlier Scottish historiographers to combat the myth of origin presented by Geoffrey of Monmouth, amongst others: Brutus, according to that version of the mythic history of these islands, became the eponymous king of Britain, and because he was a king from the southern half of the mainland, it was important for the Scots to restrict his influence to that area, thus denying the English claim of supremacy. As a result, in the eyes of the Scots, 'Albion' was the name of the mainland, not 'Britannia'. It was important for Boece to restate this, both to refute any claims made by Henry VIII to rights over Scotland and to counter John Mair's use of 'Britannia' in his *Historia* of 1521. Mair's usage is perfectly acceptable in his work, since it suits his argument, but it was open to misinterpretation.[38] The passage in Boece's work reflects Boece's concern to place Scotland in the right position in European political geography and to correct any misapprehensions caused by reading the Ancients. Boece was writing for a European audience and thus this kind of statement is vital for him;[39] for a Scottish audience, who knew where Scotland was and needed no confirmation of its standing, the passage was largely irrelevant, and therefore Bellenden shortened it greatly. Similarly, he removes all discussion of the ancient authorities and the vainglory of the Romans, leaving only a terse explanation of the debt to Tacitus, which barely applies to the translation anyway.

Without doubt, Bellenden manages to abbreviate most of Boece's episodes. This is no mean feat when translating from Latin into Scots. Sometimes, the compression does nothing to harm the sense of what is said. For instance, although the translation of this passage is very much reduced, it still conveys the gist of what Boece says:

> Erat Kynnatillo animus (uti extrema valetudine est fassus) summa se potestate abdicandi, restituendique Aidano regni. Consilium interrupit superveniens regi aegritudo. Vicesimo etenim die quam creatus est Brancho et Angina morbis correptus est, unde publico regimine Aidano permisso, in cubiculo se continere est coactus.[40]

> (Kynnatillus was of a mind to renounce the greatest office and restore the realm to Aidan, since he was tired from extreme ill-health. Sickness, overcoming the king, interrupted the plan. For on the twentieth day after he had been made king, he was seized by the diseases bronchitis and quinsy, through which he was forced to remain in his chamber, the rule of the realm having been entrusted to Aidan.)

> Schort tyme eftir ane immoderatt fluxe of caterre fell in his throitt and chastis, and causit him to resigne the gouernance of his realme to Aydane.[41]

Here is omitted quite a sizeable chunk of Boece's text, and its omission shows an easy attitude to accurate representation. An even more striking example of such abbreviation occurs in book 13, where the enthronement of Alexander III is described:

> Mortuo Alexandro secundo, filius eius Alexander huius nominis tertius priusquam in regnum reciperetur magnam inter nobiles disceptationem et contentionem ortam sustinuit, tamen eius in patris locum suffectionem non impedivit, aliis sidera, quae plurimum illis observare mos est, adversa regi creando esse dicentibus, aliis nondum equitem auratum factum esse, ac propterea a regni gubernaculis prohiberi. At nisi contemptis istiusmodi superstitionibus comes Fifensis lapidi admotum fatali puerum more prius maiorum inunctum coronasset, profectis dilatandis comitiis haud dubie res in summum evasissent discrimen. Declarato vero iam rege ac sacro peracto accessit ad eum vir quidam haud ignobili genere natus, montana Scotiae

inhabitans, qui contextam a se Genealogiam regum Scotiae omnium, ad parentem usque gentis Gathelum memoriter recitavit. Quem rex amplissime donatum ex consilio gubernatorum domum dimisit. Annum agebat Alexander, cum patri succederet, nonum, ac proinde metus erat maximus pueri rectoribus, ne contempta eius pueritia undique in regnum impetus fieret.[42]

(After Alexander II had died, before his son, Alexander (the third of this name) was admitted to the kingdom, he endured a great dispute and controversy which arose among the nobles, nevertheless it did not prevent his succession to his father's place. Some said that the stars, which it was the custom for them to observe a great deal, were against him being made king, and others said that he had not been made a knight and on account of this he was prohibited from the government of the realm. But if the earl of Fife, despising such superstitions, had not crowned the boy, after he was conducted to the chair ordained by fate, and anointed first in the manner of his ancestors, without doubt the matter would have ended in the greatest dispute as the gathering of the arguing nobles grew larger. Once Alexander had been declared king and the sacred rites performed, there came to him a certain man, born of a not ignoble house, an inhabitant of the mountainous region of Scotland, who recited from memory a genealogy of all the kings of Scotland, which he had composed, back to the founder Gathelos. With the advice of the regents, the king sent him home richly rewarded. Alexander was in his ninth year when he succeeded his father and accordingly there was a great fear among the boy's governors lest, in contempt of his youth, there would be attacks on the realms from all sides.)

Alexander the Secund berijt on this wise, his son Alexander the Thrid, havand bot ix yeris of aige, was maid king. Eftir his coronacioun come to him ane Hyeland man with ane buke, quhilk was maid schort tyme be him afoir, contenand all the genology of Scottis kingis fra the begynnyng of the realme to his dayis. This Hieland man was richelie revarditt be the king for his labouris. And becaus King Alexander had bot ix yeris in aige at his coronacioun, the pepill beleiffitt nocht bot importabill troubill and contempcioun of the Kingis autoritie in all partis.[43]

Here Bellenden repeats the age of the king at his enthronement, but fails to discuss the role of the men whom Boece calls the *gubernatores*, or 'governors', appointed because of Alexander's age. Boece repeats much more of the established tradition of the story, including the arguments over knighting the new king and inauspicious days, demonstrating the serious disquiet felt among the nobility at the prospect of so young a king. Bellenden omits all the detail of the enthroning ceremony as well as the disagreements beforehand, mentioning only the presentation of the Highlander, and attributes the unease to the people, who can do nothing to improve the situation. Reflecting perhaps the growth of a literate culture, Bellenden seems to imply that the Highlander presents 'ane buke' to Alexander, rather than an oral recitation, while Boece is familiar with the notion of an public reading, if not a recitation. Boece also emphasises the genealogical nature of the performance, which culminates in Gathelos; Bellenden, true to his geographical conception of Scotland, talks of the beginning of the realm. Finally, Boece acknowledges the Highlander to be *non ignobilis*, while Bellenden does not refer to his origin at all, which might be more typical of a Lowlander's approach. In fact, Bellenden seems unwilling to discuss any sort of Gaelic heritage for the Scots, since he also omits the use of the Stone of Destiny; Boece is generally punctilious about its presence, even though he is prone to backdate the use of a crown and anointing, as he does here. The basics of the narrative, that Alexander was a minor, which threatened the realm, but that he was still enthroned and presented with his genealogy, occur in both texts. In omitting the disquiet of the nobility and the appointment of governors, Bellenden gives a far greater sense of inevitability to his text and presents far less interaction between the different layers of government. In abbreviating the ceremony of enthronement, especially the genealogical presentation, he reduces the solemnity of the occasion as well as the antiquity of inheritance falling on Alexander's shoulders, which represents the age and identity of the Scots. As a result, although Bellenden does not change the course of the narrative in his abbreviation, he alters quite considerably the tone of Boece's original presentation.

A similar alteration can be seen in the discussion of how the Moravians became fully assimilated into the Scottish people.

> Cessere exinde Moravis Scotae virgines matrimonio, atque effectum
> brevi ut mirum in modum crescerent et augerentur. At posteritas lin-
> guam sequuta maternam, paterna oblita, aliquot post annos in unam
> cum Scotis gentem communeque linguae commercium adolevit. Man-
> sit deinde nomen ad nostram usque aetatem et populo et regioni.[44]

> (After that, Scots girls yielded to the Moravians in marriage and in a
> short time it caused them to thrive and increase in a marvel-
> lous way. But their offspring followed their mother's tongue and
> forgot their father's, and after some years they grew up as one race

with the Scots and with a common fellowship of language. Thereafter the name for both the people and the region remained until
our own age.)

Eftir this thai war marijt on Scottis virginis, and grew within schort
tyme vnder ane blude and amite with the Scottis.[45]

This passage, though short, is quite important, since it shows how
Boece sees a people fully integrating with the Scots and demonstrates
a recognition of the influence of language. Bellenden undermines Boece's
scholarship by leaving out the description of the Moravians learning
the Scots language, because there Boece shows that he has a firm grasp
on the way a common language defines a people, even if their origins
are different. Boece's perception of this was doubtless coloured by the
relationship between Gaelic and Scots, which would still have been
evident in Aberdeenshire in his own time. Bellenden, much more of a
Lowlander, may not have given this aspect of the Scottish realm any
thought at all.

Because of this passage and others like it, it is often difficult to tell
from the translation alone whether Bellenden is closely adhering to the
text he is meant to be translating, since it is not always predictable
which episode will grasp the interest of the translator most. As a result,
it is important that Bellenden should not be taken as the sole witness
for what Boece has to say.

Some of the alterations and omissions Bellenden makes, such as the
explanations of nicknames, are unimportant, since they do not change
the interpretation of the narrative. It is, for example, self-evident why
Edward I is called *Langschankis* in a vernacular text. Others, however,
point to a different reading of the text. A prime example of this is the
way in which Bellenden changes the character of John Comyn. After
the pact with Bruce, which in the *Scotorum Historia* seems much less
pre-meditated than in the *Chronicles*, Boece portrays Comyn as a man
beset by doubts;[46] this does not so much excuse his later behaviour as
make it more understandable and Comyn a slightly more sympathetic
character.

Sed Cumein facta coniuratione seu metuens ne coepta non bene
possent procedere, comparans vires suas cum tam potente rege, seu
occasione oblata, qua uno omnium in Scotia potentissimo e medio
sublato ipse caeteros omnes excelleret, ac regno proximus esset,
nuncium fidelem sibi ad regem Eduardum cum literis coniurationis
mittit, ac inita consilia aperit, ut convictus Robertus supplicio
sumpto tolleretur.[47]

(But after the conspiracy had been agreed, whether because he feared that what had been begun could not proceed well, comparing their strength with so powerful a king, or whether because the opportunity was offered by which, after the most powerful man of all in Scotland was removed from the community he would surpass all the rest and be nearest the throne, Comyn sent a messenger loyal to himself to King Edward with the letters of the conspiracy, and revealed the plan that had been entered upon, in order that Robert, once convicted, would be removed when punishment had been inflicted.)

Eftir this confideracioun the Cwmyne thoch this powere and autorite wald be of litill effect in Scotland, gif the Bruse war King, and therfor send ane secrete seruand to King Edward, schawin the writingis laitlye maid betuix him and Robert Bruse, desyring King Edward, gif he intendit to reiose Scotlannd but troubill, to put the Bruse haistelye to ded.[48]

As is clear, Bellenden omits any remotely sympathetic light and shows Comyn in the standard Scottish frame as a traitor, for not only does the alternative motive for Comyn's revelations (*seu metuens ... tam potente rege*) not appear in Bellenden's translation, but he also has Comyn deliberately ask for Bruce's death, while in Boece's version, that desire is implicit but never stated.[49] Again, when the murder of the Comyn takes place, Bellenden retains Boece's interpretation of the events as the result of a violent outburst of rage by Bruce, but he changes the attribution of the dialogue between Bruce's supporters and the wounded Comyn, introducing an almost farcical element:

Inde Dumfrens profectus duce eodem Flemein, ubi Cumein agere sciebat, deprehendit eum in choro Fratrum Minorum. Ubi cum paucis de prodita fide inter se disceptassent, negante Cumein a se factum id esse, ac Roberto asserente, tandem Robertus exemptum gladium in ventrem Cumein configit ac mox se ex templo proripit. Ibi duo eius amici Iacobus Lindsai et Rogerus Gilpatrik quid factum esset rogitantes, credere se ait, Cumein occisum esse. 'Adeo ne rem,' inquiunt, 'periculosam in incerto relinquis?' ac verbo ad Cumein accurrentes placide et velut amice rogant num letale esse vulnus crederet. Quo negante, si peritus propere adesset chirurgus, tribus eum insuper aut quatuor ictibus interimunt.[50]

(From there, after he had set out for Dumfries where he knew Comyn was, with the same Fleming as guide, he caught him in the choir of the Friars Minor. As they argued between themselves with

brief words about the betrayal, with Comyn denying that he had
done such a thing, and Robert insisting, at last Robert drew his
sword, stabbed Comyn in the stomach and rushed out of the
church. There when two of his friends, James Lindsay and Roger Gil-
patrick, asked eagerly what had happened, he said that he believed
that Comyn was slain. They said, 'Are you leaving so dangerous a
matter uncertain?' and so saying they ran to Comyn and in gentle
and apparently friendly voices they asked whether he thought he
had a fatal wound. When he replied that he had not, if an experienced surgeon came quickly, they slew him with three or four
further blows.)

Bruse, eftir that he had knawin the tenour of thir writings, inquyrit
quhair the Cwmyng was. The Flemyng schew that he was in the
Freris of Drumfress. Incontinent he slew the Flemyng for bering of
thir writingis, and come haistelye in the qwere of Drumfress, quhar
he fand the Cwmyng, and eftir that he had accusit him of his
tresoun, straik him with ane swerd in the wame; syne fled haistelye
oute of the kirk, and met Iames Lyndsaye and Rogere Kirkpatrik,
his tendir freyndis, and sayid to thame, 'I trow the Cwmyng be
slayne.' To quhom thai ansuerit, 'Has thou attemptit sa grete ane
mater, and left it vncertane?' Incontinent thai went to the Cwmyng,
inquyring him gif he had ony dede strakis, or gif he mycht recover,
havand a gude syourgiane; and becaus he ansuerit he had nane, bot
mycht recovere, thai straik him thre or foure vther strakis mair cruel-
lye, and sone eftir he gaif the gaist, the yere of God j^m iii^c & v
yeris.[51]

This is a much described episode in Scottish histories and it is not
surprising to find elements of other versions, such as Bruce's slaughter
of Fleming, creeping into Bellenden's translation. However, to have
the assassins ask Comyn if he would survive with a good surgeon, when
what they wanted to know in Boece's account was whether he was
likely to survive at all, almost renders the dialogue comical, where
Boece's is merely cruel in its portrayal of the apparently friendly attitude
of Lindsay and Kirkpatrick. Bellenden's version of the scene distracts
the reader from feeling any sympathy for the Comyn, while maintaining
Bruce's separation from the actual killing. Here Bellenden clearly puts
his own interpretation on to the events described, and lapses from the
role of a reliable paraphraser, since he fails to represent either the spirit
or the letter of the text he is translating.

Bellenden's insertions are often much easier to identify, especially the
one in book 12, which the scribe has helpfully and uniquely marked

as *verba translatoris*.[52] Unfortunately, if the note appears where the editors indicate, then it does not cover the whole insertion. The context deals with David I's over-generous foundations of religious houses. For Boece, these foundations are comparatively unimportant as deeds; he does not praise them, neither does he condemn them, which is more or less typical of his attitude to such foundations throughout the *Scotorum Historia*. In contrast, Bellenden heartily condemns them as ruining royal finances.[53] Whatever the motivation behind this outburst, it is notable for two reasons:[54] firstly, in its similarity to Mair's comments on the same topic in the *Historia* and secondly and more importantly for this article, its flagrant deviation from its original text. There is no comparable passage, where Boece makes such direct criticism in *propria persona* in the whole of the *Scotorum Historia*. Kings are criticised but only in the context of the narrative and never with such statistics at hand. While it is true that this insertion is marked and quite obvious, others are not so, and it is well to be wary of attributing to Boece Bellenden's own views.

A more minor insertion occurs in book 14, where Bellenden apostrophises Edward I after his capture of Berwick:

> Passim igitur caedes miseranda non in viros tantum, ac si qui armati occurrebant, sed etiam in pueros, senes, ac mulieres imbelles fieri coepta, quae crudelissima profecto atque inaudita amentia videtur, in eos videlicet quos non vi expugnaveris, te nulla privata irritatum iniuria, sine exceptione aetatis saevire.[55]

> Incontinent King Edward enterit in the toun with all his army, and slew nocht onlye the soidouris and weirmen, bot als barnis, wemen, and agit personis, bot ony reuth, mercy or ransoun and left na creature of Scottis blude on live within that toun. The yere that this toun was takin was fra our Redempcioun j^m ij^c lxxxxvj yeris. O Edward, maist furious tyran, how mycht thow rage in sik cruelte on the pepill, but ony excepcioun of aige, quhair na occasioun of iniuris was, and quhare the pepill was nocht subdewitt be force of armys?[56]

The use of the second person accusative pronoun *te* and the second person verb *expugnaveris* could give rise to such an translation, but it is not the most likely one. Rather, Boece is using a general construction, as occurs in modern English and which translates like this:

> that most cruel and unheard-of madness was seen to rage without discrimination of age, especially against those whom you would not attack when unenraged by a personal injury.

It is clear that Bellenden had to add the reference to Edward, which Boece does not have but which would be necessary to a Latin apostrophe.[57] Despite Boece's rhetorical tendencies, apostrophe is not one of his figures; rarely does he come so far out of his narrative to pass judgement on the characters from outside, unlike his attitude to other writers of history.[58] This is in keeping with his great classical models, for while Cicero used apostrophe frequently and effectively in his orations, neither Livy nor Tacitus made great use of it in narrative. Bellenden's direct accusation of Edward I is therefore a flourish of his own, or else a mistake in translation. It undoubtedly adds emotion to the text, but it does not reflect Boece's more restrained style.

Seton and Chambers point out another section where Bellenden interpolates material, when he discusses the rise of the house of Douglas.[59] Here Bellenden states that

> Off this Iames discendit the illustre surname of Douglass, quhilkis war evir the sikkir targe and weere wall of Scotland aganis Inglismen, and wan nevir landis in Scotland bot be thair singulare manhede and wassallage.[60]

Boece confines himself to the statement that

> ab hoc Iacobo, Douglas insignis familia, quae tametsi nonnihil ante tempus initium habuisset, primum celebre decus, accepisse ferunt.[61]

> (from this James, they say that the distinguished family of Douglas received its first famous glory, even if it had its beginnings some time before.)

Chambers and Seton believe that Bellenden's addition is a result of his association with the Douglases during James V's minority and that this is a statement of courageous loyalty, a fine example of tailoring material to suit an audience. Pleading for the Douglases directly would have been very dangerous in the early 1530s, for James was not prepared to forgive the means used by the Earl of Angus to control the realm during his minority. By inserting such a statement here, Bellenden would be able to blame it on Boece, relatively safe in Aberdeen, should the king react badly to its inclusion.[62] However, the expression of such enthusiasm for the Douglases is not to be found in the *Scotorum Historia*, and Bellenden is here frankly manipulating the text for his own purposes. He is not the reliable and neutral translator he is sometimes presented as being, but a writer with his own political perspective which he is intent on communicating.

This is of course a highly cursory account of the two texts; they are large in the extreme and require detailed study before their relationship to each other as well as to their audiences can be established. Yet even from these preliminary observations, it is evident that Bellenden's variations from his original are diverse. While some are simply the mistakes typical of any translation of this size, others are a result of Bellenden's conscious reworking of the text. The distribution of such reworking through the *Chronicles* has not as yet revealed itself in any pattern. Bellenden's tendency to abbreviate is probably consistent throughout his text and it is even more likely that where he feels it appropriate so to do, he alters the original material to suit the audience for whom he was writing. This would seem to be confirmed by the further development of the printed text, although the alterations may not be uniform in number or in magnitude throughout the translations.

What is clear, however, is that Bellenden is no more to be considered an adequate witness to Boece than he is to be considered an absolute witness to Livy, and in fact probably less so, since he appears to have a greater respect for Livy's writing than for Boece's. It is only fair, therefore, that Boece should be represented in his own words, when it is his text and his influence which are under examination. There are undoubtedly times when Bellenden's texts are more important, for example, when considering how the Scots saw themselves, but when considering how one Scot wished the scholars of Europe to see his people, Boece must be used as his own witness. The *Scotorum Historia* and the *Chronicles of Scotland* are by no means identical, in content, in audience or in author, and treating them as if they are does them both injustice.

1. John Bellenden, *The Chronicles of Scotland, compiled by Hector Boece*, ed. R. W. Chambers, Edith C. Batho and H. Winifred Husbands, STS, 2 vols (Edinburgh and London, 1938–41), II, prefatory note, p. viii, hereafter Bellenden, *Chronicles* (STS). Spellings with thorn and yogh have been normalised and abbreviations expanded.

2. The facsimile of the printed edition was published as number 851 in *The English Experience: Its Record in Early Printed Books, Published in Facsimile* (Amsterdam and Norwood, N.J., 1977); the nineteenth-century edition is John Bellenden, *The History and Chronicles of Scotland, written in Latin by Hector Boece*, ed. Thomas Maitland, 2 vols (Edinburgh, 1821), hereafter Bellenden, *Chronicles* (1821).

3. See *Accounts of the Lord High Treasurer of Scotland*, ed. Sir James Balfour Paul (Edinburgh, 1903), vol. 5: A.D. 1515–1531, p. 434 and vol. 6: A.D. 1531–1538, pp. 37 and 97.

4. See E. A. Sheppard, 'Studies in the Language of Bellenden's Boece' (unpublished doctoral thesis, University of London, 1937) pp. 107–43 and also in this volume, Sally Mapstone, 'Shakespeare and Scottish Kingship: a Case History', p. 183, n. 13.

5. See Bellenden, *Chronicles* (1821), vol. 1, p. cxii.

6. These were only printed with the second edition of the *Scotorum Historia* in 1574 under the aegis of Giovanni Ferreri.

7. For convinced judgements on this matter, see W. W. Seton and R. W. Chambers, 'Bellenden's Translation of the *History* of Hector Boece', *SHR* 17 (1919), 5–15, esp. 14–15, the appendix by E. A. Sheppard to Bellenden, *Chronicles* (STS), II, pp. 439–40, and Mapstone, 'Shakespeare and Scottish Kingship', pp. 163–8, 173–6.

8. References to *Scotorum Historiae a prima gentis origine libri xvii* (Paris, 1527) will be by the abbreviation *SH* followed by the folium number.

9. A similar statement has been made about the printed text, for although its chief supporters, W. W. Seton and R. W. Chambers, first claim that it is the more accurate of the two, they then admit that it simply diverges in different places. See 'Bellenden's Translation', 6.

10. See Brigitte Moreau, *Inventaire Chronologique des Éditions parisiennes du XVIe siècle, d'après les manuscrits de Philippe Rénouard*, 3 vols (Paris, 1985) vol. 3: 1521–30, no. 1143, under 1527, for extant copies known to be in the possession of libraries.

11. On the use of Latin instead of the vernacular, see P. O. Kristeller, 'The Moral Thought of Renaissance Humanism', in *Renaissance Thought and the Arts* (Princeton, 1990), pp. 20–68, esp. p. 28.

12. The merchant class, that is the growing burgess population, must have been an important audience for the printed text, since they would have had both the money to purchase such a book and the ability to read it. See Gordon Donaldson, *Scotland: James V to James VII*, Edinburgh History of Scotland, 3 (Edinburgh, 1990), p. 137. Bellenden's own connections with the Edinburgh merchants have been indicated by Theo van Heijnsbergen, in 'The Interaction Between Literature and History in Queen Mary's Edinburgh: The Bannatyne Manuscript and its Prosopographical Context', in *The Renaissance in Scotland*, ed. A. A. MacDonald, M. Lynch and I. B. Cowan (Leiden, 1994), pp. 183–225, esp. 185–6 and 191–2.

13. See R. J. Lyall, 'Vernacular Prose before the Reformation', in *The History of Scottish Literature: Origins to 1660*, vol. 1, ed. R. D. S. Jack (Aberdeen, 1989), pp. 163–82, esp. pp. 172–4, on the difficulties of translation.

14. John Mair, *Historia Maioris Britanniae, tam Angliae quam Scotiae* (Paris, 1521), fol. 15.

15. Robert Gaguin, *Compendium de origine et gestis Francorum* (Paris, 1495).

16. Bellenden, *Chronicles* (STS), has paragraphs as well. It is hard to tell from facsimiles of the Pierpont Morgan manuscript whether this reflects scribal practice, but some paragraph markers appear to be used. They certainly occur in the printed version. See *Ten Facsimiles from the manuscript of Bellenden's translation of the Chronicles of Scotland by Hector Boece, formerly in the possession of King James V and now in the possession of J. Pierpont Morgan Esq., by whom they are presented to members of the Scottish Text Society* (Edinburgh and London, n.d.) and *The Chronicles of Scotland*, The English Experience 851 (Amsterdam and Norwood NJ, 1977).

17. There is no complete edition of the Mar Lodge translation, and in this essay, references are made to *The Mar Lodge Translation of the History of Scotland*, ed. George Watson, vol. 1, STS (Edinburgh and London, 1946). Curiously, while Bellenden divides the *Scotorum Historia* into more manageable chapters, he does the reverse in his translation of Livy. There although the material is already divided into chapters, Bellenden frequently gathers together several to suit his own perspective on the narrative. For example, he puts the whole account of Numa Pompilius under one summary, whereas it covers five sections in the Latin text. I am grateful to Mrs Priscilla Bawcutt

for pointing out that Gavin Douglas, who certainly knew John Bellenden, provides chapter divisions in his translation of the *Aeneid*, similar to Bellenden's practice in the *Chronicles*: such editing is evidently quite widespread in early sixteenth-century Scotland. See John Bellenden, *Livy's History of Rome, the first five books*, ed. William Craigie, 2 vols, STS (Edinburgh and London, 1901-3), and Gavin Douglas, *Eneados*, ed. D. F. C. Coldwell, 4 vols, STS (Edinburgh and London, 1957-64).

18. *SH* 309 (book 14). I am very grateful to Mr Ian Cunningham of the National Library of Scotland for his assistance with the translations.

19. Bellenden, *Chronicles* (STS), II, p. 262.

20. A similar change in perspective is indicated by Bellenden's omission of the explanation of Comyn's nickname. There was, after all, no need for him to translate the word 'red' for the benefit of his audience.

21. Bellenden, *Chronicles* (STS), II, p. 264.

22. Walter Bower, *Scotichronicon*, ed. D. E. R. Watt, vol. 6 (Aberdeen, 1991), book 12, chapters 7-8, pp. 310-15, and *SH* 310 (book 14).

23. *SH* 58 (book 4).

24. Bellenden, *Chronicles* (STS) I, p. 148.

25. *SH* 304 (book 14) and Bellenden, *Chronicles* (STS), II, p. 232; *SH* 310 (book 14) and Bellenden, *Chronicles* (STS) II, p. 248; *SH* 338 (book 15) and Bellenden, *Chronicles* (STS) II, p. 332. The last two errors are corrected in the printed text, by either Boece's or Bellenden's pen. See Bellenden, *Chronicles* (1821), vol. 2, p. 379 and pp. 446-7. The first, quite possibly a result of a confusion of minims in Boece's original manuscript, remains unchanged.

26. *SH* 303 (book 14) and Bellenden, *Chronicles* (STS), 2, p. 246. Several changes in this name are evident in the development of Bellenden's translation: see Sheppard, 'Studies', p. 145.

27. *SH* 58ᵛ (book 4) and Bellenden, *Chronicles* (STS) I, p. 149.

28. *The Mar Lodge Translation*, p. 210.

29. Neither 'Galdus' nor any apparently related word appears in either the *Dictionary of the Older Scottish Tongue* or in the *Scottish National Dictionary* under the definition Boece gives it. The solution may lie in the Gaelic word 'Gall' meaning 'foreigner': Professor J. MacQueen has suggested that Boece's usage derives from the Aberdeenshire surnames 'Gaul', 'Gauld' and their more widespread variant 'Galt', which in turn derive from the Gaelic word, still familiar in sixteenth-century Aberdeenshire (private correspondence, 1996).

30. *The Mar Lodge Translation*, p. 210.

31. *SH* 59 and Bellenden, *Chronicles* (STS), I, p. 150; *SH* 174ᵛ and *Chronicles* (STS) I, p. 386.

32. *SH* 58.

33. Bellenden, *Chronicles* (STS), I, p. 148.

34. *SH* 75 (book 4).

35. *SH* 58 (book 4); Bellenden, *Chronicles* (STS) I, p. 148.

36. Bellenden, *Chronicles* (1821), vol. 1, p. 128. See Chambers and Seton, 14 and for more detail on Davidson, see R. Dickson and J. P. Edmond, *Annals of Scottish Printing* (Cambridge, 1890), pp. 105-35.

37. *SH* 273 (book 12) and Bellenden, *Chronicles* (STS) II, p. 185; *SH* 74 (book 4) and Bellenden, *Chronicles* (STS) I, p. 183.

38. For a brief account of Mair's unionist views, see Roger A. Mason, 'Kingship, Nobility and Anglo-Scottish Union: John Mair's *History of Greater Britain* (1521)', *IR*, 41 (1990), 182-222.

39. The perception of the Scots, generally by people of other, more southerly nations, and of the northern Gaelic sub-section by themselves, as savage and uncivilised was one Boece strove to overturn. For a fuller account of this issue, see A. H. Williamson, 'Scots, Indians and Empire: The Scottish Politics of Civilisation 1519–1609', *Past and Present*, 150 (1996), 46–83, esp. 46–56 and 74.

40. *SH* 173 (book 9).

41. Bellenden, *Chronicles* (STS) I, p. 384

42. *SH* 295ᵛ (the folium is actually misnumbered CCXCIIII). A very similar account can be found in Boece's sources, the *Scotichronicon* and John of Fordun's *Annalia*. See *Scotichronicon* vol. 5, ed. S. Taylor and D. E. R. Watt with B. Scott (Aberdeen, 1990), book 10, chapters 1–2, pp. 290–7 and Fordun, *Annalia* chapters 47–8 in *Chronica Gentis Scotorum*, vol. 1, ed. W. F. Skene, Historians of Scotland 1 (Edinburgh, 1871), pp. 293–4.

43. Bellenden, *Chronicles* (STS) II, pp. 229–30.

44. *SH* 58 (book 4).

45. Bellenden, *Chronicles* (STS) I, p. 148.

46. See p. 140 above.

47. *SH* 309 (book 14).

48. Bellenden, *Chronicles* (STS) II, pp. 262–3.

49. In *The Matter of Scotland: Historical Narrative in Medieval Scotland* (Lincoln, Neb. and London, 1993), R. James Goldstein argues that the portrayal of the Bruce as the favoured claimant to the throne and later of Robert I as the true and unchallenged king of the Scots constant in late medieval and Renaissance historiography is the result of what he calls 'Brucean ideology' (pp. 79–87). This leads to a necessary degradation of Comyn's character into that of a traitor, first evident in Barbour's account (pp. 172–3). While Boece is ambivalent about Bruce's character until he proves himself as king, Bellenden moves even further towards Barbour's perspective in the printed version of the text, where John Comyn in fact makes the offer of the kingdom to Bruce. See Bellenden, *Chronicles* (1821) vol. 2, pp. 378–9.

50. *SH* 310.

51. Bellenden, *Chronicles* (STS) II, pp. 263–4.

52. *SH* 273 and Bellenden, *Chronicles* (STS) II, pp. 185–6.

53. This condemnation is expressed even more vehemently in the printed text of the translation, where Mair is cited as showing a similar opinion in the *Historia Maioris Britanniae*. See Bellenden, *Chronicles* (1821) vol. 2, pp. 299–300. Such an opinion, especially from the archdeacon of Moray and the precentor of Glasgow, may have found a sympathetic audience among those with Reforming tendencies, who were particularly evident among the burgesses of Edinburgh. See Michael Lynch, *Scotland: A New History* (1991), pp. 189–91.

54. It is interesting to speculate whether such an attack, directed so specifically at the threat to the crown and thus the realm through David's overspending on religious houses, might originally have been used as justification for the appalling record of church appointments made by James IV and James V, in an attempt to divert church money back into royal coffers. See Ranald Nicholson, *Scotland: The Later Middle Ages*, Edinburgh History of Scotland, 2 (Edinburgh, 1978), pp. 556–62 and Donaldson, pp. 47–8.

55. *SH* 304ᵛ.

56. Bellenden, *Chronicles* (STS) II, p. 250.

57. Professor Michael Winterbottom is prepared to accept Boece's usage, remarking only that in good classical usage that the *te* would have been omitted. Mr Cunningham,

however, disputes the accepted currency of Boece's usage altogether. Claiming partiality, I support Boece's approach.

58. For example, see *SH* 20ᵛ (book 2) for Boece's comments on Bede and *SH* 310ᵛ for his comments on the unnamed *Scotichronicon*.

59. Chambers and Seton, 9–10.

60. Bellenden, *Chronicles* (STS) II, p. 267.

61. *SH* 311ʳ and ᵛ (book 14).

62. See Donaldson, pp. 44–5.

8

SHAKESPEARE AND SCOTTISH KINGSHIP: A CASE HISTORY

Sally Mapstone

This study is concerned with the Scottish pre-history of one particular scene in *Macbeth*, and more particularly still one episode within that scene. It is a scene that has, over the years achieved a dubious notoriety by laying claim to being the least popular, or most boring, in the play. In nineteenth-century performances it was common to cut it, or one part of it.[1] E. K. Chambers regarded it as tedious; Kenneth Muir, editor of the Arden edition which first appeared in 1951, registered that criticism and attempted to salvage the issue by claiming, 'It does not seem tedious today, perhaps ... because of the events of recent years'.[2] In the past twenty years it has been considerably rehabilitated and recognised as a significant element in *Macbeth*, but a recent commentator has still described it once again as 'the dullest scene in the play'.[3] This study's second concern is to suggest that such dullness is primarily in the mind of the beholder, and that the scene is central to the play.

The scene in question is Act IV, scene III, which opens with a lengthy dialogue on kingship between Macduff and Malcolm. Macduff, visiting Malcolm in England, urges him to return to rescue the Scotland ravaged by Macbeth. Malcolm first indicates doubts about Macduff's integrity – he could be a treacherous decoy – and then, when Macduff responds angrily, Malcolm declares himself a liability if he should assume the throne since he outdoes Macbeth in vices: lechery, avarice, and an inbuilt resistance to all 'the king-becoming graces' (91). Macduff, responding to each vice in turn, attempts to suggest that the first two failings can be accommodated, but reacts with outrage to the final catalogue: 'Fit to govern?/No, not to live.' (103–4) At this point Malcolm reveals that he has been dissembling in order to test the sincerity of Macduff's request – so often has Macbeth attempted to gain hold of him through sending duplicitous delegations of this sort. The two are reconciled; the rest of the scene consists of a brief episode involving a doctor's praise of king Edward the Confessor's touching for scrofula, which in turn is followed by the arrival of Ross with the news of the murder of Macduff's wife and children.

The accusations of boringness have most commonly been directed at the episode which will be the special subject of enquiry here, the debate between Malcolm and Macduff. Its meaningfulness in the play has of late been more readily appreciated, but it is still the case that the substance of this scene remains strikingly undiscussed in *Macbeth* criticism.[4] In a play the language of which has been lingered over with such attention, the details of the arguments in this scene are strangely unexplored. Certain aspects of it have given pause, and attracted very different explanations: the fact, for instance, that Macduff, as Malcolm reminds him, has left his wife and children unprotected in Scotland, in that 'rawness' (26).[5] It has been recognised that this issue and the conduct of the debate that follows it can be seen as highly relevant to the play's exploration of ideas of kingship, but there is still more to be said here, particularly about the actual content of the discussion between Macduff and Malcolm.[6]

Another reason why the details of this scene have been neglected is that it is perceived as the scene in *Macbeth* which is the closest borrowing from its source. That source, as is also well known, was 'Holinshed's' *Chronicle* of England, Ireland and Scotland, the second and revised edition of which, published in 1587, Shakespeare is commonly held to have used for *Macbeth*.[7] This is the main historical source; of other material on Scotland posited to have been known and used by Shakespeare, the most convincing arguments have been made for his knowledge of George Buchanan's *Rerum Scoticarum Historia* (1582), itself employed by Thynne in his revisions to the 1587 edition of Holinshed.[8]

Most recent commentators on *Macbeth* thus look little further than Holinshed's *Chronicle* when discussing Shakespeare's primary source for the text, and this is strongly the case in relation to IV, 3.[9] Some close parallels of phrasing have doubtless encouraged this view. Malcolm's description of the workings of his lechery, for example, 'there's no bottom, none,/In my voluptuousness: your wives, your daughters,/Your matrons, and your maids, could not fill up/The cistern of my lust' (60–3) obviously takes its cue from this in Holinshed: 'such immoderate lust and voluptuous sensualitie (the abhominable founteine of all vices) followeth me, that if I were made king of Scots, I should seke to defloure your maids and matrones'.[10]

It is common, however, also to remark upon the freedom with which

Shakespeare treats Holinshed elsewhere in the play, the salient features for the discussion here being as follows. In Holinshed Duncan is a younger and weaker king than he is in Shakespeare. He is indeed contrasted with Macbeth who, for all his cruel streak, has a capacity for assertive action and just rule that manifests itself both in assistance to the ineffective Duncan during his reign and in ten years of his own good rule after the murder of Duncan. Macbeth and Duncan too are figures in an onrunning Scottish dispute over the transmission of kingship, this system having been fairly recently altered under Kenneth III from one of election to become one of primogeniture. But this is not wholly endorsed by the Scottish political community and it is clear in Holinshed that Macbeth has a felt grievance against Duncan after the latter proclaims his son prince of Cumberland, an indication that he is the heir to the throne. Under the old pre-Kenneth system Macbeth would have had a claim as the closest male relative had Duncan died while his son was still a minor. These things are omitted by Shakespeare, or in the case of the prince of Cumberland reference (I, IV, 48–50) presented in extremely compressed fashion, as is the fact that in Holinshed Macbeth conspires with Banquo in the murder of Duncan, an inappropriate detail to be associated with the progenitor of the Stewart dynasty. That Shakespeare worked such extensive variations on what he found in Holinshed as a whole suggests that individual scenes are also worth examining in particular detail. We will see that derivative as it is, IV, III, is no exception here.

Those editors and commentators on the play who have gone further on the source question discuss other materials Shakespeare might have known,[11] and point out that Holinshed's own main source is Hector Boece's *Scotorum Historia*, first published in 1527 and reprinted with some revision and additional material up to 1488 by Giovanni Ferreri in 1574.[12] It is frequently stated or assumed that this chronicle was mediated to Holinshed through the translation by John Bellenden, originally composed c. 1530–1 and published in revised form c. 1540.[13] Whether Shakespeare might independently have consulted either Boece or Bellenden has received surprisingly little detailed attention, presumably because his debt to Holinshed is so conspicuous, and there is little doubt that that chronicle is the play's major source.[14] However, perhaps even more surprisingly, the transmission of the *Scotorum Historia* to the compilers of Holinshed's Scottish chronicle has received scant scholarly inspection. The reference to Ferrerius in Holinshed's list of works consulted proves that the Latin version of Boece's chronicle was available to the compilers, but it is equally clear, as the following discussion will show, that although Bellenden is not specifically mentioned as a source, it was his translation which was often closely worked from.[15] But these points need more inspection than they have generally received. What has not been appreciated in this context is the complex transmission of material from Boece's Latin version into Bellenden's translation. For another set of assumptions is commonly at work here, despite the efforts of Bellenden's editors and others to dispel them.[16] The first is that Bellenden's translation of Boece is a reasonably faithful one, an assumption that has been demonstrated to need serious and applied qualification.[17] The second is that the Scottish Text Society's edition of Bellenden's translation, the most recent available, is the correct one to cite. Thus it is that the standard guide to Shakespeare's sources for *Macbeth*, while asserting Boece's Latin chronicle to be Holinshed's main source, gives quotations from Bellenden, and from the STS edition of his translation.[18] But the STS version is based on the best manuscript version of Bellenden, rather than the earliest print. This essay will show that for an understanding of Boece's history, Bellenden's translation, Holinshed's use of Boece, Bellenden and other Scottish sources, and finally Shakespeare's working in *Macbeth*, the appreciation of the difference between the manuscript and printed versions of Bellenden's translation is fundamental.

That the compilers of the Scottish Holinshed were not for this scene working primarily from Boece's Latin text is easily demonstrated by the ways in which the structure and arguments of Boece's and Holinshed's accounts differ at various signal points. Boece's version of events in this part of his twelfth book may be summarised thus. Malcolm is moved by Macduff's account of the oppression of the Scots people under Macbeth, but prudently decides to dissemble in order to test Macduff's motives, lest he should have been sent by Macbeth to entrap him. He says (this is presented in indirect speech) that he is sorry for the country's sake, but cannot take on the government of the realm because of his irremediable vices, especially lechery, which is at present confined to his own dwelling and thus harmful only to himself. Now direct speech ensues and Malcolm describes his excesses as of a magnitude which would incite him to ravish wives and daughters in a manner even more intemperate than Macbeth's bloody tyranny. And in addition to this he has an even more unkingly vice, a pleasure in lying and deceit. Thus since constancy, truth and justice are kingly virtues, and nothing is more opposed to them than lying, it is clear how incapable he is to govern the realm. To illustrate this he tells a fable of how a fox lay wounded with flies sucking her blood. A passer-by enquires whether the fox would like the flies removed from her; to which she replies no, for the flies sitting in her wounds are full of her blood, giving her little discomfort – if they were removed others would come and suck out the rest of her blood.[19] Therefore it is better for the vicious Malcolm to remain where he is than to produce a situation where he would have to be chased from Scotland with even more shame.

Macduff's reply to this in Boece is to enquire whether Malcolm might not at least agree to be named as leader for the purpose of liberating his homeland, leaving other matters to be dealt with by him and his friends. But Malcolm, concerned to test Macduff to the utmost, rejects this too. When Macduff sees that Malcolm will not go along with this, he prays that God may either change his mind or permit him not to remain alive long as a shame to the nation. Now, devoid of hope, Macduff will not stay to see the ruin of his country, but will leave it to travel to uncivilised lands as a good Christian. As he turns to leave, Malcolm holds him back, and reassures him that he was just testing his motives; the more slow to fulfil Macduff's wishes he has appeared, the quicker he will now be to carry them out. And the scene ends with their embrace and embarkation upon discussions about how to achieve their goal.[20]

The equivalent passage is given thus by Holinshed. After the same preliminaries, Malcolm again says that he cannot take on the kingdom. Direct speech is used immediately here. Firstly Malcolm describes his lechery, in terms similar to those just set out in Boece. At this point in Holinshed, Macduff answers, saying that this is indeed an evil fault, for which many princes and kings have lost their lives and kingdoms, but there are really enough women in Scotland, and if Malcolm will become king it will be ensured that he can indulge this vice in secret. Malcolm then replies, saying that he is also the most avaricious of men; if he were king he would deceitfully seek to obtain lands and possessions from the Scots nobility; and to illustrate the point he tells the fox fable, concluding that were he to assume the throne the problems they now have would seen light in comparison to the outrages which would ensue during Malcolm's rule. Macduff immediately responds that this is a worse crime, and one through which many Scottish kings have met their deaths. Nevertheless Malcolm should still think of taking the Scottish crown, for 'There is gold and riches inough in Scotland to satisfie thy greedie desire'.[21]

Malcolm now answers this, stating that he is also inclined to lying and deceit, and since lying is anathema to constancy, truth and justice, he should not govern the realm. But perhaps Macduff can help him find some means whereby, as with the other vices, he may be able to cloak this one from public knowledge. In other words, he is ready, on these alarming terms, to take on the realm. But Macduff reacts with revulsion. This, he declares, is the worst of all vices. Poor Scotland, with one tyrant reigning over her and the man who does have the just right to the throne being 'replet with inconstant behaviour and manifest vices of Englishmen, that he is nothing woorthie to inioy it'.[22] He bids farewell to Scotland, at which point Malcolm intervenes and the two are reconciled.

While Holinshed has an obvious debt to Boece here, most noticeably in the fox and flies fable, the shape and details of his scene are also significantly different from that source. Whereas in Boece Malcolm catalogues two vices, lechery and lying, before Macduff intervenes and makes the pragmatic (if striking) suggestion that Malcolm assume the throne and let a group of nobles handle the running of the realm, Holinshed has a more dramatic dialogue between the two men, in which three vices – lechery, avarice, and lying – are listed by Malcolm and the scene builds to his own suggestion that he should assume the throne. Holinshed is clearly dependent upon another source here, and it is, primarily, Bellenden's translation of Boece, but crucially and very intriguingly, in its printed rather than its manuscript version.

It is hardly surprising of course that Holinshed should have had access to Bellenden in printed rather than manuscript form, but the nature of the intrigue lies in the dramatic differences in the narration of this episode between the manuscript and printed versions of Bellenden's translation. The manuscript version or versions are in this instance much closer to the structure and disposition of Boece's Latin, though the rendering is still far from always a close translation: material is omitted or paraphrased, and there are other changes in the narration, as indicated below. By the time of the printed version, however, this scene has been significantly revised into the form that patently lies behind Holinshed's.

Although as will be shown, the manuscripts of Bellenden's version of this passage themselves show stages of revision, it is broadly legitimate to distinguish here between the manuscript and printed versions by taking the STS's edition (from the Pierpont Morgan MS, *c.* 1531–3, the presentation copy to James V and one possibly revised by Bellenden himself) as a representative MS for the time being.[23] In the manuscript version Bellenden had already done things to enhance the dramatic quality of Boece's scene. Whereas in Boece Malcolm's opening remarks are reported in *oratio obliqua* Bellenden has them in direct speech. However, the manuscript version of his translation follows Boece in postponing all comment by Macduff until the fox fable has been told and then inserting his suggestion, but again in direct speech rather than Boece's reported speech, that Malcolm 'mak thi self King of Scotland

and latt me and vther thi freyndis haif the administracioun therof',[24] to be followed by Malcolm's swift rejection of this, Macduff's despair, and Malcolm's effecting of their reconciliation. The printed version of Bellenden, however, has Macduff respond immediately to the first admission of lechery by effectively volunteering to become Malcolm's pander in a manner that would be passed down to Holinshed: 'That is ane evill falt; for mony nobill princis and kingis bene disherist and tint baith thair lyfe and kingdomis for the samin. Nochtheles thair is gret plenty of wemen in Scotland; and thairfore, will thow do my counsall, make thyself king. I sall dres that mater sa wisely, that thow salbe satisfyit at thy pleseir, and thy vice salbe unknawin'.[25] In the printed version too the second vice to which Malcolm confesses is not lying and deceitfulness, but avarice, and it is to this that he links the telling of the fox fable. In the print Macduff's response is to acknowledge the seriousness of the vice but again to urge Malcolm in similar terms to '... mak thyself king, and do my counsall: thow sall have riches at fouth; for thair is gold and geir ineuch in Scotland to satisfie the at thy pleseir'.[26] This too is followed by Holinshed. Only after this in the print does Malcolm put forward his first vices of lying and deceit, link them to their opposing virtues of constancy, verity and justice, and make the coolly devastating request, 'And sen thow hes sa mony rameidis to colour all the laif of my vicis, I pray the to hyde or colour this vice amang the laif'.[27] Macduff responds to this with revulsion, but again in a manner different from the earlier MS account, lamenting the misery of the Scots who have the choice of being either destroyed by a bloody tyrant or being the victim of a figure 'repleit with the treasonable maneris and vicis of Inglismen',[28] again a detail that goes through to Holinshed. Malcolm then brings the scene to its conclusion as in the earlier version. One further significant thing, however, that has gone from Bellenden's account in the shift from manuscript to print is the specific offer (there in Boece of course) on Macduff's part that he and his friends would run the kingdom on Malcolm's behalf having installed him in place of Macbeth.

The marked closeness of the printed version of the scene to that in Holinshed is manifest, but what should be equally so is how very different are the character and structure of the scenes in the manuscript and printed versions of Bellenden's translation. The question that necessarily presents itself here is whether Boece or his translator Bellenden was responsible for the radical reworking of this scene.

Boece was clearly involved in the revising of Bellenden's translation for publication; what remains unclear is the precise nature and extent of that involvement. Thomas Davidson's printer's notice to the edition states that it is 'compilit and newly correckit be the reuerend and noble clerke maister Hector Boece channon of Aberdene./Translatit laitly be maister Iohne Bellenden Archedene of Murray, channon of Ros'.[29] It is uncertain whether Boece's corrections were made to his original Latin text, as published in 1527, and then passed on to Bellenden for incorporation in the revised translation, or whether Boece worked immediately from a MS of Bellenden's translation, adding his corrections and revisions in Scots. If he did revise his own Latin translation, those revisions were not preserved and passed on to Ferreri for the 1574 edition, the first seventeen books of which are identical with the 1527 text. Nor did Boece apparently supply Bellenden with the (admittedly still draft) accounts of the reigns of James II and III, completed before his death in 1536 and incorporated by Ferreri in the 1574 edition. On the other hand, there is no evidence of Boece working in the vernacular. All his surviving works are in Latin, 'not a line of Scots'.[30] The most extensive discussion of this problem to date points out that there is evidence in one of the 'intermediary' manuscripts of Bellenden's translation (between the first recension and the printed version), for contact between Boece and Bellenden over the translation of the Description of Scotland, a part of the *Scotorum Historia* not present in the first MS version but added to the printed edition. The language of this passage uses similar terms of 'compiling' and 'correction' to those found in the printer's note: 'and because the remanent ... is no^t sufficiently correckit be the first compilar we will at his desyre continew the remanent quhill efter that It may w^t better cognosance past to licht'.[31]

The implication of these various remarks is that Boece had access to Bellenden's translation during the process of its making and provided corrections to it, and it is possible to envisage a large-scale version of this process taking place when the completed translation was revised once more for printing. However when the detailed extent of the revisions is considered – 'It would be no exaggeration to say that the printed text is a version in which almost every sentence has been rewritten'[32] – it becomes apparent that Bellenden's share in this process must also have been a substantial one as he reconsidered and refined his original work. That first translation itself already exhibited considerable departures from Boece's Latin original in the form of added or omitted details, abbreviation, and occasional omission or addition of episodes or comments, along with instances of paraphrase rather than translation. And given that Bellenden made changes to the printed versions of his own prefatory and poetic material accompanying the chronicle, the extension of this practice to his translation seems entirely plausible.[33]

The process of 'correcting' Bellenden's original translation seems thus most likely to have involved the contributions of both men. But we lack a thorough-going analysis of the instances where the manuscript and printed versions of the text differ substantively and importantly in terms of content and interpretation rather than in phrasing and more minor detail, in order to attempt to distinguish the 'authorial' hand behind them.

That we cannot assume that such substantial alterations to the Boethian original stem from Boece himself rather than Bellenden is witnessed by the instances in Bellenden's manuscript translation where the translator shows himself amply capable of silently introducing material that reflects his own concerns or associations, as in his eulogistic comments on the loyalty of the house of Douglas and James Douglas in particular in book 14, chapter 8.[34] An 'intermediary' manuscript of the translation, now University College London MS Angl. 1, which contains revisions to the original manuscript version, many of which, including this one, go through into the printed edition, heightens these laudatory remarks by a quotation from what is referred to as 'Brucis buke', '"Sa mony gud as of the Dowglass hes bene,/Of ane surname wes nevir in Scotland sene"'.[35] As the decasyllabic couplets themselves suggest, however, this quotation is not from what would seem the most obvious candidate for identification with 'Brucis book', John Barbour's *Bruce*. These are in fact the first two lines of a set of eight verses charging the Douglas with the burial of Bruce's heart inscribed on the blade of a sword of state said to have been given to James Douglas by Robert the Bruce, and kept at Douglas Castle until the 1930s, but now regrettably untraced. Earlier commentators thought that the verses were probably a later addition to a possibly genuine sword,[36] which their metre would also suggest, decasyllabic verse in Scots being a feature of the second half of the fifteenth century onwards. In any event, the Douglas family connection is again strongly apparent in the context of this quotation. So too, however, is a desire still to link them with loyalty to the monarchy, and to the literary heritage of that monarchy. In a manner not unlike Richard Holland's strategy in the *Buke of the Howlat*, Barbour's poem in praise of the Stewarts is suggested in a context which is designed as much if not more to elevate the significance of the Douglases. Moreover, in the printed edition of Bellenden's revised translation a further laudatory sentence on the Douglases is added after the 'quotation': 'For thay decorit this realme with mony noble actis, and, be glore of marciall dedis, grew in gret estimation'.[37] This small stemma of Douglas additions strongly suggests that the translator was successively building onto his original, and revealing knowledge and exploitation of possible sources in the process.

This fine tuning of the printed edition is moreover followed shortly after by an even more explicit and daring addition to the opening of book 15 which in this version extends and revises the account of the story of James Douglas's mission to the Holy Land with the heart of Robert the Bruce. In this account Douglas succeeds on his mission, burying the heart in the Holy Land and only dying on the return journey while helping out the king of Spain against the Saracens. There is no precedent for these details in any MSS of Bellenden's first translation or Boece's Latin original, but notably in the revised printed version a source is again adduced, this section of the narrative being rounded off by the statement, 'He was LVII sindry times victorious on Inglismen, and XIII times on the Turkis; as is writtin at lenth in Scoticronicon. Bot we wil returne to our history'.[38] A little sleight of hand is again at work here because the unhistorical elaboration of Douglas's mission to the Holy Land with Bruce's heart as a successful enterprise is not found in Fordun or Bower (*Scotichronicon* being a possible reference to either), both of whom describe his death among the Saracens. In fact, and interestingly in the light of what we have already seen in relation to the presentation of the Douglases in book 14, it is first adduced in the mid-fifteenth-century *Buke of the Howlat*, a text of course produced under Douglas patronage.[39] But what is again striking is that whoever has made this addition to Bellenden's printed addition has been looking back to source material. Bellenden's family and personal connections with branches of the Douglas family (he 'remained a Douglas supporter all his life'[40]) make him a more likely candidate than Boece for the production of such additions. Given that James V had marked the conclusion of his minority only a few years earlier by forfeiting and exiling the Angus Douglases, advocacy of the Douglases' traditional loyalty to the crown in a translation being made at the king's instigation is in itself striking here, and clearly had to be handled with some delicacy. The presence of this pro-Douglas material in a text presented to the king illustrates a recurrent facet of earlier Scottish political writing, that texts directed towards the monarch frequently arise out of and reflect the viewpoints of an aristocratic constituency.[41]

What these additions also demonstrate is that, if they were Bellenden's, he too had been consulting the same sorts of source text that Boece himself had been reading, even if not always citing them with total accuracy. Nor was this reading necessarily confined to 'older' Scottish sources such as *Scotichronicon*. The criticisms of David I's excessive liberality in the foundations of monasteries (excessive because of its later implications for the crown's finances), which Bellenden has long been known to have added to his book 12 in its original manuscript form,[42] are successively heightened and extended in the revised MS UCL Angl. 1, and in the printed edition. The UCL MS and the print back up their remarks by reference, a genuine and verifiable one in this case, to the 'Cronikles' of 'Maister Johne Mair',[43] a Latin work printed only a few years before Boece's own chronicle. Given that this reference occurs in a section of the text already 'original' to Bellenden, it seems most likely that this addition is his rather than Boece's and confirms his reading around in other chronicle material.

Such signposting is not, however, available for other of the additions thus far detected to the printed text of the translation. No source is apparent for the anecdotes about David I and the White Hart in book 12, chapter 16 or about Archibald Douglas in book 16, but the former is an addition to the David I material already clearly expanded by Bellenden rather than Boece, and Douglas associations might again suggest that the latter is Bellenden's appropriation from family traditions.[44] Cumulatively then, the evidence assembled here would suggest that while Boece may indeed have been involved in the revisions to Bellenden's translation, the translator himself played an active and sometimes politically interventionist part in the recasting of his translation, often on the basis of consultation of a range of Scottish source material.[45] It is in this context that we must approach the transformation of the Malcolm/Macduff scene from Bellenden's earlier manuscript version into its final manifestation in the printed text.

The Malcolm/Macduff scene is actually one of the most popular and repeated episodes in Scottish historical narratives from the end of the fourteenth century until the end of the sixteenth.[46] The appeal of this scene to medieval and Renaissance writers is worth remarking upon because it goes some way towards explaining why Shakespeare was so drawn to it. The episode makes its first and, of all versions, most extended appearance in the Latin *Chronica Gentis Scotorum* of the Scottish chronicler John Fordun, which was compiled between the 1360s and Fordun's death in about 1385.[47] Fordun's version is crucially influential on the sequence of texts from Bellenden to Shakespeare with which we are concerned here, and must be treated in detail.

As far as can be told, it is from this lengthy account that all the other versions mentioned here ultimately derive. Fordun's nineteenth-century editor Skene believed that 'For the whole of this ingeniously imagined interview, I consider Fordun to be solely responsible'; he also believed him to have invented this Macduff, a point which recent scholarship seems to have confirmed, and the more interesting because in his portrayal of him Fordun seems to give us an early example of a phenomenon documented in other sources on the Macduff family, that they had the power of king-making.[48] That Macduff is not only a supporter of Malcolm but perhaps also an invested king-maker gives the whole scene an added resonance.

In Fordun the Macduff/Malcolm exchange constitutes the first six chapters of book 5 of the *Chronica Gentis Scotorum* and it is one of the most fascinating and extended pieces of deliberation on questions of kingship to be found in that work. The scene begins in the familiar manner and then takes the form of a highly charged and protracted debate between the two men, in which Malcolm reveals his three vices and Macduff responds to the description of each as it is made known to him. But there is far more complexity to it than that. Malcolm insists on the deep-set nature of his sins, which would compulsively reassert themselves were he ever to succeed to the throne. The first is lechery, and it is here that the recurrent motif of violating the beds of noble wives and deflowering virgins is introduced. But, having declared this vice, Malcolm then goes on, in Fordun, to acknowledge the full nature of its destructive potential by narrating a series of exempla of monarchs who have been brought down by lust. He begins, unsurprisingly, with Tarquin and Lucretia – a popular exemplum used to warn against lechery in advisory works, since Tarquin's violation of Lucretia was so strongly linked to the Romans' rejection of monarchy, as indeed it is here.[49] It is this association that underscores Macbeth's reference to 'Tarquin's ravishing strides' in Act 2, scene 1 (55) when he is recollecting his murder of Duncan – consciously or unconsciously, at the very point at which he stands to gain the crown he associates himself with the violation of a pure creature and the loss of a kingdom. In Fordun Malcolm's list continues with a mixture of examples from classical antiquity and the more recent past: Sardanapalus, Chilperic, king Edwy of England. Malcolm goes on to say that more recent examples in Scotland include kings Culen and Rodoric – indeed he could adduce hundreds more, many of which have produced civil strife and the loss of kingdoms.

Fordun is most probably drawing here on a repository of exempla on lust supplemented by examples from English and Scots tradition, two of which, Edwy and Culen, had been cited in the same debauched connection in book 4.[50] While the idea of the recitation of the three worsening vices may draw on popular or folk tradition[51] (compare the motif of the king's three questions used in the *Thre Prestis of Peblis*), Fordun's treatment gives it a very different and more learned character, turns it in fact into a striking inset example of advice to princes. For the potential king Malcolm is advising the king-maker on the dangers of kingly vices! In one sense, of course, Malcolm's appreciation of the dangers of the vices he attributes to himself gives the lie to his essential viciousness, but in another, the idea that he knows about its destructiveness but claims to be unable to control himself gives the scene a disturbing element, which will eventually come through to Shakespeare.

Macduff's response to the catalogue of lechers is of equal interest. He reproaches Malcolm for such an unsatisfactory response to people like himself who 'for your sake, have deserted our kingdom, and our estates, our sons and our wives and the people of our, nation'.[52] It is that detail that Boece would be the first to expand into the idea that Macbeth actually murders Macduff's wife and children. Holinshed borrows the episode, but it is Shakespeare who has it revealed to Macduff after rather than before the debate with Malcolm – thus making Malcolm's doubts about Macduff's motivation more credible. But however reprehensible Macduff here may think the vice of lechery to be, his further response is pragmatic: 'When you are king, will you not be able to have at will the most beautiful young girls in the kingdom and the most complaisant women to satisfy your lecherous lust?'[53] And he caps Malcolm's exempla with his own of the emperor Octavian, who had the habit of disporting himself with a dozen women he had seduced on one side and a dozen virgins on the other, but who also nevertheless managed to strengthen and extend the empire.[54]

Malcolm now says he has a worse vice, he is an avaricious thief. And this time he supports the argument not with exempla, but with sententia-like remarks: 'The downfall of a distinguished person always far, far exceeds the descent into vice of a more obscure person in the degree of scandal involved.'[55] With this Macduff agrees, adding again his own: a prince who descends into vice is doubly a wrong-doer because the fickle mob will imitate him. Malcolm is breaking two of the commandments already; nevertheless God established these precepts because they were possible, not impossible, to keep. And since the desire to thieve arises primarily from need, Malcolm should still aim for the kingdom for 'When you are king, you will lack for nothing ever'.[56]

For Fordun's Macduff the idea of Malcolm managing his vices as ruler is essentially linked to a basic premise of good kingly self-government, that kings should endeavour to contain their failings within a right-minded regime. What is being posited here is a variant on the common medieval theme that one could fight against one's physiognomy and its attendant vices or failings.[57] Thus Macduff seeks to claim that great qualities can be set against vices and that a king equipped with these and with the advantages of kingship has all the more reason and ability to endeavour to contain his failing.

But, Fordun goes on, Malcolm wished to test Macduff yet further and he now confesses that he is thoroughly false, devious and lying, brilliantly achieving this by seeming genuine but being duplicitous – a terrifying suggestion in the particular context of this dialogue, of course. He concludes, 'And on that account, just as in the preceding vices, come to my aid in this fault also, and please delicately draw over it some veil devised by your keen mind, and whatever the purport of your proposal demands, I offer myself with all my resources for its implementation'.[58] Shocked for a while into a stunned silence, Macduff then responds with a series of apostrophes on the misery of the country, which now confronts three potential horrors: that its men must lose wives and children and undergo exile; or serve an avaricious and usurping tyrant in Macbeth; or serve the legal king, who has all these terrible vices. Finding the last two notions intolerable, he claims he will choose banishment – at which point Malcolm intervenes. But it takes, in fact, quite a long speech for Malcolm to convince Macduff, who then replies with exultation but still with a slight degree of doubt, 'If what you say is indeed true you restore me from death to life'.[59] The resolution to this scene, as in Boece, Bellenden and Holinshed, and the many versions of it between them and Fordun, is a rapid reconciling embrace. But the strong moment of doubt that Shakespeare's Macduff expresses at the end of the dialogue, 'Such welcome and unwelcome things at once/Tis hard to reconcile' (138–9) has its emotional precedent in the original version of the scene.

What should now be clear is that although, as we shall see, there are other candidates for the source of the revised form of this scene in the printed version of Bellenden's translation, there are very close similarities between the structure and character of the Fordun/Bower rendition and that in the revised Bellenden. In that rendition the exempla from antiquity are cut out and the Boethian fox fable is retained, but in order of dialogue, disposition of vices, and particular details the scene now unmistakably resembles the earlier Latin chronicle versions. In both versions Macduff now responds to the first two vices by promising Malcolm that he will be able to indulge them once king. And notably only here in the Bellenden print and in Fordun/Bower does Malcolm conclude his litany of corruption with the request that Macduff aid him by further concealing the vice of deceit as he has concealed all the others – a detail that of course goes through to Holinshed. Macduff's contrasting of the terrible options of Macbeth's tyranny or Malcolm's treachery is also appropriated from Fordun, though in Bellenden Malcolm's vice now has the added slur of being of a particularly English complexion. As we noted earlier, one particularly striking detail that is now lost from the Bellenden manuscript version is Macduff's suggestion, inherited from Boece, that he and his friends should have the running of the kingdom on Malcolm's behalf. We shall need to consider the full implications of this below.

It seems extremely likely then that it is from a manuscript of either the *Chronica Gentis Scotorum* or the *Scotichronicon* that the reviser of the printed edition of Bellenden's *Chronicle* got his material. There are two other possible sources that could have been consulted in the revision, but both may be reasonably briefly and easily discounted. The earlier is the version of the scene in book 6 of Andrew Wyntoun's *Original Chronicle* of Scotland, composed during the 1420s.[60] Because some of Wyntoun's Macbeth material is not found elsewhere earlier than his chronicle, he is often deemed to be drawing on popular sources independent of (among others) Fordun,[61] but his rendition of this particular scene reads like a highly abbreviated form of Fordun's. The construction of the dialogue and the nature of the vices is the same, but there is little of the reflective quality of Malcolm and Macduff's remarks, writ large in Fordun/Bower and still present in Bellenden, and none of the direct parallels that we have already noted. The scene between the two men is altogether gruffer and far more condensed.

The other candidates is the version in John Mair's *Historia*, a work we have already seen consulted and cited in the revised Bellenden. Mair also treats the scene in a highly compressed manner, but he does have the three-fold catalogue of vices in the right order, though the disposition of speeches is different. This version is short enough for the core of it to be quoted:

> Malcolm ... declared that for three reasons he should prove himself an unserviceable king: first of all, that he was by nature voluptuous, and by consequence would deal wantonly with the daughters and (what is much greater wrong) the wives of the nobility; secondly, that he was avaricious, and would covet all men's goods. To these two objections Macduff makes answer: 'In the kingdom of Scotland, all northern and cold though it be, you shall find a wife, the fairest you will, who shall alone suffice for your needs. There is no prince, whether in England or Scotland, who will not readily give you his daughter in marriage. And for avarice, you shall use as your own the whole possessions of the realm; and there is nothing that the people will deny you if you but ask it in the way of love and with no desire for strife.' To all this Malcolm then made yet a third

objection, saying, 'I am a liar, a man of deceit, unstable in all my ways.' And then to him Macduff is said to have made this answer, 'Dregs of the race of man, begone; begone you monster among men – unfit for any realm.' [62]

The reconciliation then follows as usual. Here, then, Macduff does not make his response until the first two vices have been set out (something Mair's scene actually shares with Boece and the earlier version of Bellenden); and he proposes coping with them not by a process of pragmatic adaptation to the situation, as in Boece and the earlier Bellenden, but by eradicating them through marriage – the English and Scottish context here nicely bringing in Mair's particular hobbyhorse of Anglo-Scottish union – or by a generous relationship between king and people. Boece or Bellenden could certainly have consulted Mair for the revision to the scene in the printed Bellenden, but it is abundantly clear that the dominant influence upon that revision was a manuscript of the *Chronica Gentis Scotorum* or the *Scotichronicon*.

This brings us back once more to the question of whose hand is at work in the revision. A copy of the *Chronica Gentis Scotorum* owned by Boece survives, and it and the *Scotichronicon* were of course sources for the *Scotorum Historia*.[63] But we have already noticed references to *Scotichronicon*, if not wholly truthful ones, in parts of Bellenden's translation that have a good likelihood of having originated with the translator.

It is here perhaps that the intermediary manuscript recension of the translation may be of help. A consistent element in manuscripts in this intermediary group between the presentation manuscript and the print is two particular additions to the earlier version (that is, before the scene is radically revised for the print), within a couple of sentences of each other. One, however, gets through to the final printed version; the other does not. The first is the one that does: Malcolm's remarks at the end of the fox and flies fable are extended by a clause, 'and think the displeseir now regnand amang yow ar bot small in respect of sic terrible outragis quhilkis sall appeir sone be my cuming'.[64]

This in fact looks like an effort to express in more extended (if not still absolutely accurate) form the sentiments of the Latin original.[65] The second addition, however, is particular only to the revised manuscripts and does not go through to the print, and thus expands the original version which was soon to be so dramatically restructured. The passage in question extends Macduff's response to the narration of the first two of Malcolm's confessed crimes. In the earlier manuscript account he responds, 'Howbeit thir maneris be repugnant to ane prince, yite mak thi self King of Scotland, and latt me and vther thi freyndis haif the administracioun therof'.[66] As was noted earlier, Bellenden's rendering is already more dramatic here than its Latin original by the use of direct rather than indirect speech. In the revised manuscripts Macduff is now given a further comment: 'and we sall dress all materis sa prudentlie that all thir vices salbe hide'.[67] There is really no precedent in the original Latin for this addition, though it is certainly in keeping with the tenor of Macduff's approach to the issue. What it does is to heighten the ambiguity of the presentation of Macduff by assigning to him a willingness to dissemble which is clearly corrupt even within the context of the removal of the tyrant Macbeth. It could also, of course, suggest that what matters in kingship is less the kingly individual exercise of power than the presence of a king as a focus for an administration composed by the political community. As we have several times noted, this alternative is not posited in the final version. Rather, the emphasis on the cloaking of vices there is Malcolm's: the king wants the help of his magnates in this respect rather than their running of the country in his stead.

What we can see here is that after the first manuscript version there was some move towards revising the original rendition, along lines which could have been a response to an initiative from either Boece or Bellenden, since in both cases there is precedent in the original Latin for what is then developed. But in the second example, the precedent is in the sentiments expressed rather than in the actual words of the Latin itself, and thus is possibly more likely to have originated with the translator Bellenden. Between this revision and the print, however, a major alteration takes place, in which the first piece of that material is admitted and the second dropped, but in which the scene is also given a dramatically different character because of the powerful influence of extraneous and new source material. Fine tuning is replaced by substantial rewriting. The source is not signalled here as it is in some of the other additions which we can assign with confidence to Bellenden, but the revisions take the text further away from the Latin original in a manner that is consistent with the recasting we can see to have been most probably at his initiative.[68]

At this point the dramatic and political character of the recast scene should also be considered. One of the most conspicuous formal distinctions between the manuscript and printed versions may also have some ideological bearing to it. In the printed version the disposition of speeches between the two protagonists achieves a much greater balance. Malcolm's accounts of his vices are virtually matched in length by Macduff's response to them, and his intervening, medial example of the fox fable is matched by Macduff's longish added speech reviling the corruption of both Macbeth and Malcolm. Moreover, both speakers recognise the cumulatively worse quality of the catalogue that Malcolm presents, and Macduff on the first two occasions draws attention to the prevalence of these failings amongst kings and in Scotland, in a manner that keeps step with Malcolm's own appreciation of their profound inappropriateness to kingly rule. Both men, however, are apparently willing to take on board lechery and avarice as part of Malcolm's kingly baggage. But we have also observed that in this later version detail that would implicate Macduff more fully in this is now omitted: it is Malcolm who requests that his final vice be cloaked, rather than Macduff volunteering to rule with friends in his stead and hide the presence of these vices in their king. The highly intelligent and in its own way quite chilling blending of Boece and Fordun is nowhere better pointed up than in the way in which in the printed version of Bellenden the sentiments on the values necessary for good kingship and the vices antithetical to it are firstly relocated from before to after the fox fable, secondly revised to a balanced group of three virtues and three vices, and thirdly linked up with the Fordunian request that Macduff and his friends assist with the concealment of this foulest vice with the others: 'And sen na thing semis mair ane prince than constance, verite, and justice; and nathing sa unsemand as falset, treason, and lesingis: thow may consider how unabil I am to govern ony province or cuntre. And sen thow hes sa mony rameidis to colour all the laif of my vicis, I pray ye to hide or colour this vice amang the laif.'[69]

The effect of these changes is several fold. The sense of kingly rule as predicated on an accord between king and political community, of whom Macduff is the representative, is increased; but the emphasis on the responsibilities of the monarch is also heightened. The idea of tokenism in kingly rule is not admitted – rather it is horror of the idea of a country without a strong and judicious ruler that is emphasised in Macduff's concluding remarks.

Let us remember that the precedent for that speech lies in Fordun's *Chronica Gentis Scotorum*. Writing during the opening years of the Stewart dynasty, against a backdrop of civil and English wars only recently resolved, Fordun made a powerful case for unifying judicious kingship, a case no less relevant during Bower's revision of this work into the *Scotichronicon* during the disrupted years of James II's minority rule in the 1440s.[70]

Whereas Boece's *Scotorum Historia* had been dedicated to a king who was also very much still in his minority in 1527, by the time Bellenden's translation was being produced and revised during the mid-1530s that same king, James V, was 'now effectively and vigorously in power.'[71] Those adjectives, however, should remind us of another recurrent feature of active Stewart rule: all the kings who bore the names of James were characterised by an assertive mature rule that at its worst could lead to conflict with the political community, as it did perhaps most memorably with James III. The complexion that is given to this recast scene participates in the sense of a number of possibilities available in kingship: tyranny, treachery, strikingly evoked now in terms that bring in an English connection, or a good kingship that looks, as Bellenden puts it towards the 'common weil'.[72] The removal from the printed versions of that idea of a kind of regency run by Macduff and his friends in Malcolm's stead that had featured in Boece's Latin and been extended in Bellenden's MS revisions, has an acquired but ambiguous relevance here as well. It removes the suggestion that magnates might push a little bit too far into the reaches of kingly power – something that James V would, after all, be sensitive too given the struggle with the Douglases at the end of his minority. Once more this could reflect the fine balancing political act that a Douglas supporter such as Bellenden had to make. It also places even more explicitly on the king the responsibility for the harmony of the realm. The positive outcome of the Malcolm/Macduff encounter here should not obscure the fact that, together with the pronounced element of dissembling in this scene, this sense of the equally great potential in kingship for tyranny or virtuous rule makes it a remarkably disturbing one, and in this instance it would seem unwise to suggest that the concern of the printed edition is (as it has been argued to be in relation to the presentation of Bruce) to 'resolve ... the ambiguities in Boece's account'.[73] Rather it seems – at either Boece or Bellenden's behest – to draw them out in a manner that heightens the element of potentiality for good or evil in Scottish kingship.

This is possibly why it appealed to the compilers of Holinshed's Scottish chronicle who, as we have seen, are following here the printed Scots translation by Bellenden rather than the Latin original of Boece which was apparently also available to them. Perhaps one reason why the compilers, if they compared Boece and Bellenden, would have found Bellenden's version of the scene acceptable is that they could check its elements elsewhere. 'Iohannes Fordon' is one of the authors cited in the prefatory material as having been consulted[74] – this would have to have been in manuscript, of course, but, given that the *Chronica Gentis Scotorum* or the *Scotichronicon* still survive in a fair number of copies it is not impossible that the compilers did indeed read one of the best known Scottish chronicles rather than merely citing its author for authenticating effect.

The compilers, moreover, did not for this scene make recourse to other Scottish sources either cited in the prefatory material or known to have been additionally consulted. This goes for both the 1577 and 1587 editions of Holinshed, in which the episode remains unchanged, and means that, in addition to discounting the version which we have already seen from John Mair's *Historia*, the revisers of 1587 also chose to ignore the version given in George Buchanan's *Rerum Scoticarum Historia* which had been published in 1582.[75] Like several of its predecessors, Buchanan's treatment of the scene is concise in comparison to Bellenden and particularly Fordun. It reads in fact like a condensed amalgam of Mair and Boece. Like Mair, he has Macduff suggest that 'licentious desire after variety might be counteracted by a lawful marriage',[76] but the slightly more extended exposition of dishonesty that follows this looks more indebted to Boece or Bellenden.

In preferring the Bellenden version of the scene the compilers of Holinshed were surely also responding to the fact that it is by far the most narratively dramatic version of those available. The debt to Bellenden is also there in the run-up to the exchange between the two men. Readers of Holinshed would know, as they read, and as Bellenden's readers had known, that Macduff has come to England distraught at the ravaging of Scotland by Macbeth which has included the murder of his own family; they also know that Malcolm's purpose is to test Macduff's loyalty and sincerity. But within this framework, as we have seen, Malcolm is made to seem to desire the throne even while perceiving the full profundity of his depravity; and Macduff, until his breaking-point is reached, urges him on to that desire even while acknowledging the dangerous character of the vices Malcolm describes. It is to these potential ambiguities, created primarily for Holinshed by the fusion of Bellenden and Fordun, that Shakespeare so powerfully reacts in his own revision of this scene. To say, as is so often said, that Holinshed is just working from Bellenden's Boece here, is to miss the signal point of the suggestively hybrid nature of the recasting of the scene in the printed edition of Bellenden.

The transformation of this scene from chronicle to drama imparts one decisive change to it. Chroniclers can set up the way to read an episode in advance by outlining the motivation of the protagonists, as we have just seen in relation to both Bellenden and Holinshed. In Shakespeare's *Macbeth* we are deprived of that assurance. Certainly the course of the drama thus far is strongly to suggest that Malcolm and Macduff are, as it were, to be trusted. The spectator of the play, moreover, approaches this scene with knowledge that neither of its two protagonists possesses – that Macduff's wife and children have just been massacred by Macbeth's men. Malcolm and Macduff are thus linked in a manner of which they are as yet unaware by both having had their families savaged by the tyrant. But that very detail imparts a degree of ambiguity to the presentation of Macduff, as witnessed by Malcolm's early question to him 'Why in that rawness left you wife and child/(Those precious motives, those strong knots of love),/Without leave-taking?' (26–8), the question which Macduff notoriously does not directly answer.[77] As a young man deprived of a parent himself, Malcolm is doubly aware, clearly, of the predicament of fatherless children, but his anxiety here is of a piece with an ambiguity, an element of doubt in his own presentation in this part of the play. Malcolm is not only young, he is also unwilling for action. His opening remark in the scene, 'Let us seek out some desolate shade, and there/Weep our sad bosoms empty' (1–2), is immediately contrasted with Macduff's more willing and active 'Let us rather/Hold fast the mortal sword, and like good men/Bestride our downfall birthdom' (3–5). It is possible to see this scene as charting a kind of coming of age in Malcolm, but it remains the case that the full expression of his successful monarchy remains a potential rather than an achieved one in the play.

In his version of the dialogue, Shakespeare makes the first two vices to which Malcolm 'confesses' lechery and avarice as before, and has Macduff respond to them in turn. As we have noted, on one level the debts to Holinshed are conspicuous. Even here, however, the tenor can be altered. Shakespeare's Macduff's 'We have willing dames enough; there cannot be/That vulture in you, to devour so many/As will to greatness dedicate themselves,/Finding it so inclined' (73–6) puts a slightly different and that bit still more unattractive gloss on the provision of women for Malcolm than Holinshed's briefer 'nevertheless there are women enow in Scotland and therefore follow my counsell'.[78] And in the Shakespearean version, moreover, the third vice to which Malcolm admits is not simply lying and deceit but a massive rejection of all the kingly virtues and a gleefully destructive criminality which would 'confound/All unity on earth' (98–9). Within this narration the fox fable is omitted. And Shakespeare does not have Malcolm volunteer to take on the kingdom in quite the same way – a point to which we shall return. In omitting the fox fable and having Macduff fall silent and then still seem uncertain at the end of the episode, Shakespeare unknowingly actually restores to the scene outlines and details it had in Fordun.[79] This is an interesting comment on his aesthetic sense – the fox fable is actually the most extraneous element in Bellenden and Holinshed, and Shakespeare manifestly felt it to be so.

But as radical is the new context in which this episode is situated.

The scene has a kind of double envelope structure to it. We have already remarked that the Macduff family murder precedes it but is unknown to Macduff; it thus indeed also succeeds it, as the scene ends with the revelation of that massacre to Macduff. In between comes the exchange with the doctor about Edward the Confessor's healing of scrofula. Within that framework are also Macduff's two farewells to Malcolm. For Macduff's actual response to the question about abandoning his family is to take it as an accusation of treachery and to bid farewell to his country in terms similar to those in which he will react to the revelation of Malcolm's own treachery (31–7; cf, 103–13). These structural doublings heighten our sense in this scene of not knowing quite how to judge either man, whether they are completely as they say themselves to be.

Another aspect to this reshaping has been well put by Goldberg:

> [When] one looks to the most apparently straightforward scene of
> the transmission of source – the recasting of Holinshed's conversa-
> tion between Macduff and Malcolm ... what one discovers is that
> something has come between the source and the scene. What blocks
> the way of transmission is the text of *Macbeth* itself: Malcolm and
> Macduff repeatedly echo words and phrases that have come before,
> words most often heard in Macbeth's mouth.[80]

It has been perceptively remarked by Norbrook that 'it is only by modelling himself on Macbeth's own strategies of dissimulation that [Malcolm] can prove Macduff's virtue'.[81] But it is also the case, to bring these points together, that Malcolm can only define himself as one who should *not* be king by again defining himself in relation to Macbeth – as worse than Macbeth, in a reversal of the traditional notion that the good subject defines his virtues in relation to those of the king. Here in another extension of the potential of the source, Shakespeare has Malcolm attribute to Macbeth all those vices to which he says he himself is more severely prone. The notion that these abuses exist in Malcolm gains credibility precisely because he declares them to be present in the known tyrant. Thus the point that has troubled scholars about the lack of evidence of Macbeth's lecherousness in the play is much less important than the fact that Malcolm claims his own manifestation of the vice to be so appalling in comparison to it.[82] And there is in Malcolm's assimilation of himself to Macbeth's vices something very troubling. The speech in which Malcolm eventually reveals his honesty to Macduff contains the statement, 'my first false speaking/Was this upon myself' (130–1). He is not what he has said himself to be – but he has also potentially taken a step towards it in this first false speaking. For

Malcolm is an untried ruler and an inexperienced man: 'I am yet/ Unknown to woman; never was forsworn' (125–6). In this, his most dominant scene in the play, he gives us an idea of what he is, only immediately to take it away again, and to leave his full potential as something felt to be good but never fully defined in the manner in which his fictitious evil self has been set out. Moreover, his definition of himself, 'What I am truly,/Is thine, and my poor country's to command' (131–2), is a statement of his willingness virtuousness, but also of a certain lack of assertiveness. This is a point that is perhaps also hinted at in the way in which Shakespeare replaces Holinshed's Malcolm's request to be given the throne as a corrupt ruler (the detail that goes back to Fordun) with a different kind of question, 'If such a one be fit to govern, speak' (101–2).

Macduff's 'Such welcome and unwelcome things at once/Tis hard to reconcile' (138–9) leaves indeed the whole episode on the verge of being unreconciled, leaves Malcolm, as it were, still undefined, poised between good and bad kingship, his own 'Well, more anon' (139) apparently accepting Macduff's authority to leave the matter unfinished. The problem of how it is to be resolved is not coped with in the traditional manner of the according embrace, established by Fordun and marked in all versions up to Holinshed, but rather through a less conclusive conjunction of plot and symbol. As Macduff and Malcolm prepare to leave the matter alone the doctor appears with the description of the off-stage healing powers of kingship, in the form of Edward the Confessor. This is then followed by Ross's miserable embassy with the news of the murders. Malcolm at first seems not to recognise Ross, which editors have found odd [83] – not least, perhaps because he so obviously recognises him in Act I, scene II – but the moment has a rather symbolic character, as Malcolm seems not quite to appreciate the full weight of his kingly responsibilities, the need for his own assertiveness. But his reaction to the fact of the murders, the prospect of which he had earlier associated with Macduff's possible treachery, is to respond with a new decisiveness: 'Be comforted:/Let's make us medicines of our great revenge/To cure this deadly grief' (213–14). The allusion to medicines picks up the idea of the healing powers of royalty just seen in the English king,[84] as plot and symbol now come together to carry the scene on to a conclusion in which Malcolm assumes some maturity: 'This tune goes manly./Come, go we to the King [highly ironic, of course]: our power is ready' (235–6). He is ready at last, but the embrace that marks the reconciliation of the scene in Holinshed and his predecessors is still not there; events, rather than debate, have forced the resolution.

Why should that be? A fully working, successful Scottish king is not figured in *Macbeth*. Duncan is good but deceivable, and is murdered. Macbeth is a tyrannous usurper. Malcolm is potentially a good king, but also potentially not one, and he is still not king at the play's end, which marks the prospect of his coronation, but not its actuality. It is often observed, as we noted earlier, that Shakespeare ignores Holinshed's depicting (inherited from Bellenden) of Macbeth as more of a mixture of a ruler, as a figure capable of just government after the removal of Duncan for as long as ten years, before lapsing into tyranny.[85] Shakespeare makes him more immediately corruptible and tyrannical. But something perhaps of the sense in this part of Holinshed, of no one Scottish kingly figure encapsulating what good kingship should be, comes out in a play in which assertiveness is at times more associated with Macbeth and Macduff, and goodness but possibly also weakness and fallibility associated with Duncan and Malcolm.

None of these kings was of course James VI and I's ancestor. But the play does also contain Banquo, the originator of the Stewart dynasty invented by Boece in the *Scotorum Historia*. Yet Banquo too is a figure murdered in the play, and his son Fleance, from whom the Stewart line was said to come down, an even less realised figure than Malcolm. But that very point is one to pause on. For James VI does of course himself appear in *Macbeth*, as one of the eight kings descending from Banquo whom the witches make appear to Macbeth in IV, I. The idea for this surely comes from Holinshed's own description of how the Stewart line came to descend from Fleance.[86] In this respect, Shakespeare's figuring of James VI has its own ambiguity. For James, whose political writings insisted so much on the value of divine right and hereditary kingship, is depicted in the play as descending from a man who was not himself king. For all the play's overt concern to assert the reimposition of order and the just removal of tyranny, for all its apparent endorsement of the Stewart line in Macbeth's recoil from the apparition of a dynasty that so crushes his desires – 'Horrible sight!' (122) – James's own origins are associated with a period of chaos and uncertainty, and in which the potential for good to turn bad or be otherwise removed seems marked.

The first version of *Macbeth* was composed in 1606, that is within a few years of James I's assumption of his English throne.[87] As a play, it clearly manifests many anxieties about the capacity of rulers to go in the direction of tyranny, for power remorselessly to corrupt;[88] the idea of a Scottish king, of a presence known but also unfamiliar, gave Shakespeare perhaps the opportunity to figure those questions with some sharpness. But if in this respect the play articulated concerns about the nature of James I's kingship in England and provided a corrective anti-type for him in the figure of Macbeth, it is hardly the case that Malcolm, the new Scottish king at the play's conclusion is a wholly endorsed figure. Nor should it be assumed that such anxieties were only those of James's new English subjects. As we have found in analysing this scene, these concerns have their roots in the Scottish historiographical and advice to princes tradition itself. Had he been aware, or more aware of that, Shakespeare would not probably have been displeased by it. For he altogether omits the comment by Macduff that in Holinshed is inherited from the printed version of Bellenden, that Malcolm 'is so replet with the inconstant behaviour and manifest vices of Englishmen, that he is nothing woorthie to inioy [the crown]'.[89] To suggest that these vices were English was not Shakespeare's project. To situate them in Scotland was not, quite, to suggest that they were Scottish, but it drew attention to their Scottish heritage. In 1606 James was still a relatively new king in England – hardly a Malcolm figure, nor indeed a Macbeth one; but still to his English subjects a relatively untried one, and one who had, after all, shown the characteristically ambiguous Stewart assertiveness in much of his Scottish rule. In its mixed Scottish and English heritage 'the dullest scene in the play' is in fact the key to its political importance.

1. M. C. Bradbrook, 'The Sources of *Macbeth*', *Shakespeare Survey*, 4 (Cambridge, 1951), 35–48 (36). Rptd (as 'The Origins of *Macbeth*') in *Shakespeare: Macbeth*, ed. J. Wain, Casebook Series (rev. edn, 1994), pp. 236–57.

2. *Macbeth*, ed. K. Muir (1984), p. 122; see also the comments in the revised introduction, pp. lxiii-lxiv. Quotation is from this edition.

3. L. Mackinnon, *Shakespeare the Aesthete: An Exploration of Literary Theory* (1988), p. 280. Compare A. F. Kinney's description of the scene as 'the crucial scene of the play', in 'Scottish History, the Union of the Crowns and the Issue of Right Rule: The Case of Shakespeare's *Macbeth*', in *Renaissance Culture in Context: Theory and Practice*, ed. J. R. Brink and W. F. Gentrup (1993), pp. 18–53 (42), and 'once thought disgressive and expendable, but actually the core of the tragedy', 'Rehistoricising *Macbeth*', in *Sacred and Profane: Secular and Devotional Interplay in Early Modern British Literature*, ed. H. Wilcox, R. Todd and A. MacDonald (Amsterdam, 1996), pp. 93–103 (102).

4. The best analyses of the ideological context of the play are by David Norbrook, '*Macbeth* and the Politics of Historiography', in *Politics of Discourse: the literature and history of seventeenth-century England*, ed. K. Sharpe and S. N. Zwicker (Berkeley, 1987), pp. 78–116, though even here the scene receives compressed discussion (111), and Kinney, 'Scottish History', pp. 42–9. For more extended consideration of it see A. Sinfield, '"Macbeth": History, Ideology and Intellectuals', in (ed.) *Macbeth*, New Casebooks (1992), pp. 121–35 (128–30; rptd from *Critical Quarterly*, 28 (1986) 63–77); J. Goldberg, 'Speculations: "Macbeth" and Source' in Sinfield (ed.), *Macbeth*, pp. 92–107 (longer

version in *Shakespeare Reproduced*, ed. J. E. Howard and M. F. O'Connor, 1987, pp. 242–64).

5. For very different interpretations of the significance of the act and Malcolm's enquiry see Bradbrook, 36 (another reference to the Second World War), and Goldberg, 104; also Kinney, 'Rehistoricising *Macbeth*', 98.

6. Norbrook and Goldberg, as n. 4; Bradbrook also argues that this scene is one of the *'political* highlights of the play' (39). A more specific explanation for Malcolm's allusions at 97–100 to concord, peace and unity is offered by H. N. Paul in *The Royal Play of Macbeth* (New York, 1950), pp. 359–66. For other, still largely generalised interpretations, see the comments in Muir, pp. lxii–lxiv. Earlier generations of critics were often bothered by Malcolm's attribution to Macbeth (58) of the vices of lechery and avarice, characteristics not evidently demonstrated by him in the play. See e.g. the comments by A. C. Bradley (from *Shakespearean Tragedy*) and G. Wilson Knight in Wain, pp. 125, 155. A more politicised interpretation of this element is argued in Kinney, 'Scottish History', pp. 43–7.

7. G. Bullough, *Narrative and Dramatic Sources of Shakespeare*, vol. 7 (1973), p. 447. Citation in this essay from the 1587 edition of *Holinshed's Chronicles* is from H. Ellis's 1808 edition (vol. 5), hereafter Holinshed. Reference to the 1577 edition is given in the form Holinshed (1577). 'Holinshed' should be understood here as a collective term for the various collaborators and revisers who, as Annabel Patterson has demonstrated, were involved in the project along with Raphael Holinshed from its origins but particularly in relation to the 1587 edition: *Reading Holinshed's Chronicles* (Chicago and London, 1994). The prime reviser of the Scottish material for the later edition was Francis Thynne. For the argument that Shakespeare also knew and was influenced by the illustrations in the 1577 edition of Holinshed, Kinney, 'Scottish History', pp. 28–41.

8. Bullough, pp. 438–40, on detail; on Shakespeare's reception of Buchanan's arguments against hereditary succession and Thynne's ambiguous response to Buchanan see Norbrook, pp. 80–2, 87–93, 102–3, Patterson, pp. 36–7.

9. See e.g. the comments by Nicholas Brooke in (ed.) *The Tragedy of Macbeth* (Oxford, 1990), 'Shakespeare derived the dialogue between Malcolm and Macduff from Holinshed's second major digression ... where [Holinshed] found it I do not know', p. 70.

10. Holinshed, p. 275.

11. The Scottish texts most frequently cited (after Buchanan) as possible sources are William Stewart's *Buik of the Chroniclis of Scotland*, an often very free verse translation of Boece's *Scotorum Historia* (completed in 1535 and surviving in one sixteenth-century manuscript ed. William B. Turnbull, Rolls Series, 3 vols, 1858); and John Lesley's Latin chronicle *De Origine Scotorum*, published in 1578. In neither case can borrowing be definitely proven. See the discussion in Bullough, pp. 438 and 441, and Muir (ed.), pp. xxxix–xli.

12. Hector Boece, *Scotorum Historiae a prima gentis origine cum aliarum et rerum et gentium illustratione non vulgari* (Paris, 1527); *Scotorum Historiae ... libri xix. Hectore Boethio Deidonano auctore. Duo postremi huius Historiae libri nunc primum emittuntur in lucem. Accessit & huic editioni eiusdem Scotorum Historiae continuatio, per Ionnaem Ferrerium Pedemontanum* (Paris, 1574). The most recent studies are N. R. Royan, 'The *Scotorum Historia* of Hector Boece: A Study' (unpublished D.Phil thesis, University of Oxford, 1996), and J. H. Burns, *The True Law of Kingship: Concepts of Monarchy in Early Modern Scotland* (Oxford, 1996), pp. 75–92.

13. *Croniklis of Scotland with the cosmography and dyscription thairof, compilit by the noble clerek maister Hector Boece, chanoune of Aberdene, translatit laitly in our vulgar and common language be maister John Bellenden* (Edinburgh ?1540; facsimile edition,

English Experience 851, Amsterdam and Norwood NJ, 1977). The precise dating of the printed edition (or editions, as there may have been more than one issued) remains unclear. See Sheppard in Bellenden, *Chronicles* (STS), II, pp. 441–3. The most recent (and slightly normalised) edition is by T. Maitland, 2 vols, Edinburgh, 1821. Quotation of the printed text is from this edition, henceforth Bellenden, *Chronicles* (1821). The first version of the translation was completed in 1531. The Scottish Text Society edition is from a manuscript of this version: *The Chronicles of Scotland compiled by Hector Boece, translated into Scots by John Bellenden 1531*, ed. R. W. Chambers, E. C. Batho, and H. Winifred Husbands, STS, 2 vols, Edinburgh and London, 1938–41, henceforth Bellenden, *Chronicles* (STS).

The most detailed survey of manuscripts of Bellenden's translation of Boece remains the part of E. A. Sheppard's doctoral thesis, 'Studies in the Language of Bellenden's Boece' (University of London, 1937) that was not published in the appendix to the STS edition of the *Chronicles*. Sheppard discusses the nine MS then known: (i) New York, Pierpont Morgan Library, now M 527, *c.* 1531–3 (M); (ii) Auchinleck, now University College London, MS Angl. 1, *c.* 1533 (A); (iii) Trinity College Cambridge MS O.3.21, *c.* 1533 (C); (iv) the Bath MS, *c.* 1537, still at Longleat (B); (v) the Scottish Record Office MS, now RH 13/10, late sixteenth century (R); (vi) Edinburgh University Library MS Laing III. 205, a late sixteenth-century copy of M (L); (vii) National Library of Scotland MS Adv. 33.4.15, an early seventeenth-century copy of A or a MS closely resembling it (E); (viii) the Brown MS, now NLS MS 5288, possibly copied from the print and with a continuation from Lindsay of Pitscottie's chronicle to 1565 (the NLS catalogue notes, however, that 'in places it differs substantially from other texts'); (ix) the Neilson MS, now NLS MS 2766, copied in 1641 from the printed text, with a continuation from Holinshed's *Chronicle* and Robert Burel's diary up to 1594 (N).

Sheppard's researches demonstrated that of the MSS surviving there were five with considerable independence, 'of which M represents the translator's first version, and C, B, A, and R, different stages in the revision of his work. C is appreciably nearer to M than the rest of the MSS ... MSS R and A are very closely allied; and B is in many respects similar to these. All three represent a further stage in the revision, which reaches its final stage in D[avidson] ... Of all the MSS, R and A approach most closely to D[avidson]. Of the final stage of the revision, however, no MS copies seem to have been made or at least none survive' (pp. 142–3). These comments occasionally need some qualification. My limited researches suggest that A is often closer to the print than R, which does not always follow it. See for instance note 43, below.

Two further MSS in the National Library of Scotland, should now be added to this list: (x) MS 3146, a mid-seventeenth century copy, earlier thought to derive from a printed edition, but the NLS catalogue entry for (xi) below, states that it probably derives from one of the manuscript recensions. It should be noted that its version of the Malcolm/Macduff interview (fol. 279^r) is incomplete, though the text here more closely resembles that of the printed edition; (xi) MS 21244, copied in 1636 possibly from the print, but according to the NLS catalogue with substantial differences from it (the Malcolm/Macduff interview, fols 274^v–5^r is as the print).

Another scholar who did considerable work on the MSS of Bellenden's *Chronicle* was Denton Fox, whose interest in them related to Bellenden's poetry, and who thus also consulted other MSS containing versions or parts of the *Ballat apone the translatione; Proheme of the History*, and *Proheme of the Cosmographe* not listed here. I am grateful to Mrs Priscilla Bawcutt for allowing me to see Professor Fox's notes on this material.

14. Neither Bullough nor Muir, for example, tackle this question. For a recent suggestion by a Scottish scholar that Shakespeare could have gone directly to Boece or

Bellenden for some details in the play (particularly in relation to Lady Macbeth) see Kenneth D. Farrow, 'The Historiographical Evolution of the Macbeth Narrative', *SLJ*, 21 (1994), 5–23 (esp. 12–13). On the scarcity of copies of Bellenden's translation, however, see n. 15, below.

15. Paul (pp. 209–12) claims that Holinshed asked William Harrison to translate Boece into English, but that Harrison worked from Bellenden's translation. In fact Harrison's dedication to the Scottish part of Holinshed's *Chronicle* makes it clear that what he translated was Bellenden's 'description of Scotland' as a preface to the Scottish chronicle, on the model of his work for the English one. However, Harrison's remarks in his preface to the Description of Scotland also indicate that while Boece was readily available and well known, Bellenden's translation had received far less circulation (*The Historie of Scotland*, pp. v–vi): 'How excellentlie if you consider the art, Boetius hath penned it, and the rest of his historie in Latine, the skilfull are not ignorant: but how profitablie and compendiouslie Iohn Bellenden archdeacon of Murrey his interpretor hath turned him from the Latine into the Scotish toong, there are verie few Englishmen that know, bicause we want the books.' There is, regrettably, no discussion of Boece or Bellenden as sources for Holinshed's *Chronicles* in Patterson; rather she mistakenly asserts that Major was Holinshed's 'one primary authority' (p. 57). For a detailed account of the relation of Harrison and Holinshed's work see also Stephen Booth, *The Book Called Holinshed's Chronicle* (San Francisco, 1958), pp. 28–31.

16. See the discussion of the differences between the MS and printed texts in Bellenden *Chronicles* (STS) I, pp. x–xii and II, pp. 435–49 (appendix by E. A. Sheppard) and two articles with the same title by R. W. Chambers and Walter W. Seton, 'Bellenden's Translation of the History of Hector Boece', *SHR*, 17 (1920) 5–15, and 19 (1922), 196–201. As noted in n. 13, the most detailed comparative discussion is in Sheppard's thesis.

17. See the essay by Nicola Royan ('The Relationship between the *Scotorum Historia* of Hector Boece and John Bellenden's *Chronicles of Scotland*') in this volume, pp. 136–57.

18. Bullough, p. 436.

19. For the background to this story and other Scottish examples, see Farrow, 18–19.

20. *Scotorum Historia*, book 12, fols cc[x]lxii–cc[x]lxiv (the folios are incorrectly numbered for these pages). For a text and translation see the appendix to this essay. I am grateful to Dr Doreen Innes and Dr Nicola Royan for advice on this translation.

21. Holinshed, p. 275.

22. Ibid., p. 276.

23. For descriptions of the MS see Chambers and Batho in Bellenden, *Chronicles* (STS) I, pp. viii–ix, and (with more detail) Sheppard, 'Studies', pp. 109–16.

24. Bellenden, *Chronicles* (STS), II, p. 160. Bellenden of course has also divided Boece's books into chapters, and this scene is taking place in chapter 7.

25. Bellenden, *Chronicles* (1821), vol. 2, p. 271.

26. Ibid., p. 272.

27. Ibid.

28. Ibid.

29. Bellenden, *Chronicles* (STS), II, p. 439 and (1821), vol. 1 p. cxii; and cf. Sheppard's comments in *Chronicles* (STS), II, pp. 440–3, and Royan, 'The Relationship', p. 136–7.

30. Sheppard, in Bellenden, *Chronicles* (STS), II, p. 441. It is sometimes also suggested that the printer Thomas Davidson may have been involved in 'modifying and "popularising" the opinions of both the "first compilar" and his "translatoure"' and this is certainly worthy further investigation. The comment here is Sheppard's (Bellenden, *Chronicles* (STS), II, pp. 442–3). See also Royan, 'The Relationship', p. 144.

31. Sheppard, in Bellenden, *Chronicles* (STS), II, p. 440.

32. Chambers and Seton, 'Bellenden's Translation' (1922), 199; cf. Chambers and Batho in Bellenden, *Chronicles* (STS), I, p. x. See also n. 68 below.

33. See Royan, 'The Relationship', pp. 138–9; Sheppard, in Bellenden, *Chronicles* (STS), II, pp. 448–60. Some corrections to Sheppard's remarks on the revisions to the *Proheme* are to be found in the unpublished notes by Fox cited in n. 13, above.

34. Bellenden, *Chronicles* (STS), II, p. 267; Royan, 'The Relationship', p. 152.

35. University College London, MS. Angl. 1, fol. 283ᵛ. I am grateful to the Librarian of University College London Library for permission to quote from this MS. As Chambers and Seton noted ('Bellenden's Translation', 1920, 7), this intermediary MS contains no preliminary reference to being corrected by Boece, as the later print will.

36. For transcriptions of the full text and discussion see W. Fraser, *The Douglas Book*, vol. 1 (Edinburgh, 1855), p. 184, and Sir H. Maxwell, *A History of the House of Douglas*, vol. 1 (1902), pp. 64–5. This couplet is also quoted at the opening of David Hume of Godscroft's *History of the House of Douglas*: see *David Hume of Godscroft's 'The History of the House of Douglas'*, ed. D. Reid, 2 vols, STS (Edinburgh, 1996), I, p. 11, II, p. 460.

37. Bellenden, *Chronicles* (1821), vol. 2, p. 383. Cf. the discussion in Chambers and Seton, 1920, 9–10, who do not note the further added sentence in the printed version.

38. Bellenden, *Chronicles* (1821), vol. 2, p. 410.

39. *Longer Scottish Poems Volume One, 1350–1650*, ed. P. Bawcutt and F. Riddy (1987), p. 331. The episode was interpolated into editions of the *Bruce* only from Lekpreuik's 1571 print onwards.

40. T. van Heijnsbergen, 'The Interaction between Literature and History in Queen Mary's Edinburgh: the Bannatyne Manuscript and its Prosopographical Context', in *The Renaissance in Scotland*, ed. A. A. MacDonald, M. Lynch and I. B. Cowan (Leiden, 1994), pp. 183–225 (192); also A. A. MacDonald, 'William Stewart and the Court Poetry of the Reign of James V', in *Stewart Style 1513–1542: Essays on the Court of James V*, ed. J. Hadley Williams (East Linton, 1996), pp. 179–200 (185, 190–1). Bellenden's mother was a Douglas; he is also found witnessing a contract with Gavin Douglas in 1520.

41. See S. Mapstone, 'Was there a Court Literature in Fifteenth-Century Scotland?', *SSL*, 26 (1991), 410–22.

42. Bellenden, *Chronicles* (STS), II, pp. 185–6, and Royan, 'The Relationship', p. 151.

43. UCL, MS Angl. 1, fol. 253ʳ; Bellenden, *Chronicles* (1821), vol. 2 pp, 299–300. MS R here (see n. 13) does not contain the revised version found in A. For Mair's comments see John Major, *A History of Greater Britain as Well England as Scotland*, ed. A. Constable, SHS, 10 (Edinburgh, 1892), pp. 136–8.

44. Bellenden, *Chronicles* (1821), vol. 2 pp. 297–9 (not found in any of the MSS); ibid., p. 479 (also not found in any of the MSS). Another addition to the print in book 16 is the charter of king William added in chapter 5 (ibid., p. 460).

45. For discussion of other revisions in the printed version in relation to the Bruce see Chambers and Seton, 1920, 10–13, 1922, 200–1; Sheppard, 'Studies', pp. 147–53; and Burns, pp. 86–9.

46. Observed by Paul ('The scene ... transmits to us the most ancient and fixed tradition concerning the Macbeth story'), though with the familiar judgment of its tediousness, pp. 359–60. Also Farrow, 18–19.

47. Johannis de Fordun, *Chronica Gentis Scotorum*, 2 vols, ed. W. F. Skene (Edinburgh, 1871–2), The Historians of Scotland, I, pp. 197–203, II, pp. 184–91. The most recent research on Fordun's sources is a product of the re-editing of Bower's *Scotichronicon*, the text of which follows Fordun for this passage. See Walter Bower, *Scotichronicon*, vol. 3, ed. J. MacQueen, W. MacQueen, and D. E. R. Watt (Edinburgh, 1995), pp. 2–15, 179–84.

48. *Chronica Gentis Scotorum*, II, p. 422. For the ideological project behind Fordun's adaptation of sources and invention of material see R. J. Goldstein, *The Matter of Scotland: Historical Narrative in Medieval Scotland* (1993), pp. 104–32. On Macduff, J. Bannerman, 'MacDuff of Fife', in *Medieval Scotland: Crown, Lordship and Community*, ed. A. Grant and K. J. Stringer (Edinburgh, 1993), pp. 20–38 (21–7); see also Walter Bower, *Scotichronicon*, vol. 2, ed. J. MacQueen and W. MacQueen (Aberdeen, 1989), p. 509.

49. Still extremely useful for the Middle Ages and Renaissance remains H. Galinsky, *Der Lucretia-Stoff in der Weltliteratur* (Breslau, 1938), esp. pp. 7–54.

50. For instance, both the Lucretia and Sardanapalus examples figure in Book VII, the advice to princes book, of Gower's *Confessio Amantis* (in place of lechery in the penitential schema of this work, VII, 4314–43, 4672–5130). For Edwy and Culen in the *Chronica Gentis Scotorum* and (following it) the *Scotichronicon*, see *Chronica Gentis Scotorum*, I, pp. 169–70, II, pp. 161–3; *Scotichronicon*, vol. 2, pp. 354–6. The source is William of Malmesbury (ibid., p. 482).

51. Bannerman, p. 27.

52. As the texts of the *Scotichronicon* and *Chronica Gentis Scotorum* are identical here, quotation in translation and Latin is from the most recent edition, of the *Scotichronicon*, vol. 3, p. 7; 'omnibus, qui pro te regnum et predia deseruimus, filios et uxores, ac nostri generis nacionem', ibid., ibid., vol. 3, p. 6; cf. *Chronica Gentis Scotorum*, I, p. 199.

53. *Scotichronicon*, vol. 3, p. 7; 'Numquid et tu rex existens ad tuam explendam libidinis luxuriam, pulcherimas regni virgines ad libitum ac placidissimas habere poteris mulieres?' ibid., vol. 3, p. 6; cf. *Chronica Gentis Scotorum*, I, p. 199.

54. The *Scotichronicon* editors note that while Suetonius ('Divus Augustus') is the source for some of the material on Octavian here, the origin of the more licentious episodes has not been identified; vol. 3, p. 183.

55. Ibid., vol. 3, p. 9; 'Excellencioris persone semper casus in vicium minoris lapsum, comparacione scandali, multo longius antecedit.'; ibid., vol. 3, p. 8; cf. *Chronica Gentis Scotorum*, I, p. 200.

56. Ibid., vol. 3 p. 11; 'Nichil umquam tibi rex existens'; ibid., vol. 3, p. 10; cf. *Chronica Gentis Scotorum*, I, p. 201.

57. See S. Mapstone, 'The Scots *Buke of Phisnomy* and Sir Gilbert Hay', in *The Renaissance in Scotland* (as n. 40), pp. 1–44 (18). In William Stewart's 'translation' of Boece, precisely this idea is introduced into the scene, in Malcolm's second response to Macduff, 'I haif hard sa that greit terrour and dreid/Causis ane man mak vertu of neid; For quhair ane man standis grit dreid or aw,/Hydis his vice, and wilbe laith to schaw;/Suppois natuir constranye him thairto' (40,245–49), *Buik of the Croniclis*, II, p. 652.

58. *Scotichronicon*, vol. 3, p. 11; 'Et ideo sicut in precedentibus viciis, et in hoc eciam crimine michi subveniens, illud queso subtiliter aliquo tui sagacis ingenii velamine pallias; et quicquid tue proposicionis tenor exigerit, me totis offero viribus ad implendum.'; ibid., vol. 3, p. 12; cf. *Chronica Gentis Scotorum*, I, p. 201.

59. Ibid., vol. 3 p. 15; 'Si quidem hec vera sunt que loqueris, ad vitam de morte me reducis'; ibid., vol. 3, p. 14; cf. *Chronica Gentis Scotorum*, I, p. 203.

60. Andrew of Wyntoun, *Original Chronicle*, ed. F. J. Amours, 6 vols, STS (Edinburgh and London, 1902–14), IV, pp. 292–7.

61. *Scotichronicon*, vol. 3, pp. 179–81; cf. E. J. Cowan, 'The Historical Macbeth', in *Moray: Province and People*, ed. W. D. H. Sellar (Edinburgh, 1993), Scottish Society for Northern Studies, pp. 117–41 (129–31).

62. *A History of Greater Britain*, pp. 122–3. John Mair, *Historia Majoris Britanniae*

tam Angliae quam Scotiae (Paris, 1521), '[Malcolmus] ob tria dicebat se regno inutilem: primum, quod luxuriosus erat, et per consequens principum filiabus, et fortasse (quod est multo deterius) conjugibus abuteretur. Secundum, quod auarus esset, et omnia cuperet. Ad quae duo Makduffus: in Scotiae inquit regno septentrionali et frigido, formosissimam habebis conjugem, quae sola tibi sufficiet. Nullus est in Anglia aut Scotia Princeps, qui non libenter suam filiam tibi conjugem tradet. Pro auaritia potes omnibus bonis regni, prout voles uti, amore et pace quicquid petieris populus tibi non negabit. Ad haec tertium Malcolmus obiecit, inquiens, sum mendax, dolosus et instabilis. Cui tale responsum, Makduffus dedisse fertur, Abito ergo faex generis nostri, abito hominum monstrum, regno quolibet indignum.' (fol. xliiiʳ) William Stewart's translation of Boece also alters this passage to suggest that Malcolm's lecherous desires will abate when he matures (*Buik of the Croniclis*, II, p. 652).

63. Trinity College, Cambridge, MS Gale, O. 9.9. On the *Chronica Gentis Scotorum* and *Scotichronicon* as sources for the *Scotorum Historia*, Royan, 'The *Scotorum Historia*', pp. 214–20.

64. UCL MS Angl. 1, fol. 244ʳ; also Trinity College, Cambridge, MS O. 3.21, fol. 251ᵛ; and SRO, MS RH 13/10, fol. 127ʳ. I am grateful to the Master and Fellows of Trinity College, Cambridge and to the Scottish Record Office, Edinburgh for permission to cite these MSS. Cf. Bellenden, *Chronicles* (1821), vol. 2, p. 272.

65. 'ne vota vestra, quae tantis nunc precibus optatis, in diuersam convertantur partem, ac quae nunc tanto desiderio aduocatis non minore indignatione ac iniuria eiiciatis postea turpissime', *Scotorum Historia*, fol. cc[x]lxiv. (… 'so that your requests, which you have made just now with so much longing be not thrown out afterwards with no less outrage and wrong').

66. Bellenden, *Chronicles* (STS), II, p. 160.

67. UCL MS Angl. 1, fol. 244ʳ; also Trinity College, Cambridge, MS O.3.21, fol. 251v; and SRO, MS RH 13/10 fol. 127ʳ.

68. Sheppard rather surprisingly notes that 'As a rule, the printed edition follows the Latin texts more closely than do the manuscript versions', something that should certainly be closely checked. But she also remarks that 'equally the printed edition departs from the Latin on occasions where the manuscripts are faithful to it' (Bellenden, *Chronicles* (STS), II, p. 442. This is certainly the case with the majority of examples discussed in this esssay.

69. Bellenden, *Chronicles* (1821), vol. 2, p. 272; cf. Bellenden, *Chronicles* (STS), II, p. 160; here the one vice mentioned is 'lesyngis'.

70. See S. Mapstone, 'Bower on Kingship' in *Scotichronicon*, vol. 9, ed. D. E. R. Watt (Edinburgh, 1998), pp. 321–38.

71. Burns, p. 87.

72. Bellenden, *Chronicles* (1821), vol. 2, p. 273; on the connotations of this term see R. Mason, 'Covenant and Commonweal: The Language of Politics in Reformation Scotland', in N. Macdougall (ed.), *Church, Politics and Society: Scotland 1408–1929* (Edinburgh, 1983), pp. 97–126 (108).

73. Burns, p. 89.

74. Holinshed, p. 1; also Holinshed (1577), sig. A1ᵛ.

75. Ibid., for citation of 'Iohannes Maior'. On the use of Buchanan in the 1587 edition see Norbrook, pp. 81–4, 87–93, 102–6, 114–16. The only textual differences for this scene between the 1587 edition and the 1577 one (p. 250), beyond minor orthographical ones, are the replacement on two occasions of the adverb 'right' with 'verie' in the later edition.

76. G. Buchanan, *The History of Scotland*, ed. J. Aikman, 4 vols (Glasgow, 1827), I,

pp. 335–6. For the Latin text from the *Rerum Scoticarum Historia*, see George Buchanan, *Opera Omnia*, ed. T. Ruddiman, 2 vols (Edinburgh, 1715), I, p. 114 ('Multorum libidinem liberali conjugio solvi'.)

77. See p. 159 and n. 5 above. Macduff's early comment 'Each new morn,/New widows howl, new orphans cry' (4–5) strikingly looks at the idea from the perpective of his own possible murder.

78. Holinshed, p. 275; and see n. 82 below.

79. That Shakespeare might have seen the *Chronica Gentis Scotorum* or the *Scotichronicon* in manuscript can not be totally ruled out but seems extremely unlikely.

80. Goldberg, in *Shakespeare Reproduced*, p. 250.

81. Norbrook, p. 111.

82. See n. 6 above. On Macduff's role in this see also Goldberg, 'He allies himself with Malcolm in a scene in which the future monarch displays his credentials first be presenting himself as extremely libidinous – and Macduff willingly responds as a virtual procurer to satisfy his lust – and then as excessively chaste; either way masculinity and power are directed against women.' (*Shakespeare Reproduced*, p. 259.)

83. For instance Muir, pp. 131–2.

84. On the further connotations of the royal touch in relation to James I, see Kinney, 'Scottish History', pp. 40–1, and 'Re-Historicising *Macbeth*', pp. 101–2.

85. See Holinshed, pp. 269–71, and Bellenden, *Chronicles* (1821), vol. 2, pp. 261–4; Norbrook, pp. 88–9.

86. Holinshed, pp. 271–5; Holinshed (1577), pp. 247–8. Also suggested by Kinney, 'Scottish History', pp. 19–21; cf. Paul, p. 18.

87. For the political context here see also Arthur F. Kinney, 'Shakespeare's *Macbeth* and the Question of Nationalism', in *Literature and Nationalism*, ed. V. Newey and A. Thompson (Liverpool, 1991), pp. 56–65.

88. For discussion see the studies in n. 4, above.

89. Holinshed, p. 276.

APPENDIX

Hector Boece, *Scotorum Historiae a prima gentis origine libri xvii* (Paris, 1527), fols cclxii–cclxiv

Haec vbi Magduffus adhortandi Malcolmi gratia dixisset fuit certe pro rei acerbitate commotus Malcolmus, tamen cuncta primum dissimulauit, vt animum hominis experiretur, verus ne esset, an (vt frequentes ad ipsum alias Maccabeus miserat ad tentandum hominus animum)[1] falsus ac subdolus vt in discrimen perduceret, atque tandem ad necem traderet Maccabeo. Respondit autem patriam quidem cordi sibi esse, dolereque eorum sese vicem qui, vt dicebat, a tyranno crudelissimo vexabantur, tamen spei in ipso illis nihil esse, nec aptum se regno. Multis se, vti fingebat, et grauissimis obnoxium vitiis, quae ipse in se agnosceret quidem, curare tamen nequiret; adeo vt si bene constitutum regnum ab aliis maxima omnium beneuolentia accipiat, tamen propter illa tueri illud se non posse. Ac praecipue propter vitiorum omnium teterrimum ac reliquorum quasi fontem immoderatam libidinem, quae etsi tunc etiam mala, perniciosaque esset, tamen eam intra aedium suarum parietes contineri, nullamque ex ea communitatem malum aliquod sentire, sibi dumtaxat vni esse pestiferam.

Quod si eam (inquit) potestatem rerum adeptus, eam omniumque agendorum licentiam quae regibus datur accipiam, multo grauiorem fortassis subditis futuram illam experiemini intemperantiam quam vt eam foribus vestris excludere possitis, quae per coniuges, per filias, per honesta atque inhonesta peruagaretur omnia insolentius quam nunc Maccabaei sit cruentus in vos gladius. Insuper (inquit) quod ab regia maxime abhorret dignitate, plurimumque populum in prauos adducit mores, mendacio intantum gaudeo, adeoque me oblectat animus subdolus, vt quantumuis graui in re, tamen me falli ac decipi aliosque, fallere et decipere gestiam. Quamobrem quum in rege nihil magis decorum sit constantia, veritate, iustitia, et toto denique virtutum illarum choro pulcherrimo quumque eas omnes vna complectantur veritas, mendaciumque ea omnia subuertat, vides quam sim ineptus ad ea quae me gerere vultis obeunda, quantoque me malo vestro in vestras vocatis ceruices. Quamobrem vti vos consoler illud accipite, eiusque memores este, quod in fabulis fertur de vulpe ab examine muscarum sanguinem ipsius exugentium oppressa, quae quum rogaretur viatore² quopiam abigi ne eas cuperet? Respondit, succi illas ac sanguinis plenas esse, ac segnes iam saturitate corpori i[n]sidere, quod si eas abegisset, alias recentes ac famelicas protinus aduolaturas, et quod reliqui sanguinis priores fecissent id omne illas exhausturas.

Proinde me vt sum sinitote ne vota vestra, quae tantis nunc precibus optatis, in diuersam convertantur partem, ac quae nunc tanto desiderio aduocatis non minore indignatione ac iniuria eiiciatis postea turpissime.

Ad ea Magduffus, saltem id patriae concedere velit, rogat, vt se ducem nominare liberandae patriae permittat, reliqua sibi ac amicis curae fore. Et quum id quoque renueret, explorare tentans quid ad extremum Magduffus acturus esset, an etiam constans permansurus (nondum eum certo animo persuasum habebat, non esse subdola fictitiamque quod ageret).

Ergo, inquit Magduffus, si nec patriae te charitas mouere, neque tuorum nefanda mala quae quotidie perpetiuntur, in sui miserationem trahere te valent, nec vllis precibus flecteris, opto, vt deus tibi mentem aliquando meliorem det, aut ne diutius in gentis tuae contumeliam superesse te finat. Quod vero ad me attinet, quando ab omnibus desertus sum, ne casum patriae videam, quam longissime hinc me in exteras proripiam terras, ac quod patriae praestare non possum, nomini prae-stabo Christiano, quo omnes eadem veluti continemur patria, atque hoc corpusculum hostibus nostrae religionis obiiciam, quoad lucem his oculis intueri potero.

Iamque discedere cum indignatione parantem, Malcolmus syncere illum quae agebat, atque ex amino et facere et dicere tandem persuasus, comprensa toga retinet, Magduffe, inquiens, quae optas effecturus sum, bono animo esto. Quod ita tergiuersatus sum experientia me facere docuit, cum huiusmodi verbis saepe mihi struxerit insidias Maccabeus. Itaque quanto tardius quae orabas pollicitus sum, tanto maiori cura ac vigilantia prosequar.

Deinde iunctis dextris et data atque accepta fide, quoniam pacto rem peragerent inter sese consultant, et rebus constitutis Magduffus ad regni oras proficiscitur atque illinc literas ad primates per fidos mittit nuncios, certiores eos faciens de coniuratione in Maccabaeum facta, et ad nouas res incipiendas hortatur, Maccabaeumque expellendum et Malcolmum verum regni recipiendum haeredem.

When Macduff had said this for the sake of encouraging Malcolm, Malcolm was certainly agitated in keeping with the dreadfulness of the situation. However he initially concealed this entirely, so that he might test the mind of the man, whether he was genuine, or (like the many

Macbeth had sent to him on other occasions to test out his intentions), false and deceitful, to lead him into danger, and finally hand him over to slaughter at Macbeth's hands. He replied that although he was indeed attached to his homeland, and he grieved for the sake of those who as he said were persecuted by such a cruel tyrant, yet there was no hope for them in him, and he was not suitable for the realm. He was enslaved to the practice of many grave vices, which he did indeed recognise in himself, but which he could not cure all the same. So much so, that if he were to receive a realm well established by others with the greatest good will imaginable, still he would not be able to hold on to it on account of them. And especially, on account of his unrestrained lust, the most loathsome of all vices and the fountain of the others, which even if it was now a foul and pernicious thing, it was however contained within the walls of his own dwellings, no community suffered any ill from it; it was so far harmful to him alone.

'But if', he said,' I acquired control of the realm, and received the licence given to kings to do everything, you will have imposed upon you an intemperance perhaps far greater than you would be able to exclude from your doors, which would range through wives, daughters, and through all that is honourable and dishonourable, more arrogantly than now Macbeth's sword stains you with blood. Moreover', he said, 'what is utterly inconsistent with royal dignity and leads a great part of the people into deprived habits – I take great pleasure in falsehood, and a cunning mind delights me so much that no matter how grave the concern still I long to be deceived and tricked and to deceive and trick others. On account of this, since nothing is more proper in a king than constancy, truth and justice, and the whole beautiful chorus of those virtues, and since truth brings those together and deceit overturns all of them utterly, you see how unsuited I would be to undertake what you want me to do, and at the cost of how great a disaster to yourselves you call on me to take on your yoke. On account of this, so that I might console you, hear this and take it to heart, what is said in fables about the fox overwhelmed by a swarm of flies sucking her blood which, when she was asked by a passer-by whether she would like them driven away somewhere, replied that those who had sucked and were full of blood sat now lazily and gorged on her body, but if he drove them away other new and hungry ones would immediately fly up to him, and drain what blood the earlier flies had left behind.

'Just so, leave me as I am, so that your requests, which you have made just now with so great prayers, be not altered into something else, and what you now advocate with so much longing be not thrown out afterwards with no less outrage and wrong.'

In response to this Macduff asked whether he would not at least be willing to agree to this for his homeland, that he would permit himself to be named as leader for the liberating of his homeland, and everything else to be the concern of him [Macduff] and his friends. And he rejected this also, testing what in the end Macduff would do, whether he would still remain constant (for he was not yet firmly persuaded that he was not acting out a cunning fiction).

'Therefore', said Macduff, if love for your homeland is not enough to move you, or the unspeakable evils which your people daily suffer may not draw you into compassion for them, and if you do not bow to any prayers, I hope that God will some time give you a better spirit, or not allow you to survive any longer in the face of the insult to your people. Truly when I am abandoned of all hope, my concern will be to take myself to unknown lands as far as possible from here so that I do not see the ruin of my homeland, and as I cannot devote myself to that homeland I will devote myself to the name of a Christian, in which all are contained in one country, and I will cast this feeble body against the enemies of our religion, until I will be able to look upon the light with these eyes.'

And now as he was preparing to leave in indignation, Malcolm, at last persuaded that he acted sincerely, and that what he said and did came from his heart, held him by the sleeve, saying, 'Macduff, what you ask I will make happen, be of good heart. For I refused you because of what experience has taught me, because Macbeth has often laid traps for me with words of this kind. And so the slower I have been to make you this promise, the more I will pursue what you ask with attention and care.'

Then having joined their right hands and given and received oaths of loyalty, they discussed between themselves by what means they would accomplish their goal, and when they had decided these matters Macduff set off for the borders of the country and there sent letters by faithful messengers to the nobles, informing them of the conspiracy against Macbeth and urging them to begin revolution, to expel Macbeth and to receive Malcolm as true heir of the realm.

---

1. The printed text has the second parenthesis after *miserat*, but *ad tentandum hominus animum* goes best here with what precedes it and refers to Macbeth's testing of Malcolm; the fact that Boece has used a similar phrase only a couple of lines earlier (*vt animum hominis experiretur*) to describe Malcolm's testing of Macduff may be a deliberate echo.

2. Text *aviatore*, but as Bellenden's translation 'ane passingere be the gaitt' indicates, emendation to *viatore* is necessary.

INDEX